The Artistic Activism of
ELOMBE BRATH

The Artistic Activism of

ELOMBE BRATH

Edited and annotated by Thomas Aiello

University Press of Mississippi / Jackson

The University Press of Mississippi is the scholarly
publishing agency of the Mississippi Institutions of Higher
Learning: Alcorn State University, Delta State University,
Jackson State University, Mississippi State University,
Mississippi University for Women, Mississippi Valley State
University, University of Mississippi, and University of
Southern Mississippi.

www.upress.state.ms.us

The University Press of Mississippi is a member
of the Association of University Presses.

All images courtesy of the family of Elombe Brath
and the Elombe Brath Foundation

First printing 2021
∞

Library of Congress Control Number available
Hardback ISBN 978-1-4968-3536-9
Trade paperback ISBN 978-1-4968-3537-6
Epub single ISBN 978-1-4968-3538-3
Epub institutional ISBN 978-1-4968-3539-0
PDF single ISBN 978-1-4968-3540-6
PDF institutional ISBN 978-1-4968-3541-3

British Library Cataloging-in-Publication Data available

Contents

Part Four
MISCELLANEOUS ART AND ESSAYS

Preface

In 1963, at the height of the southern civil rights movement, Cecil Brathwaite, under the pseudonym Cecil Elombe Brath, published a satire of Black leaders called *Color Us Cullud! The American Negro Leadership Official Coloring Book*. In Brathwaite's day job, he worked as a graphic artist for ABC television. Outside of that framework, he was a Black nationalist thinker who participated in (and created) a variety of Pan-African causes, including the Patrice Lumumba Coalition. He helped found the African Jazz-Art Society & Studios, through which he published *Color Us Cullud!*

The book pillories a variety of Black leaders, ranging from political figures like Adam Clayton Powell and Whitney Young to civil rights activists like Martin Luther King Jr., Bayard Rustin, and John Lewis, and even entertainers like Sammy Davis Jr., Lena Horne, and Dick Gregory. It takes on Elijah Muhammad and Malcolm X, A. Philip Randolph, and Roy Wilkins, along with several others. The illustrations are strong. The commentary is unique. The book also includes a satirical poem about the integration of Ole Miss. It has, however, virtually disappeared from the historiography. This volume restores *Color Us Cullud!* to a place of prominence in the historiography of the Black left, along with the full catalog of his activist art.

Elombe Brath, born Cecil Brathwaite, had a long and accomplished life. He fought for Black rights in the United States and around the world. From a family that originated in Barbados, he was an acolyte of Carlos Cooks, part of a strain of Caribbean radicalism that influenced many in New York in the twentieth century. Brath would be responsible for carrying that radicalism into the twenty-first. He was an advisor to governments and royalty in several African nations, and a champion of a variety of civil rights causes in the United States. In his later life, he did the bulk of that work with his typewriter and with his feet, but in his early adulthood, he did it with his comic and artistic skill.

Brath's first published artistic work came in 1957 in a collection of jazz album reviews for *Down Beat* magazine. He then published a series of cartoons pillorying much of the scene and culture that surrounded jazz music. It was in 1960, however, that his comic artwork addressed itself specifically to the subject of his activism. That year, he began publishing a comic strip, "Congressman Carter and Beatnick Jackson," in the short-lived New York *Citizen-Call* newspaper, which lasted until 1961. Three years after that, Brath published his most enduring work, *Color Us Cullud! The American Negro Leadership Official Coloring Book*, critiquing what he considered to be the inauthenticity of movement leaders while urging a more radical approach. And he did so with a comic sense and an artist's eye. His work presents a version of Black radical critique that is not often included in broad-brush approaches to civil rights, one that puts, for example, Martin Luther King Jr. and Malcolm X on the wrong side of the same coin. It was an effort that, in the heart of the civil rights movement, required audacity and truth-telling in the face of what would be understandable opposition, as he took on many of the movement's most sacred cows.

What follows here is a depiction of that audacity and truth-telling. It begins with an analysis of Brath's influences. A full biography of the vast scope and breadth of Brath's remarkable life has yet to be written, but this first section describes the development of the particular strain of Caribbean radicalism that often receives short shrift in studies of the Black left, but that was vital for the development of that left in urban hubs like Harlem. It describes the life and work of Brath himself. And it describes the history of the Black satire of which Brath made himself a vital part. The second section features the artist's early work, his illustrations for *Down Beat* magazine and *Beat Jokes, Bop Humor, & Cool Cartoons*. The third section emphasizes the full flowering of his comic radicalism. It features the full run of Brath's comic strip "Congressman Carter and Beatnick Jackson" from the New York *Citizen-Call* and a complete edition of *Color Us Cullud!* itself, the most influential outgrowth of Brath's early artistic production. It is followed by annotations that frame and contextualize each of the coloring book's entries. In the volume's final section, there are several miscellaneous examples of the intersection of his art and his political thinking recovered from archival material, followed by several representative examples of Brath's written work, particularly as it relates to the domestic politics presented in the coloring book.

In the process of that presentation, and already in this short preface, this narrative makes liberal use of terms like radicalism, nationalism, and Pan-Africanism, which often become sites of contestation in discussions of Black thought. Even those historical actors who used such terms did so at variance with one another, making any kind of definitional consensus difficult to attain. For the purposes of this book, then, the definition of radicalism will follow that of the *Journal for the Study of Radicalism*, which distinguishes "radicals" from "reformers." Radicals in the journal's formulation "seek revolutionary alternatives to hegemonic social and political institutions," whether violently or nonviolently.[1] This book's definition of nationalism will adhere to the work of William Van Deburg. In *New Day in Babylon*, one of the first and best historical studies of the Black Power movement, Van Deburg argues that nationalists "are suspicious that radically divergent groups long can live in peace and on the basis of equality while inhabiting the same territory or participating in the same societal institutions." When one of those groups is forced to assimilate, its culture is subsumed into that of the dominant group. "To advert this end, nationalists seek to strengthen in-group values while holding those promoted by the larger society at arm's length" and seek to "maintain sociocultural autonomy." Brath would embody various forms of nationalism. His interest in African repatriation represented what Van Deburg calls a "territorial nationalism" while his work with groups like the African Jazz-Art Society was a manifestation of "cultural nationalism."[2]

Finally, the book's references to Brath's Pan-Africanism follow that of Peter Olisanwuche Esedebe's popular account. Esedebe's Pan-Africanism "is a political and cultural phenomenon which regards Africa, Africans, and African descendants abroad as a unit." That emphasis on the diaspora then combines with a desire "to regenerate and unify Africa and promote a feeling of oneness among the people of the African world. It glories the African past and inculcates pride in African value."[3]

Brath undoubtedly gloried in the African past. He advocated pride in African value. And he left his modern readers a complicated legacy. He was a fierce opponent of white supremacy and a critic who demanded accountability of Black leaders. At the same time, he promoted racial essentialism, gender policing, and occasional anti-Semitism.[4] He demonstrated a clear skepticism regarding celebrity activists and movement figureheads. His work provides a unique perspective on the civil rights movement from someone who watched as it happened, a perspective often omitted from the historiography but one vital to understanding its full scope. It is also, importantly, funny. Elombe Brath was a philosopher and activist for most of his life, but he was also an entertainer, and his work in this collection is undoubtedly entertaining. It is comedy in service to civil rights, presented together in this complete form for the first time.

And it is a project that could not have been completed without the vital help of Cinque Brathwaite, Elombe's son, and the Elombe Brath Foundation. The organization provided guidance, points of clarity, and permissions for much of the material presented herein. I cannot thank them enough.

Part One

ELOMBE BRATH IN CONTEXT

1

THE CARIBBEAN ORIGINS OF ELOMBE BRATH'S RADICALISM

Cecil Brathwaite, the future Cecil Elombe Brath, was born in Brooklyn in September 1936 to parents who had immigrated to the city in the 1920s from Barbados, and his thought through the bulk of his life would rest at the intersection of New York and the Caribbean.

Barbados was a hotbed of Garveyite radicalism in the 1920s. "In the Caribbean," notes Glenford D. Howe, "national identity, national and nation-state processes historically emerged out of a response to territorial, military, economic, political and cultural forms of domination." It was, however, a process with starts and stops. In Barbados, there was the early Bussa Revolt in 1816, the Confederation Riots of the 1870s, then another series of uprisings as late as 1937. "In tracing the lineaments of Barbadian nationalism, one discerns a single theme of freedom, an empowering impulse, running through popular conceptions of nationhood," Howe explains, "sometimes sitting uneasily alongside elite perceptions of the national interest."[1]

The migration of the West Indian population in the early twentieth century was vast, but despite the colonial conflicts of the nineteenth century, it began relatively slowly. At the turn of the century, there were merely a few hundred Caribbeans in Harlem. By 1924, the year that Brath's father arrived in New York, there were more than 12,000. By 1930 the Caribbean population was almost one quarter of the total Harlem population.[2]

It was a migration fueled by a variety of interrelated hardships back home. In Jamaica, a crippling tenant labor system and the collapse of farm prices in the 1890s and early twentieth century left few options for those unwilling to travel outside its borders. The outmigration from Barbados was even starker. Between 1881 and 1921, Barbados lost more than 82,000 people, roughly half its 1881 population. When the bottom dropped out of the sugar market in the 1880s, islands like Jamaica diversified their farming, but Barbados continued stubbornly with its sugar production, slashing the wages of the poor tenant farmers to compensate for the difference. Then there were a series of droughts, earthquakes, and hurricanes. Those who might seek other avenues of work in the face of such calamities were stymied in 1911 when the colonial government ended competitive civil service exams, ensuring that qualified Black applicants would be passed over for white-collar work in favor of white and light-skinned people. It would have a cutting effect on all of the British West Indies. Marcus Garvey's first published article was an attack on this policy.[3]

The two places that disaffected Black Caribbeans found open to them were the two places closest to the island chain, Central America and the United States. The first massive wave of emigration led to Panama, where West Indian migrants formed much of the labor that built the Panama Canal from 1904–1914. After that, World War I became the dominant pull factor, but the historical assumption that the trajectory of migration shifted to the United States after 1914 is incorrect. As Winston James has explained, "the migration from the Caribbean to the United States was simultaneous with the migration to Panama between 1904 and 1914." The United States obviously became a more important destination after the guaranteed work of the canal was complete, "but there was no sudden or dramatic increase in the number of Caribbeans entering the United States," he notes. "The trend was upward, but not markedly so." After

World War I, however, the paradigm completed its shift, and "New York was the primary destination of the migrants to the United States."[4]

But the conditions that led to emigration were also the conditions that radicalized the migrants. According to Glenford Howe, the modern outgrowth of Barbadian nationalism developed in World War I. While the British demanded much of its colonial population, for example, it did not want Black soldiers serving in forward areas. What recruitment that did happen belied both class and color divisions within West Indian society. Segregated white units included fair-skinned Black citizens, leading to a variety of colorist reprisals. Black soldiers from the islands were treated categorically poorly as unequals. Meanwhile, domestically, labor strikes predominated throughout the Caribbean, demonstrating unrest even among those not directly participating in the war effort. In July 1919, the first of a series of Caribbean uprisings occurred in British Honduras, with returning soldiers and civilians combining to attack edifices of whiteness. In Barbados, white authorities imposed a harsh rule to ensure that similar events didn't happen there. Former members of the military who returned to Barbados tried to join groups like Garvey's Universal Negro Improvement Association but tended to find themselves punished for their efforts. As Howe explains, "The war stimulated profound socioeconomic, political and psychological change and greatly facilitated protest against the oppressive conditions in the colonies and against colonial rule by giving a fillip to the adoption of the nationalist ideologies of Marcus Garvey and others throughout the region."[5]

One of those returning servicemen from Barbados was Clennell Wilsden Wickham, a cousin of the future Brath who became a writer and editor for the island's *Herald* newspaper, using this platform to relentlessly attack the ruling minority on the island. Like so many African American soldiers after serving in World War I, Wickham had fought with the British

West Indies Regiment in Egypt and Palestine during the Great War and returned radicalized, ready to work to better the situation of Black Barbados. In 1919 he began writing for the *Herald*, founded by Clement Innis, and used his position to stump for rights groups like the Democratic League, of which he was a founding member. The ruling elite, he argued in the pages of the *Herald*, needed to "get in touch with the hopes and aspirations of the common people like myself, and find out why we are dissatisfied and what we want. It would be a very dangerous thing if it should become generally accepted that the legitimate aspirations of the working classes are always to be opposed by those higher up." Wickham's first candidate for the Barbados assembly under the Democratic League banner was another Brath relative, Christopher Augustus Brathwaite, and after constant stumping in the *Herald*, Brathwaite and the League won the seat. It was a sea change in Barbadian politics, but it was also a threat to the white establishment. A libel case brought against Wickham in 1930 bankrupted the paper and forced it to cease operations. In the 1930s, he would move to Grenada and edit the *West Indian* newspaper there in the last decade of his life. By that time, however, the Brathwaites had already gone north to the United States.[6]

It was at the end of the war, in 1919, that Barbados developed its first chapter of Garvey's Universal Negro Improvement Association (UNIA). In response, the Barbados government enacted a Seditious Publication Ordinance in 1920, particularly to crack down on the UNIA's *Negro World* (see below), and law enforcement monitored UNIA branch activities. The organization faltered in the face of such oversight and in response to Garvey's arrest in the United States. In 1926, to fill the void, the island developed the Workingmen's Association, which carried many of the same goals of the UNIA. "We (the black race) will not be satisfied until we walk on the continent of Africa," wrote Moses Small, one of the Workingmen's Association founders, "then we will be able to sing 'lusty.' We are clamouring for better conditions for our people. We are scattered all over the world and not represented. The time will come when God said that we will rebuild the temple." The Workingmen's Association and the UNIA would work together through the remainder of the 1920s and 1930s.[7]

There were, by that time, however, more than 100,000 West Indian migrants in the United States, and the most common destination for them was New York. "Harlem has, in this century, become the most strategically important community of black America," wrote Harold Cruse. "Harlem is still the pivot of the black world's quest for identity and salvation. The way Harlem goes (or does not go) so goes all black America." He argued that "this community still represents the Negro's strongest bastion in America from which to launch whatever group effort he is able to mobilize for political power, economic rehabilitation and cultural reidentification." Though Harlem was unique, and though most Americans didn't have the kind of shared experience of Harlem, Harlem created the cultural identity for Black America, and "without a cultural identity that adequately defines *himself*, the Negro cannot even identify with the American nation as a whole."[8]

It was a place that, much like Caribbean islands to its south, was created by waves of political and economic upheaval. The Dutch had arrived in what would become Manhattan in the 1630s, and New Haarlem was officially established in 1658. It was rural. It was outside the bounds of the larger New York City. It remained a farming village for a long time, and even into the nineteenth century it remained largely separated from Manhattan. Beginning in the 1840s and 1850s, Irish immigrants moved into the region, which only made the area even less desirable for most Protestants and vastly reduced property values. It was a poor region in massive decline, and in an attempt to fix that, Harlem was incorporated into Manhattan in 1873.[9]

What brought the region to life was the advent of public transportation, which had begun to develop in the 1870s. Elevated trains reached the Harlem section of Manhattan in the 1880s, and when the city was planning its subway system, Harlem was a proposed stop on the route, as well. As was common in many areas across the country, the advent of transportation led to massive, swift urbanization. Businesses, ornate housing, and tenement slums all developed quickly. The Polo Grounds went up as a place where people could play polo. Seven years later, the New York Giants began playing baseball there. The Harlem Opera House opened in 1889. The section had its own newspaper, its own periodical press. One of those magazines, the *Harlem Monthly Magazine*, wrote in 1893 that "it is evident to the most superficial observer that the centre of fashion, wealth, culture, and intelligence, must, in the near future, be found in the ancient and honorable village of Harlem."[10]

When Jewish immigrants from Eastern Europe began moving into the neighborhood after subway delays again dropped real estate prices, the residents of Harlem worked to keep them out. There were also Latinos, Italians, Finns, and Irish at various points in the second half of the nineteenth century and early twentieth, but they too eventually moved on.[11]

There had been a small number of Black residents ever since the first tenement housing went up in Harlem in the 1880s, but it was the first early wave of the nascent Great Migration, beginning in the 1890s, that fed the first new numbers of Black residents to New York. But those early migrants couldn't, for the most part, get into Harlem. White residents didn't want a Black presence in the neighborhood any more than they wanted a Jewish or immigrant presence, and remained relatively successful in keeping them out, even through the rough economic times brought by the Panic of 1893. Continued financial difficulties, however, combined with the subway suffering constant building delays, made it harder and harder to fill houses and apartments in Harlem. In the words of Cruse, whites used "all means—legal, persuasive, and conspiratorial—to stem the negro influx which assumed mass proportions around 1905."[12]

It was going to take work to defeat this kind of intransigence. And the base of that work began far, far away in Alabama, where Booker T. Washington founded the National Negro Business League in 1900. Among his acolytes were Charles W. Anderson, a Republican politician appointed collector of internal revenue of New York by Teddy Roosevelt, and Philip A. Payton, a real estate salesman. Together, along with T. Thomas Fortune, editor of the *New York Age*—the oldest Black newspaper in the city—they created the Afro-American Realty Company (AARC). The AARC would lease or buy apartments that had either been abandoned by whites or weren't being rented, then rent them to Black residents.[13] Black migrants in need of a place to live didn't mind white neighbors, but established whites certainly did mind Black neighbors. As James Weldon Johnson noted, "The whole movement, in the eyes of whites, took on the aspect of an 'invasion'; they became panic-stricken, and began fleeing as from a plague. The presence of one colored family in a block, no matter how well bred and orderly, was sufficient to precipitate a flight. House after house and block after block was actually deserted."[14]

And the AARC was profitable. The group incorporated with $500,000 at $10 per share, hoping to expand not only to the renting of available space but the building of new apartment buildings. The AARC only technically lasted about five years. Most Black migrants moving to the area didn't have the kind of available money to capitalize such an endeavor, and therefore weren't able to add to the coffers. But it spurred similar action outside of its corporate bounds. Payton combined with a colleague to buy two five-story apartment buildings. John E. Nail, the investor who really took the real estate mantle from Payton, bought a series of houses and apartment buildings in

Harlem. But it wasn't just leading real estate investors who made it their duty to create a place for Black migrants to Harlem. The congregation of St. Philips Episcopal Church bought a row of thirteen apartment buildings, for example. The AARC, in other words, spurred others to action. It wasn't simply civil rights activism that won Harlem for New York's Black residents; it was also what Cruse described as "black economic nationalism."[15]

Many of the Caribbean radicals who came north to New York, suffering as they had under the colonial thumb of England, brought a version of that nationalism with them. But not all of them did. Radicalism from the West Indies was multifaceted in its public display, but those differences tended to cluster into two broader groups, the first making a nationalist argument stemming from the intellectual lodestar of Marcus Garvey. Born in Jamaica in 1887, Garvey grew up in economic depression and under the colonial thumb of England. He dropped out of school at an early age to earn money for his family and found work in a print shop. It was there that he first became involved in radical politics and was fired after trying to lead a strike and attempting to publish his own reform newspaper. So in 1910, like so many others in the region, he left, traveling with tens of thousands of others to Central America. From there he traveled to Europe, learning along the way of the plight of Black people throughout the world. In London he came under the influence of the Sudanese-Egyptian Pan-Africanist Dusé Mohamed Ali, a polymath who at the time was engaged in publishing the nationalist *African Times and Orient Review*, as well as Booker T. Washington, with whom he developed a correspondence. He returned to Jamaica in 1914, as so many others were returning after the completion of the Panama Canal, to start an organization that would both uplift the race all over the world and promote a kind of Washingtonian self-help ethic, one built on a fusion of the ideologies of Ali and Washington—the Universal Negro Improvement Association.[16]

The general goal of the UNIA was "to work for the general uplift of the Negro peoples of the world," but its activities in Jamaica for its first two years were largely limited to trying to establish educational and industrial colleges on the model of Washington's Tuskegee in an effort to develop a path out of tenancy in the wake of the British government's elimination of the competitive civil service exam. In the hopes of raising funds for his fledgling organization and starting a UNIA branch in the United States, Garvey came to Harlem in March 1916, again following the path of so many of his countrymen. His success was limited for his first three years in New York, but the galvanizing upheaval of World War I and the increasing migration from the West Indies led the UNIA to fully find its footing in 1919 and 1920, when it began developing chapters across the United States, the Caribbean, and Latin America. Garvey also created the *Negro World*, a weekly paper published in Harlem and distributed throughout the world through the UNIA. Its estimated circulation at its height was around 200,000, but it was banned by many colonial governments for its uncompromising Black nationalist message.[17]

Garvey's was a complete Pan-Africanist vision, arguing that colonization affected all Black and brown peoples, whether under the thumb of a traditionally conceived colonial government or not. The unity of the Black world was not just theoretical for Garvey. He hoped to develop Liberia as a permanent home for people of African descent in the Western world, to create a legitimate homeland in Africa. He also began conceiving a variety of businesses that would help generate insular economies among colonized peoples. In August 1920, the UNIA held its international convention in Harlem and announced the creation of the Black Star Line, a shipping company designed to compete with white importers. That summer, the UNIA was at the height of its power. But while sale of company stock brought hundreds of thousands of dollars into the UNIA, the company failed in 1922, and Garvey and other UNIA leaders were jailed and convicted on mail-fraud charges.[18]

There were legitimate accounting irregularities with the Black Star Line, but his arrest and incarceration were more complicated than that. His closest supporters claimed that the arrest was politically motivated by white officials, and concern about government collusion still exists on the part of many activists. What is certain, however, is that Garvey's arrest was, in fact, aided by Caribbean immigrants, those radicals from the islands whose ideology formed the other dominant group, moving along a parallel trajectory—those advocating communism. Garvey did not support communism, arguing that it was an economic system designed to benefit white people over and against the victims of colonialism. "It is a dangerous theory of economic and political reformation because it seeks to put government in the hands of an ignorant white mass who have not been able to destroy their natural prejudices towards Negroes and other non-white people," he wrote. "While it may be a good thing for them, it will be a bad thing for the Negroes who will fall under the government of the most ignorant, prejudiced class of the white race."[19]

That would necessarily put him at odds with Caribbean communists like Cyril Briggs, leader of the African Blood Brotherhood. The Brotherhood was founded in New York, but Briggs was another West Indian migrant, born in Nevis in 1888 and arriving in Harlem in 1905. Initially, Briggs had argued for African repatriation and a version of Black nationalism, but his ideology evolved to adopt a radical socialism as the best method of Black liberation.[20] His conflict with Garvey really began after trying to recruit communist supporters from within the UNIA. He would continue to grow more critical of Garvey as time passed, in particular scoffing at the handling of the Black Star Line. It was Briggs and fellow Caribbean socialist ally W. A. Domingo who first published exposés of what they described as fraudulent business dealings by Garvey and his UNIA. Their reports, published separately in their respective publications, the *Crusader* and the *Emancipator*, did not lead postal inspectors to Garvey, but their work bolstered the government's case and helped land the Pan-Africanist leader in prison.[21]

It was a demonstration in microcosm that West Indian radicalism was not monolithic, and in fact developed on two distinct and parallel tracks, one advocating socialist economics and the other trumpeting Black nationalism. Both, however, were seeking the death of colonialism in the Caribbean and in Africa. When both strains of that activism arrived on the shores of the United States, they began working for Black liberation in their new country, as well.

One of the most influential of those activists was Hubert Henry Harrison, who A. Philip Randolph called the "Father of Harlem Radicalism." Originally from St. Croix, Harrison arrived in New York at age seventeen in 1900. Over the next three decades, Harrison would be an author, labor organizer, and street speaker. Harrison became an intellectual lodestar for many because his thinking served as a big tent that included both of those intellectual strains. He helped edit the socialist *Messenger* magazine of Randolph and Chandler Owen, for example, and he also helped edit Garvey's *Negro World*. "Harrison occupied a very unusual position intellectually and politically," argues Winston James. "He was a major inspiration for two powerful and seemingly incompatible currents of black radicalism in Harlem: revolutionary socialism, on the one hand, and radical black nationalism, on the other."[22]

Brathwaite's parents were among a cluster of Caribbean immigrants finding a home in New York during the era of the Harlem Renaissance and using their new surroundings as a base of activism for a distinctly West Indian vision of Black nationalism. The most influential of those immigrants was Marcus Garvey, but he was not alone. Joel Augustus Rogers, for example, was, like Garvey, a Jamaican by birth who came to the United States in 1906. Like Garvey, he also wrote vigorous denunciations of the elimination of Jamaica's competitive civil service exam. In 1917 he published *From Superman to Man*, which uses a debate between a Black Pullman car porter and a white southern politician to make the case against assumptions of Black inferiority. He also wrote regularly for Black newspapers, including Garvey's *Negro World*, and even interviewed Garvey in prison in 1926. The Jamaican icon told Rogers that he planned even more efforts like the Black Star Line upon his release and criticized mainstream civil rights organizations. "The NAACP encourages Negroes to move into white neighborhoods," said Garvey, "then turns around and cashes in on them." After Garvey's release and deportation, Rogers covered his European travels for the *Pittsburgh Courier*. Rogers also wrote as an amateur historian, publishing several books highlighting historical Black achievements, influencing a generation of Harlem leaders and using his version of the Talented Tenth to give lie to theories of white superiority.[23]

Then there was Richard B. Moore from the Brathwaites' native Barbados. Moore came to New York as a teenager in 1909. He was the educational director for Cyril Briggs's African Blood Brotherhood, as well as secretary of the Harlem Educational Forum and director of the Institute for Social Study. In 1915 he even founded a cooperative grocery. It was an interesting alliance, as it was Briggs and the African Blood Brotherhood whose reporting on Garvey's shipping program validated his arrest and helped lead to his imprisonment. Moore, in fact was part of the effort to expose fraud in Garvey's organization, putting him, at various points, on the opposite political side of his West Indian compatriots.[24]

Or at least some of them. Moore's role is chronicled most effectively and comprehensively by historian Joyce Moore Turner, who is Moore's daughter. She has claimed that though Moore disagreed with Garvey, he did not have any role in the effort to jail and deport him. That is not true. It was the work of Briggs and W. A. Domingo that exposed the reality that Garvey had been claiming ownership of shipping vessels he didn't technically own when he began selling stock in the Black Star Line. Moore and Thomas Potter were the ones who investigated the ownership claims and fed the information to publications like Briggs's *Crusader* and Domino's *Emancipator*, which ultimately led to Garvey's indictment. Briggs and Moore, along with Domingo and Potter, and others not from the Caribbean like A. Philip Randolph, believed that socialism, not separatism, was the key to Black salvation. Theirs was a vision, then, opposed to that of their West Indian counterpart. Moore later claimed that the schism began when Garvey met with leaders of the Ku Klux Klan and endorsed a statement made by then-president Warren G. Harding that fundamental differences between the races would always make it impossible for Black and white residents to live together on equal terms. The African Blood Brotherhood and the Black socialists condemned both Harding and Garvey, and many among them began working for Garvey's deportation, thereby creating the two parallel tracks of West Indian thought in Harlem, one advocating versions of socialism built on the work of leaders like Briggs and the other advocating versions of nationalism built on the work of leaders like Garvey.[25]

Moore, a longtime representative of the former, was a popular street speaker; in 1926 he was arrested in a police crackdown against street speaking, and more than five hundred people rallied in a demonstration against the arrest. Two years later he unsuccessfully tried a run for Congress.[26] Moore joined the Communist Party during the Great Depression but was later expelled for his nationalism. He worked for the next four decades for unity among the West Indian population in New York and colonial independence for Caribbean nations as part of groups like the United Caribbean American Council. He also owned and operated Harlem's Frederick Douglass Memorial Book Store, creating a repository of literature on the experiences of African American, Caribbean, and African peoples. Moore was an author, a historian, who also worked to expand that literature. In so doing, he joined a contingent of West Indian immigrants that shaped a new international socialist radicalism in Harlem. Moore joined A. M. Wendell Malliet, Cyril Phillips, Captain Hugh Mulzac, Reginald Pierrepointe, Sudia Masoud, Otto and Hermina Huiswoud, and others to shape a new Black left fundamentally contingent upon a radical economic thought crafted from experiences with colonialism and poverty in the Caribbean.[27]

Then there were the West Indian immigrants who didn't necessarily identify as decidedly socialist or nationalist. Arthur Schomburg, Hubert H. Harrison, Claude McKay, George Padmore—each evolved varying theories of rights advocacy over time. None of this should be surprising. The Caribbean was no monolith. Domingo and Garvey had been involved in trade unions on the home islands. Claude McKay and Charles Petioni had been influenced by British Fabians. Samuel Haynes had been disillusioned while serving in the British military. Then there was the variance in experience in Harlem itself. As Winston James has noted, Caribbean migrants had "a long and distinguished tradition of resistance" and "a sense of self-confidence and pride that would have predisposed at least some of them to radical activity." That radicalism came in a variety of forms, often opposed to one another, as were the socialists and the nationalists.[28]

It was the nationalist track of radical West Indian thought, however, that would be most influential to Brath, the line feeding from the fount of Marcus Garvey's influence and given its longtime twentieth-century representation by Carlos Cooks. Cooks immigrated to New York from the Dominican Republic in 1929. Even before his move to the United States, he attended meetings of the Garvey-led UNIA with his father, who was devoted to

Garvey's cause. At age nineteen, he joined the Universal African Legion of the Garvey Union and began making his name as a street preacher and activist. He enrolled as a correspondence student with Garvey's School of African Philosophy in the 1930s, and in 1939, he lobbied Congress on behalf of Garvey, even meeting with Mississippi's Theodore Bilbo and giving Garveyite approval to the senator's infamous Liberia repatriation bill. (J. A. Rogers, meanwhile, thought the alliance a dangerous one, arguing that "Garvey's biggest mistake" was "his flirting with the Klan. His theory was that he and the Klan could work together, because even as the clan wanted to make America a white man's land so he wanted to make Africa a Black man's land. This was as lunatic a piece of logic as could be found inside or outside an insane asylum." This new alliance with Bilbo was simply Garvey's mistake rehashed.)[29]

Like so many other nationalists, Cooks walked a fine line between influence and ignominy. He first came to wider attention in the city in 1936. Cooks staged a street meeting in front of the Bella Restaurant, an Italian eatery, in response to Italy's attack on Ethiopia. The police predictably attacked, leading to, in the words of the *Amsterdam News*, a "sidewalk riot" that injured several, including three policemen. Cooks was arrested.[30] At the same time, however, he was part of a delegation of Black city leaders meeting with New York mayor Fiorello LaGuardia, another representative of Italian America, to discuss racial problems in the city and issues of police brutality. He was only twenty-three that summer, but he was able to move relatively seamlessly between the worlds of protest and politics.[31]

The year after Garvey's 1940 death, Cooks created the African Nationalist Pioneer Movement, which he envisioned as a logical extension of the UNIA. The group was dedicated to "bringing about a progressive, dignified, cultural, fraternal and racial confraternity amongst the African peoples of the world." Early in the war effort, however, those ideals manifested themselves in praise of Hitler. "Personally," he announced, "I admire any white man who can organize white people to kill each other. The white race should produce more Hitlers. If there were more Hitlers we wouldn't have a damn thing to worry about."[32] It was a similar way of thinking that made allying with Bilbo possible. And it led Cooks to anti-Semitism. "Jews are all Communist," John Roy Carlson reported Cooks as saying in one of his well-attended street speeches, "I wouldn't life my finger to save a Jew." Other of his statements were more defensible. "We came here against our will," he told that same audience. "They brought us here as slaves and they've treated us as slaves. We owe nothing to America. America owes everything to us. This isn't my culture. Cooks isn't my name. This isn't my home. My home and my culture and my name are in Africa." He also published a newsletter, the *Street Speaker*, to codify his ideas and provide another avenue to get them to the Harlem public.[33]

The magazine's first edition appeared in April 1940. In it, Cooks wrote about the early history of the slave trade. There were small bits of domestic news and broadsides to encourage readers to "patronize Negro business." Cooks wasn't the only author, but he was the principal author. In one article on Garveyism, Cooks explained that "Garveyism advocates the universal confraternity of all Negroes irrespective to where they may be born, what language they may speak or what nationality they may claim as long as their pigmentation is black or their ethnological characteristic is that of the member of the African race." Advertisements for Harlem businesses framed accounts of the Advance Division of the UNIA. It was a small publication, and it didn't last long in its initial incarnation.[34]

After the war, Cooks joined the Universal African Nationalist Movement as its international organizer. He also devoted much of his time to "Buy Black" campaigns, which encouraged Black residents of Harlem to only patronize stores owned by Black entrepreneurs. It was an economic nationalism that accompanied the cultural nationalist efforts to convince African Americans to wear natural hairstyles and to reject the term "Negro." In 1949 he revived his original African Nationalist Pioneer Movement, pushing his "Buy Black" campaign, organizing celebrations of Garvey's birthday, and hosting beauty contests that celebrated natural Black beauty standards—all of which Brath would revive. In 1955 Cooks reformed the *Street Speaker*, which in its second run focused far more on the politics of African colonialism than it had previously.[35]

Cooks was also a substantial influence on Malcolm X, and his ANPM often worked with the Nation of Islam, particularly in the late 1950s during celebrations of Marcus Garvey Day, when Cooks and Malcolm shared the speaking stage, and in 1960 when both the Congo's Patrice Lumumba and Ghana's Kwame Nkrumah visited Harlem. Nkrumah had been educated at Pennsylvania's Lincoln University. He proclaimed that independent Ghana would show the world that Africans could take the "lead in justice, tolerance, liberty, individual freedom and social progress" and publicly called for African Americans to help Ghana's development, tapping into the Pan-Africanism of Garvey. Two years later, Cooks sought to capitalize on that momentum. He broke ground on the Marcus Garvey Memorial Building, intended to memorialize Garvey and provide a permanent home for the ANPM. The construction was beset by controversies and delays, and was never completed, but the effort demonstrated the scale of Cooks's thinking. He died in May 1966 after complications from a stroke.[36]

One of his most devoted allies was Professor Rayfus Waldo Williams, who served as the education leader of the African Nationalist Pioneer Movement. "By controlling the education of our race, the whites have succeeded in keeping from the minds of Black People in America, any knowledge of their long and glorious past," Williams argued in Cooks's *Street Speaker*. "We of the African Nationalist Pioneer Movement, know that if our race is to be free, we cannot entrust the training of our minds to those who have enslaved us. For only a foolish jailer would give his prisoners the key." Williams was not from the Caribbean but was still a migrant, from Columbia, South Carolina, part of the Great Migration that came to Harlem. Involved in the West Indian community as he was, Williams married a Jamaican woman, tying himself directly to the community. "When the true forces of nationalism assume the reins of Africa's destiny," he argued in 1962, "every enemy of her freedom, every traitor bearing guilt of participation, aiding or abetting the rape of the Congo and the murder of Patrice Lumumba, will face a day of reckoning. Eventually, justice will write their epitaphs on the tombstones of oblivion."[37] He was known as a forceful critic of the *New York Times* as a paper that upheld white supremacy and became a philosophical inspiration for the principles of Kwanzaa.[38] Williams's most well-known work was a poem published in the ANPM's journal, *Black Challenge*:

Hail Lumumba! Man of Africa
Who stands like a mighty dam
Against the floods of oppression
A granite wall of reality before
The white man's dream of madness.
To keep the African his slave and Africa
His feasting ground of exploitation.

Hark! The Congo is free
The heart of Africa beats again at last
The pulsating throb of Freedom is felt
Throughout the land
The giant awakens and lifts His mighty hand
To smite the leeches who sucked
His blood while so long he slept.[39]

It was this emphasis on "the pulsating throb of Freedom" that maintained a consistent line through all Caribbean radicalism that was such an influence on Elombe Brath, whose life embodied that pulse, that devotion to Patrice Lumumba, to African liberation, and to Black internationalist politics. And it was his artistic talent that gave that embodiment its earliest, loudest voice.

2

THE LIFE AND WORK OF ELOMBE BRATH

Brath, born in 1936 to Barbadian parents steeped in the radical postcolonial politics of the Caribbean and never able to meet Marcus Garvey himself, was a devoted follower of both Cooks and Williams. "Our father was a tailor on Seventh Avenue at 134th Street and we used to leave there at night and head for the crowds at 125th Street and Seventh Avenue" where Cooks was speaking, remembered Brath's brother, Ronnie Brathwaite. "We couldn't leave. We'd stay there all night, listening to these men speak. You could actually learn world history on that corner." Cooks "could do fantastic things on that ladder."[1] The West Indian strain of Black radicalism would not be an island unto itself, its adherents in New York interacting with other Black radicals seeking equalization efforts on various fronts. There was, for example, Cooks's substantial influence on the thinking of Malcolm X, and though Brath criticizes Malcolm and Elijah Muhammad in *Color Us Cullud!*, he too had a working relationship with Malcolm. But the nature of Caribbean radicalism was different from other US-based nationalist Black thinking. It was more rooted in Africa, in global thought, and in racial politics as a form of anticolonialism. It was more secular than more traditional rights movements stemming largely from the American South prior to the advent of the Black Power movement after 1965. It was, in other words, an ideological third way between traditional Black middle-class politics—represented by the NAACP and what would become the classical civil rights movement—and the radicalism of groups like the Nation of Islam and what would become Black Power, a non-aligned movement that maintained the legacy of Garvey and provided an international framework through which African Americans could interpret their own struggle for rights.

Perhaps fittingly, a broader international nonaligned movement developed in the wake of the post–World War II bipolar politics of the Cold War. In 1955, when Brath was still young eighteen-year-old Cecil Brathwaite, the Afro-Asian Conference convened in Bandung, Indonesia. It was a year after Malcolm's move to Harlem, just months before the onset of the Montgomery Bus Boycott that would make Martin Luther King a household name. Convened by the prime ministers of Indonesia, India, Burma, Ceylon, and Pakistan, the conference featured representatives of twenty-nine nonwhite nations whose populations totaled more than a billion people. Its message was a radical anticolonialism and a dedication to national self-determination. Attendees challenged racism and imperialism in all their forms, breaking the bipolar geopolitical model that reigned during the Cold War.[2] As the plotting of that global third way took root, it mirrored that Caribbean radical strain in Black politics from the 1920s onward, providing a third way between the traditionally understood though functionally ahistorical poles of the civil rights movement, which tracked Malcolm and his acolytes on one side and King and his acolytes on the other, thus keeping radical African American eyes on Africa.[3] Though Brath was born in Brooklyn, he was born to both biological and ideological West Indian parents and would always carry that strain of activism, which began by pivoting on a distinctly Harlem-Caribbean axis (on the Garveyite nationalist side of those parallel Caribbean strains) and ultimately witnessed its maturation rotating on a distinctly Harlem-African axis, into the twenty-first century.

Cecil T. Brathwaite and Margaret Etelka Maloney-Brathwaite, Brath's parents, migrated to Brooklyn in the 1920s from Barbados, part of the broader migratory wave affecting the bulk of the Caribbean after World War I. His mother was born in 1905 and came to United States in 1922. The elder Cecil Brathwaite was born in Barbados in 1896, and like so many other migrants, he first traveled to Central America and Cuba before finally arriving in New York in 1924, where he established himself as a tailor, opening two stores in Harlem. His Day Star Cleaners and Dryers became a Harlem institution, often catering to a variety of celebrities. Ten years after his arrival, in 1934 he would marry his fellow Barbadian Etelka. Brathwaite's first child and namesake would be born on September 20, 1936, and would be raised in the Bronx in a diverse migrant culture. While his father was a tailor by trade, he was also a talented artist and taught all three of his sons the fundamentals of composition. Building off his father's early teaching, the younger Cecil Brathwaite studied at the High School of Industrial Art and the School of Visual Arts.[4]

Along with his artistic pursuits, however, the young Brathwaite also became involved in radical politics. In 1956 he joined his brother Kwame and several others to form the African Jazz-Art Society and Studios (AJASS), an organization originally designed to reclaim jazz as an authentically African art form, but soon to branch out to defend a variety of cultural forms in the United States and to use them to promote Garveyite Pan-African nationalism.[5] But his focus was also on Africa. In 1960 he began a long relationship with the South West African People's Organization (SWAPO), the liberation movement for the occupied nation that would later become Namibia. Members of the group were "the sole and authentic representatives of the Namibian people," he argued, and defended SWAPO and their fight against South African occupation at both American and African events, as well as at the United Nations, remaining a vocal supporter until Namibia finally achieved its independence from South Africa in March 1990.[6] That work would lead to a lifetime of effort to aid African liberation movements. He worked with leaders like Samora Machel of Mozambique, Thomas Sankara of Burkina-Faso, Kanyama Chiume of Malawi, and Robert Mugabe of Zimbabwe. He served as Gil Noble's consultant on African affairs for his television program *Like It Is*, airing on WABC in New York from 1968 into the twenty-first century. He also hosted his own radio show, *AfriKalidescope*, on New York's WBAI, a program that highlighted postcolonial problems throughout the world.[7]

His AJASS aided the Nigerian independence movement in 1970. "We believe in a united Nigeria," he told the *New York Times* in response to the Biafran War. European nations were interested in seeing it balkanized because it was "the largest black nation in Africa" with "vast potential wealth and the largest standing black army."[8] When a group of protestors from the South African Students Organization (SASO) were arrested in Durban to a surge of international outcry, Brath became one of their loudest defenders in the United States. Working with the SASO Nine Defense Committee, he participated in press conferences and worked for the release of the students. He also served as a representative for the Federation of Pan-Afrikan Nationalist Organizations, which advocated tirelessly for an end to colonialism in Africa. "We hope," said Brath in founding the organization, "to politicize the masses of black people to put pressure on black politicians to get them to speak up in America for Africa the way Jewish politicians speak up for Israel."[9]

He traveled regularly to the continent in service to postcolonial governments as a representative of the United States. The southern region was of particular importance to Brath, and he worked with a variety of groups and in a variety of settings to help end colonial regimes in places like South Africa. He was careful to emphasize, in nationalist fashion, that domestic race relations needed to be analyzed in relation to international imperialism and white supremacy, and that the struggle in South Africa was less a struggle against apartheid and more a struggle for control of land. In the 1980s, Brath never hesitated to criticize the Reagan administration's friendly relations with South Africa. "It is a known fact that many of the men around the President, and even he himself, have no great sympathy for Black people," he explained in 1982, "but are very understanding of the plight of the white community in South Africa." In 1990 he even helped bring Nelson and Winnie Mandela to Harlem. His work in the region would earn him dozens of honors from African nations and a place in the history of anticolonialism on the continent.[10]

Much of that work was funneled through the Patrice Lumumba Coalition (PLC), founded by Brath in 1967. Named after the Pan-Africanist independence leader and first prime minister of the Republic of the Congo (to whom Brath also co-dedicated *Color Us Cullud!*), the Coalition was designed to be a clearinghouse for political advocacy for anticolonial movements in Africa. The death of Lumumba affected Brath greatly. After his assassination in 1961, the African Jazz-Art Society presented *A Portrait of Patrice Lumumba*, a theatrical performance coauthored by Brath.[11] The PLC, the organizational extension of that reverence, also hosted weekly forums on Friday evenings at Harlem's Harriet Tubman School. "Our purpose from the very start was to have an organization and forums that would advocate an African internationalist perspective," Brath explained. "That is, we saw a need to have a Pan-Africanist outlook with a class component."[12] In 1975 the PLC began advocating against colonial efforts in Angola and for the independence effort in that nation, the People's Movement for the Liberation of Angola (MPLA). But the group's efforts also emphasized the African National Congress in South Africa and similar groups in Mozambique and Zimbabwe, along with its continued support of SWAPO in Namibia.[13]

It was vital work that would define much of Brath's later life. *Color Us Cullud!*, however, deals more comprehensively with Brath's thinking about domestic policy. Beginning in 1962, Brath and his African Jazz-Art Society began organizing a series of fashion shows designed to highlight Black feminine beauty in its natural state, without playing to dominant mainstream tropes of white beauty—an effort feeding from that of his mentor Cooks. The shows featured a group of Black women known as the Grandassa Models, who demonstrated Black beauty in its natural state. The event was, according to the AJASS, "the original African coiffure and fashion extravaganza deigned to restore our racial pride and standards." It was an effort that generated the "Black Is Beautiful" campaign in the 1960s and 1970s, the germ of another idea presented by Carlos Cooks while a younger Brath watched from the street corner. Cooks turned to a group of women in the crowd, shouting, "Your hair has more intelligence than you," referring to their straightened and colored hairdos. "In two weeks, your hair is willing to go back to Africa and you'll still be jivin' on the corner." It was a problematic display of gender policing, but it was also a pronouncement that always stuck with Brath and helped influence the AJASS fashion shows. They were, in a sense, the domestic outgrowth of his work with Africa and part of his Garveyite nationalist legacy. Brath even credited the phrase "Black Is Beautiful" to his mentor. "The original statement of the aforementioned wording can be traced back to the philosophy of Marcus Garvey," he explained. He referenced a 1927 *Amsterdam News* account describing Garvey's appeal: "In a world where Black is despised, he (Garvey) has taught them that Black is Beautiful."[14]

"We believe in, what I like to call 'ethnicticity,' that is to say, the purest form of authenticity in anything we do, that is ethnic," Brath wrote in promotional materials for the fashion shows. "We feel that our race has reached a new low point, in racial integrity, and its highest point in ridicule," he explained, so "we have designed a show, which we believe reflects favorably upon our pride and beauty." He and those who worked with him wanted to restore pride in natural Blackness as an antidote to media teachings that physical features associated with Blackness were to be hated. "Slowly but surely, we will restore dignity to the words kinky . . . wooly . . . nappy and most of all, the word BLACK."[15]

And the effort was having its intended effect. "The black man here is now proud of his blackness," he explained in 1970. "He's starting to wear African clothes, he's trying to speak the language, he's calling himself an African and he is eating African foods. The only thing left is for him to be in Africa."[16]

The group accompanied the fashion show with a theatre production, written by Brath, that satirized civil rights issues and other race-related current events. As the 1960s wore on, the AJASS added more events surrounding the fashion show. There were African dances, there were art exhibits. The group also began developing other kinds of shows. In October 1969, Brath produced *Of Land, Lunatics & The Cosmos*, a dramatic program designed to merge the thinking of Frantz Fanon and Marcus Garvey. In publicity for the show, Brath discussed Fanon's concept of African revolution, "the conquest by the peoples of the lands that belong to them. If we truly understand what Dr. Fanon meant," he argued, "and weigh it against Marcus Garvey's call to hitch our hope to the stars—Our Star of Destiny . . . then we can really begin to put together and into effect a dynamic program to solve the universal Black plight of injustices, and coordinate the international African Revolution." Brath was an activist and an artist, who understood that art, by way of cartoons, fashion, painting, dance, or jazz, could precipitate revolution. "We're hoping to develop a working coalition among as many Brothers and Sisters in the Black Movement," he said in a description of one of the AJASS fashion shows, "to politicize the masses of our people into a practical and honest relationship with Africa."[17]

It was also the fashion show that would lead to a milestone in Brath's personal life. Nomsa Helene White was the president of the Grandassa Models and close contact with the founder ultimately blossomed into love. Brath and White were married on August 23, 1964. They would have seven children. Perhaps more importantly to Brath's activism, his wife would be a substantial collaborator on what would become the family's varied projects.[18]

Brath also worked tirelessly on issues of criminal justice. In 1987 he helped found the December 12 Movement in response to the murder of Caribbean-born Michael Griffith in Howard Beach, Queens. Griffith had been hit by a car and killed after being chased onto the highway by a group of white youths. The movement was designed, as Brath described it, to carry on the ideology represented by the Patrice Lumumba Coalition, but to do so "on the political action front."[19]

He also advocated tirelessly in the case of Larry Davis, arrested after shooting six police officers in a November 1986 raid on his sister's Bronx apartment. Brath, Davis's lawyers, and many others in the community made the case that Davis shot in self defense—that the raid was a staged attempt to murder the suspect because he knew about drug deals that white cops were facilitating in Black neighborhoods. After being captured, authorities intentionally placed Davis in dangerous situations while in custody, and many charged that law enforcement was still trying to kill him while in jail. Davis was ultimately acquitted of three different murder charges. "Most people can appreciate that the juries in three separate trials have seen through the police scheme to convict Davis on bogus charges to cover up their role in pushing drugs in our neighborhoods," Brath explained. "If the cops are successful in killing Davis, his blood will not only be on the hands of those who actually carried out the act, but it will be equally on the hands of those leaders who did not speak out in his defense." Eventually, Brath's fears would be realized.

Davis was finally convicted on a fourth murder charge in 1991 and was killed in prison in 2008.[20]

Along with the Griffith and Davis cases, Brath also worked with activists to protest the perceived racial injustice in the case of Tawana Brawley, who accused four white men of a racially motivated rape in Wappingers Falls, New York, in November 1987. Brawley was later determined to have lied about the assault, but prior to new revelations that seemed to disprove her claims, the case had rallied many in the Black community, including both Brath and perhaps her loudest defender, Al Sharpton.[21]

Brath and Sharpton were both staunch initial defenders of Brawley, but whatever relationship existed between them would be quickly strained. Brath would become one of Sharpton's most vocal Black critics. His December 12 Movement would denounce Sharpton as a "traitor" and opportunist who collaborated with white law enforcement when it suited his interests. Both leaders rejected the grand jury's supposition that Brawley had staged her assault. Brath rebuked the state attorney's investigation, but also "ludicrous statements and demagoguery remarks" made on Brawley's behalf by Sharpton. The relationship didn't get better with time. Sharpton was "a known and admitted federal informant" in league with white leaders, Brath claimed. As late as 1990, he expressed his frustration with the Black press for continuing to publicize Sharpton's antics over and against his own more substantive protests. In response to Sharpton's plans for a protest march in Teaneck, New Jersey, after the April 1990 police killing of a teenage boy, Brath boldly claimed that the only way such acts of police brutality would end was if minority groups "fight back vigorously and take a life for a life."[22]

In 1989 that fight led him to become one of the organizers of events to protest on behalf of the innocence of the Central Park Five, a group of five teenagers charged with raping a white jogger in Central Park. The youths confessed, but continuously argued that their confession was coerced. Despite the fact that an FBI rape kit proved that none of the five had committed the crime, the district attorney charged and convicted them anyway. "This case reminds me of the 'Scottsboro Boys' case," Brath told reporters soon after the arrests in April 1989. "Tawana Brawley could talk and identified her attackers, and they arrested nobody. This woman can't even talk and they arrested everybody." Brath worked tirelessly for the boys, speaking on behalf of the families and drawing the kinds of comparisons—like that of Scottsboro—that would demonstrate the bias at the heart of the case. "It's the same old story," he told the *New York Times*. "The press is trying to make our youth out to be some kind of animals, some vicious 'wolf pack.'" When the trial judge seemingly showed favoritism to the prosecution, he was not shy about pointing out the disparity. He attended marches and rallies on behalf of the defendants. He even testified in the trial as a character witness for Kharey Wise, one of the accused.[23]

Such activism kept him in the sights of Justice Department officials. In June 1991, for example, he was pulled from a group of passengers returning from Paris at Newark International Airport, frisked, and interrogated about a trip he had made to Libya back in 1987. Officials told him he was on a list of "suspect individuals" and persons of interest kept by Treasury and Justice. "I am an international activist as well as a journalist," he told reporters, "and have the right to travel without fear of being harassed by the US."[24]

Throughout all these efforts, Brath supported his family as a graphic artist for ABC Television, where he worked from 1962 to 1999. It was his artistic ability, along with his unrelenting effort on behalf of the dispossessed at home and abroad, that defined his life, and in discussions of Brath's activism, that artistry is often subsumed into discussions of his organizing, if not completely overlooked. But it was central to the way he expressed himself. In early 1960, for example, Brath got his first publication, producing a series of twenty cartoons for a book called *Beat Jokes, Bop Humor, & Cool Cartoons*. It was a lighthearted publication, to be sure, but Brath's cartoons pilloried what he saw as white cultural appropriation, as white jazz enthusiasts used the language of jive and beat to simulate an authenticity in the culture that did not exist. The sanctity of jazz and its culture as decidedly Black spaces was obviously important to the co-creator of the African Jazz-Art Society and Studios, and in *Beat Jokes* Brath's cartoons criticize what he sees as the stupidity and drug abuse of a group of interlopers who are, in essence, colonizing something that does not belong to them. For the first time in almost sixty years, those cartoons are reprinted in this edition.[25]

Later in 1960, as he mentions in his introduction to *Color Us Cullud!*, Brath developed a comic strip for short-lived Black newspaper the *New York Citizen-Call*. The strip alternated between two featured characters, Congressman Carter, a Black politician in the mold of Adam Clayton Powell that allowed Brath to critique current political issues, and Beatnick Jackson, an everyman Harlemite who gave voice to a street wisdom about the state of race and civil rights. Like his later work in the coloring book, Brath occasionally used the strip to critique actual political figures, including John F. Kennedy, Malcolm X, and Sammy Davis Jr. It was a step in both Brath's political and comic development, and it was that cartooning ability that ultimately led him to expand his critique in the form of *Color Us Cullud!* The full run of Brath's work for the *Citizen-Call* is also reprinted for the first time in this edition.

Regardless, Brath continued writing, along with his art, often publishing journalism in the New York *Amsterdam News*. He was also a poet.[26] And even in his other endeavors, the language of the coloring book never left Brath and his efforts. In 1973 he helped host Marcus Garvey Jr. at Liberty Hall, Harlem's UNIA headquarters. A decade after the publication of the coloring book, Garvey seemed to mimic its language. Integrationists, entertainers, and popular athletes propped up as Black leaders were part of the problem, he told his audience. "Court jesters who entertain the wealthy whites are always paid well," said Garvey Jr., "but are clowns allowed to lead the white race?"[27]

Brath continued such critiques, combining them with his anti-colonial African activism, until his death on May 19, 2014. The sadness of his death demonstrated the influence of his life. Representatives from the United Nations, American and African governments, and the music industry all attended Brath's funeral. Maya Angelou, herself just days from death, sent a video message, as did Mumia Abu-Jamal. The daughter of Malcolm X read a letter from South African President Thabo Mbeki. Brath was "a true champion of African liberation, who lives his Blackness—walks and talks his Blackness like a robe of honor," said Empress Phile Chionesu, convener of the historic 1997 Million Woman's March.[28]

A year prior to his death in May 2013, Congressman Charlie Rangel, who served Adam Clayton Powell's former district, read a biographical tribute to Brath into the congressional record. Brath was "a living hero of Harlem and an international warrior for the African people."[29] In 2017 officials in New York City named the corner at 125th Street and Adam Clayton Powell Jr. Boulevard "Elombe Brath Way" in recognition of his service to Black rights in the United States and Africa. "Elombe spoke truth to power unrelentingly," said New York councilman Charles Barron. "He gave us the courage and truth we needed in our fight against white supremacy and imperialism."[30]

3

THE RHETORICAL ORIGINS OF ELOMBE BRATH'S SATIRE

"The function of humor and the therapeutic value of the accompanying laughter, inside safe, communal black spaces—whether Granny's front porch or center stage at the Apollo—spoke to specific black experiences," explains historian Bambi Haggins. "Black comedy, in its literal and literary construction, has always overtly and covertly explored the trials, tribulations, and triumphs of African American communities." Haggins describes a transition from the late nineteenth century to the late twentieth wherein a Black humor rooted in laughter "to keep from crying" began to change, became an active agent of protest. "Black humor's potential power as an unabashed tool for social change, for the unfiltered venting of cultural and political anger, and for the annunciation of blackness," began to be realized during the civil rights movement. "The humor, as conceived and received within the community, spoke to a deep cultural impulse," Haggins argues, "extending beyond articulating suffering in muted tones to howling about oppression and subjugation, as well as the victories in survival and amidst strife."[1]

Terrence Tucker has described what he calls comic rage, a form of humor that "centralizes African American experience and, fueled by militant rage, uses a comic lens to examine the complexities and inconsistencies in the American national narrative." It was a humor that, in the words of Glenda Carpio, "functioned as a way of affirming [Black] humanity in the face of its violent denial."[2]

Darryl Dickson-Carr has placed the substantive beginnings of Black satire in the late nineteenth and early twentieth centuries in the novels of authors like Charles Chesnutt and Pauline Hopkins. It was muted satire, to be sure, but Chesnutt used his protagonist and narrator Uncle Julius McAdoo "to undermine common, humiliating literary and cultural stereotypes and to lampoon whites' romantic view of slavery after the peculiar institution's demise."[3] Hopkins was more overt in her satire than Chesnutt. Her novel *Contending Forces: A Romance Illustrative of Negro Life North and South* (1900) satirized anti-miscegenation laws, and *Of One Blood: Or, the Hidden Self* (1903) skewered pseudoscientific academic racism.[4]

Neither of the two, however, were representatives of the radical or nationalist strain in Black literary thought. In the United States, instances of Black nationalist thinking that constitute the genesis of that strain can be seen as early as Benjamin Bannaker's 1791 correspondence with Thomas Jefferson. In the following generation, David Walker became infamous for his 1829 *Appeal*.[5] The physician, journalist, and novelist Martin R. Delany took up the nationalist cause in the antebellum era, as did activists like Paul Cuffe and Daniel Coker, Black proponents of colonization to Africa. Delany was a doctor and a novelist, born free in western Virginia in 1812. He grew up in Pennsylvania and by the 1840s clearly saw Black self-reliance as the only avenue to real freedom. Though he worked at times with Frederick Douglass, who was no nationalist, on his *North Star* newspaper, Delany wanted migration. "We must MAKE an ISSUE, CREATE an EVENT, and ESTABLISH a NATIONAL POSITION for OURSELVES," he said in 1852. By far the most successful Black novelist of the period, his *Blake, or the Huts of America*, a story of the emerging racial consciousness in the southern states, was published as a serial in 1859.[6]

The radical nationalism of Delany, however, did not manifest itself in satire. Thus it was that the mantle of the subtle, more muted satire of Hopkins and Chesnutt would be taken up by those not necessarily part of the nationalist tradition. Nine years after the publication of Hopkins's *Of One Blood*, James Weldon Johnson published *Autobiography of an Ex-Colored Man* (1912).[7] The story describes the life of a mixed-race musician who experiences the white supremacy of the Gilded Age and seeks to pass as white as a result. "The impetus fueling Johnson's narrative experiment seems clearer if one summons to view the African-American male writers tradition," writes Heather Russell Andrade. "Although Johnson's ironic title borders on satire, the discursive subversion marked by satire is meaningless without a clear contextualization of the black male literary enterprise upon which satire would, as it were, 'signify.'"[8] While the irony of the title does frame a form of satire, the violence and racism that the protagonist experiences are all too real. It isn't, in other words, a funny story. That kind of more subtle satire steeped in a form of literary realism, however, would soon give way to more direct forms.

And those direct forms would come within the spectrum of a broader movement with which Johnson is often associated: the Harlem Renaissance. This postwar literary and artistic movement featured the first full reconception of Black literature, but at the same time it produced a literary critique of the movement itself. Wallace Thurman, for example, was, along with other authors like George Schuyler, one of the loudest critics of "of the tenets held by the Negro bourgeoisie." Renoir Gaither has argued that "satire and social realism became for Thurman the chief means by which he attempted to identify, explore, and replace the values associated with the New Negro." Gaither explains that one of Thurman's most common targets was the gentility that underlay the presentation of those antiquated values. For Nathan Irvin Huggins, Thurman "of all the Harlem literati, contained within him the paradoxes of Negro art."[9] And that often made his satire difficult for its targets to see. W. E. B. Du Bois, Eunice Carter, and Sterling Brown, for example, all negatively reviewed Thurman's *The Blacker the Berry* seemingly without an understanding of its ironic tone. *The Blacker the Berry* tells the story of Emma Lou Morgan, a dark-skinned Black woman who experiences colorism in a variety of forms and in a variety of places, on the West Coast during her collegiate years and in Harlem after that. Perhaps his most devastating satire, however, and the one most closely mirroring the work of later artists like Elombe Brath, was his novel *Infants of the Spring*, which pillories Alaine Locke's concept of "the New Negro" and describes the artists of the Harlem Renaissance as living in an apartment building called "Niggerati Manor." There they drink gin and talk about their collective talent without really demonstrating it. Meanwhile, Thurman also takes on himself, describing a character named Raymond Taylor, who unlike many of the others actually does have talent, but takes himself far too seriously to relate to the others in his particular tribe.[10] The principal difference between the characters of *Infants* and those featured in Brath's *Color Us Cullud!* is that those in the former are given pseudonyms and couched in the narrative fullness of a novel, but the trajectory of the criticism and the comedy of its presentation are much the same.

The first half of Richard Bruce Nugent's *Gentleman Jigger* does much the same thing, using satire to pillory the main drivers of the Harlem Renaissance and the assumptions of the Talented Tenth. Like Brath, Nugent was a visual artist, but his painting went in a decidedly different direction, emphasizing graphic depictions of sexuality intended largely to celebrate the act rather than to satirize the libidinousness of the era.[11]

Another author to riff on the same themes presented by Thurman and Nugent was Dorothy West, though her signal work in this regard, *The Living Is Easy*, did not appear until 1948.

West had been a young author during the Harlem Renaissance, a cousin of Helene Johnson and friend of Thurman and Langston Hughes, but by 1948 she demonstrated the ironic, critical eye of her forebears. *The Living Is Easy*'s protagonist, Cleo Judson, is the daughter of sharecroppers who becomes part of the Great Migration and seeks for her family to become part of the Boston elite. West had grown up in that Boston elite, attending Boston University and Columbia before moving to nearby Harlem in the 1920s.[12] Her novel, then, was a takedown of Black upper-class mores and pretensions that dominated the accounts of some of her fellows and would also be present in the work of Brath.

Another of the female writers of the Harlem Renaissance, Nella Larsen, could also claim at least a measure of this satiric bent with her novel *Passing* (1929), a bent that engages the same thing as many of the other satires of the period. While it is ostensibly a story of Clare Kendry, who uses her light skin to enter white society and thus loses much of her cultural Blackness in the process, Mary Mabel Youman has argued that the real protagonist is Clare's childhood friend Irene Redfield, who has the ability to pass but almost always chooses not to. It is Redfield, in this interpretation, who "has more truly lost her heritage than Clare who literally removes herself from Black life and lives as a white among whites. The title *Passing* is thus ironic, for it is Irene who 'passes.'" By hoping to rise within the social strata of the Black community rather than hiding away in the white one, "Irene's major concerns in life are security, middle-class morality, and middle-class standing. Anything that threatens these values must be destroyed. In turn, Irene has lost her Black heritage of spontaneity, freedom from convention, and zest for life."[13] It is thus through a complex satire cloaked in a seemingly melodramatic novel that Larsen makes much the same critique as West and Thurman.

The year prior to the publication of Larsen's *Passing*, Rudolph Fisher published *The Walls of Jericho* (1928), which satirizes both classism and colorism within the Black community of Harlem. It was a full-length version of a critique first presented in his short story "The City of Refuge," first published in 1925. That story describes a southern migrant to Harlem who is early enraptured by the city upon arrival, but is eventually duped into becoming a drug dealer by the narrative's end. Fisher's critical lens was not the only element that placed him in this particular line. He was also, like Martin R. Delany a century prior, a medical doctor as well as a novelist. Like both Delany and Brath, Fisher was a devotee of Pan-Africanist thought, an early version of Black nationalist advocacy.[14]

Much of this criticism is embodied directly in Richard Wright's 1937 essay "Blueprint for Negro Writing," in which he argues that "Negro writing in the past has been confined to humble novels, poems, and plays, decorous ambassadors who go a-begging to white America." Those authors "were received as poodle dogs who have learned clever tricks." It was a conclusion with real consequences. The work of Black authors "should have been something of a guide" for the lives of Black readers, but it never reached that plateau. Thus "Negro writing became a sort of conspicuous ornamentation," Wright argued. Black writing "on the whole has been the voice of the educated Negro pleading with white America. Rarely has the best of this writing been addressed to the Negro himself, his needs, his sufferings, and aspirations. Through misdirection Negro writers have been far better to others that they have been to themselves."[15] This essay is a distillation of much of the criticism that had been leveled satirically by so many before him, encapsulating the lament that ironically emanated from the very writers who were the subject of his criticism.

Of course, it was professional critics who often embodied much of this larger critique. Theophilus Lewis, for example, published most of his criticism in A. Philip Randolph and Chandler Owen's magazine *The Messenger*. A drama critic by trade, his work ventured into every area of Black cultural life. "[Lewis's] fundamental theme that the primary need of blacks in establishing their own cultural independence," explains Theodore Kornweibel, "was for a national black theater grounded in the works of black playwrights, was a justifiable criticism." Lewis reviled what he saw as the duplicity of elite Black attitudes, particularly when it came to drama. "When the higher type of Negro goes into the theater, he commonly ignores his own tastes," Lewis wrote in 1926, "and demands that the performance be adjusted to a set of standards alien to birth."[16] Through much of his career Lewis would work closely with the man who would become the most notorious satirist in the generation prior to the appearance of Brath's comic illustrations, George Schuyler.

George S. Schuyler was both a journalist and satirist. He worked with Lewis during his time at the *Messenger* but would later move away from both the socialist periodical and socialism altogether. He was known for his conservatism and for his gleeful willingness to provoke. After World War II, he would even become a vigorous anticommunist and a sometimes opponent of the civil rights movement. Schuyler argued that the best way to speed acceptance by whites was in part by limiting the tendency of Blacks to segregate themselves through outsider art and culture.[17] His satirical masterpiece and most complete novelistic demonstration of his thinking was his novel *Black No More* (1931). In the novel, an African American scientist invents a procedure to turn Black people white, a procedure that becomes so popular with so many that it begins to erode Harlem's economy. It also, however, begins to erode the southern segregationist system, used partly to mistreat Black southerners but also to convince poor whites of their place in the system. The criticism of the procedure leads to strange bedfellows among both the Harlem and white southern elites. The novel is a scathing satire of American racial assumptions in the 1920s and the stakes in maintaining racial categories for both Black and white culturemakers.[18]

Five years prior to the publication of *Black No More*, Schuyler published in the *Nation* another among many controversial essays, "Negro-Art Hokum," in which he advocates Black artists hewing to a standard set by mainstream Western European culture. "The Aframerican," he argues, "is merely a lampblacked Anglo-Saxon" after hundreds of years of close contact with those of European descent. "Negro art 'made in America' is as non-existent as the widely advertised profundity of Cal Coolidge," wrote Schuyler, "or the reported sophistication of New Yorkers. Negro art there has been, is, and will be among the numerous black nations of Africa; but to suggest the possibility of any such development among the ten million colored people in this republic is self-evident foolishness."[19]

In the next issue of the *Nation*, Langston Hughes brutally rebuked Schuyler's claims. In his influential "The Negro Artist and the Racial Mountain," Hughes created a precedent document for the ideology of the Harlem Renaissance. "I am ashamed for the black poet who says, 'I want to be poet, not a Negro poet,' as though his own racial world were not as interesting as any other world," he lamented. "I am ashamed, too, for the colored artist who runs from the painting of Negro faces to the painting of sunsets after the manner of the academicians because he fears the strange un-whiteness of his own features." It was that kind of assumption that created the class of Black leaders that had been lambasted by Thurman and Nugent and West and Larsen. "We younger Negro artists who create now intend to express our individual dark-skinned selves without fear or shame. If white people are pleased we are glad. If they are not, it doesn't matter. We know we are beautiful. And ugly too."[20]

Hughes was perhaps the most successful of the Harlem Renaissance writers. Yet another participant in the Great

Migration originally from Joplin, Missouri, he became one of the most successful authors of the period, merging modernist poetics with jazz. That interest in jazz, and the illustrations that accompanied some of his work as a result, would itself become a precedent for the artistic work of Elombe Brath.[21] But it would be after the Renaissance, during the lean years of World War II, when the author would create his most influential fictional character, one that can serve as a fitting comparative model for the kind of satire in which Brath would engage: Jesse B. Semple.

The character, envisioned by Hughes in 1943 after overhearing a conversation in a Harlem bar, represents, in the words of Donna Akiba Sullivan Harper, "the Negro everyman."[22] He is, like so many others, a southerner who came to Harlem in the Great Migration and has experienced the different kinds of racisms that define the two regions. Semple is estranged from his wife, Isabel, and has a classy girlfriend, Joyce, who is regularly frustrated with the simple pleasures of beer and conversation at the local bar, frustrated with Semple's small salary from his menial job, and frustrated that he cannot or will not get a divorce and marry her. As Harper notes, many of the leading characters in Semple's life are women, but his principal foil is Ananias Boyd, an erudite, college-educated bar patron. If Semple is Hughes's Beatnick Jackson, Boyd is his Congressman Carter. (See the Brath comic strips in Part 3.) He is not, however, a disconnected snob, as the college-educated or middle class might be expected to be portrayed. "Simple not only tolerates the foil's education, he draws upon it," Harper explains. "On the other hand, he feels comfortable reprimanding his bar buddy when he perceives an exaggerated erudition or any other offensive air surfacing. The foil, then, emerges as a sympathetically presented upwardly mobile, college-educated persona."[23]

Their interaction did not play out on the comics pages, but it did play out in the newspaper. Hughes's first Semple column appeared in the *Chicago Defender* in February 1943 as part of the author's weekly column. It was popular and, encouraged by *Defender* publisher John Sengstacke, he continued the episodes regularly. He published his first collection of the stories in 1950, the first of what would be six such collections spanning to 1965 and encompassing the period of Brath's most strident comic output.[24]

Hughes was able to portray Semple, an ordinary working-class man, with dignity. "It is impossible to live in Harlem and not know at least a hundred Simples," he said.[25] As Blyden Jackson has explained, it was an important effort because the assumptions of white America tend to see Black lives as either exceptional, the supposed Talented Tenth, on one hand, or abject failures on the other. "At the very heart of American racism," Jackson writes, "there seems to be an assumption of the most dangerous import: to wit, that there are no Negroes who are average people."[26] And Semple was an average person. "I am what folks calls an ordinary citizen," he said in one of Hughes's columns. "Me, I work, pay my rent, and taxes, and try to get along."[27] Semple is, in that sense, intended to be a stand-in for the average Harlemite. The "Harlemite endures being fired, jim crowed, insulted, eliminated, called black, blackjacked, caught in raids, false arrested, third degreed, caught with another man's wife, and near about lynched," explains Julian Carey. He is a Black man, and "a black man, in order to endure in racist America, must be lonesome inside himself, realizing that as soon as he leaves the third floor rear, Paddy's Bar, and the Harlem sanctuary, he becomes a pariah. Simple, however, is not defeated; nor is he destroyed."[28]

Very much in the style of Brath's characters, Semple criticizes white society and white supremacy; but he also criticizes, in the words of Charles Watkins, "the foolish social climbing, moral hypocrisy, and spiritual emptiness" of Black leaders.[29]

Like Congressman Carter and Beatnick Jackson, the Semple stories, then, feature "two men from different educational and cultural backgrounds" who "meet on an equal plane, exchange ideas, develop a friendship, and bridge the gap between them," largely because the one commonality they share is that "they are both black in a radically unbalanced society."[30]

It was a formula, as it would be for Brath, that allowed Hughes to use satire to comment on the racial issues of the day. He was not the radical that Elombe Brath was, but his work was a precedent document that allowed for the creation of Brath's comic work in his strips and in his comic opus *Color Us Cullud!* When taken together with his individual biography and the influence of Caribbean radicalism on his thought, the development of Black satire, and the work of Langston Hughes in particular, created the possibility of an Elombe Brath, of a fundamentally unique voice in the narrative of Black rights and the push against white supremacy.

Finally, there was a long history of Black cartoonists who used their drawings and humor to provide commentary on contemporary racial situations. As early as the 1880s, the Black press began including cartoons to help make racial points. With the creation of major Black weeklies like the *Baltimore Afro-American* in 1892, the *Chicago Defender* in 1905, the New York *Amsterdam News* in 1909, and the *Pittsburgh Courier* in 1910, the demand for Black cartooning only grew and spread throughout the nation. Comic strips like "Bungleton Green," illustrated by Leslie Malcolm Rogers, debuted in the *Defender* in 1920 and became one of the longest-running comic strips drawn by African Americans and featuring African American characters. Such strips were bolstered over the years by editorial cartoonists who used their work to respond more directly to the news of the day. Such work provided the seedbed for the art of Elombe Brath.[31]

EDITORIAL NOTE

Brath's writing was rarely professionally edited. Its original presentation included spelling errors, inclusions of excessive commas, and other minor grammatical and typographical errors. I have cleaned up those errors without using brackets or *sic* designations in order to keep the author's intended flow. Nothing of substance that would fundamentally alter the meaning of any sentence or phrase has been changed.

Part 2

BRATH'S EARLY WORK

4

DOWN BEAT JAZZ RECORD REVIEWS ILLUSTRATIONS, 1957

In 1957, *Down Beat* magazine released the first in a series of annual collections of jazz record reviews from 1956, and as Christopher Hall notes in his "About the Author" commentary in *Color Us Cullud!*, illustrations for the volume were drawn by Brath. It was his first published work, and it featured caricatures of a variety of jazz stars of the mid-1950s, including Cannonball Adderley, Buddy Arnold, Django Reinhardt, Count Basie, Ella Fitzgerald, the Modern Jazz Quartet, and others. Just as Langston Hughes's satire served as a comparative model for Brath's activist art in the early 1960s, his emphasis on jazz can serve as a comparative model for Brath's jazz caricatures. Two years prior to the publication of *Down Beat*'s first comprehensive record review issue, Hughes published *The First Book of Jazz*, a children's book that described the history and theory of the genre. The illustrations were drawn by Cliff Roberts and served as comical scenes of jazz performances. Much earlier, his book jackets for *The Weary Blues* (1926) and *Not Without Laughter* (1930) also included musical imagery.[1] Of course, actual representations of jazz artists in Hughes's children's book were presented as photographs, but the illustrations of jazz life and the images of jazz performers presaged the caricatures of Brath, spaced intermittently throughout the record reviews.

As Hughes was publishing those works during the Harlem Renaissance, the imagery of painters like Jacob Lawrence and Aaron Douglas presented a vibrant jazz life that properly centered the jazz experience in Black venues with Black performers and demonstrated the power and joy of the music and the clubs where it was performed.[2]

Of course, jazz was also a substantial part of the white imaginary. The book jacket for F. Scott Fitzgerald's *Tales of the Jazz Age* (1922) featured caricatures of jazz scenes. Everyone, both the musicians and those dancing to the music, was white.[3] Perhaps even more problematic were the short film cartoons that featured jazz. In 1936 MGM presented "Old Mill Pond," an incredibly popular cartoon nominated for the Academy Award, which featured Black jazz musicians as frogs in a bayou. The following year, the jazz frogs returned in "Little Ol' Bosko and the Pirates," featuring a young Black child drawn in minstrel style in conflict with the frogs.[4]

It was a legacy of jazz caricature that was inherently racially problematic, countered at the time by the imagery of the Hughes book jackets and the art of Lawrence and Douglas. These works, however, were about jazz life in general rather than caricatured portraits of individual performers. Brath's illustrations for *Down Beat* are among the first comprehensive efforts to depict the stars of the age in caricature. The year prior to publication, Brath and several others created the African Jazz-Art Society and Studios to push back against problematic racial codings of jazz in illustrations, cartoons, and other forms. Jazz was an authentically African art form, the organization argued, and should be represented as such.[5] Brath's cartoons for *Down Beat* do not include any political statements, of course. His was an illustration job, and he performed it by caricaturing both Black and white performers, highlighting the leading figures in the scene. His efforts are included here as demonstrations of the individualized continuation of the efforts of those like Hughes, Lawrence, and Douglas and of Brath's earliest published work.

––––––––––––––

Images from Jack Tracy, ed., *Down Beat Jazz Record Reviews, 1956* (Chicago: Maher Publications, 1957).

Cannonball Adderley

Charlie Parker

Paul Chambers

Fats Waller

Vince Guaraldi

Art Blakey

Ella Fitzgerald

J.J. Johnson and Kai Winding, known as Jay and Kai

Lester Young

Stan Kenton

Art Tatum

Jerry Mulligan

Billie Holiday

Chet Baker

Buddy Arnold

Modern Jazz Quartet

Bud Powell

Billy Taylor

Dizzy Gillespie

Django Reinhardt

Gene Krupa

5

CARTOONS FROM *BEAT JOKES*, *BOP HUMOR*, & *COOL CARTOONS*, 1960

Brath's artistic ability received its largest early national audience in the first months of 1960, prior to the debut of his strip in the New York *Citizen-Call*, with a series of cartoons in the book *Beat Jokes, Bop Humor, & Cool Cartoons*, edited by Bob Reisner and published by the Citadel Press.

Robert Reisner's life was devoted to jazz and jazz culture. In 1951 he formed the Institute for Jazz Studies at Brooklyn College. He also operated a series of Greenwich Village jazz clubs, including the Pad and the Open Door. In 1962 Reisner would publish a biography of Charlie Parker, but prior to that much of his writing centered around humor. In 1958 he published the joke book *Captions Courageous, or Comments from the Gallery* with Herb Kapplow, which became a bestseller. *Beat Jokes, Bop Humor, & Cool Cartoons* combined Reisner's love of humor and his love of jazz culture, playing on the idiosyncrasies of the culture for laughs. "Well, I admit he doesn't blow very well on any of those instruments," says a jazz fan in one of the book's early jokes, "but the guy's quite a showman. Like, you know, he can dance and he's a ventriloquist." His companion replies, "Why doesn't he try that ventriloquist bit on his horn?"[1]

Brath, too, had an abiding interest in jazz and jazz culture. Five years after Reisner founded his Institute for Jazz Studies and four prior to the publication of *Beat Jokes*, Brath had co-founded the African Jazz-Art Society and Studios. His participation with Reisner was an opportunity to publicize his work and make a paycheck through his art, but it also allowed him to ridicule what he saw as white interlopers and phonies moonlighting in jazz culture. In one of his panels, two "jazz" fans decide to start a commotion by playing a record of Guy Lombardo and Lawrence Welk. In another, a worshipful portrait of Jack Kerouac is on the wall, with two white beatniks claiming to be more authentic than him. The group is pilloried as a collection of ignorant, drug-using white dilettantes who don't understand jazz culture and so play on its peripheries with slogans and catchphrases they assume to be keys to the kingdom. It is humor with a different trajectory than that of the coloring book or the *Citizen-Call* comics, but an effort clearly in line with those later, more fulsome and nuanced works. Presented here is the full group of Brath's twenty cartoons originally published in the 1960 collection.

"Man, what a high!"

"Like help!"

"What delegation do you think he's with?"

"I'd do anything for you, Lenora—beg—steal—go com-mercial!"

" 'Take me to your leader'? Man, like take me to your tailor!"

"This ought to shake my man up!"

"All off, baby, all off—bald heads are in this year."

"Lawrence here is a linguist—knows how to make out in nine languages."

"You'll really go for these cats, baby—they're really far out."

"Say, man, did you dig my old lady make her crazy break?"

"*Me and my man here would like to join. We feel that during our experiments we have obtained some highly useful informations.*"

"Dig those crazy ash trays."

"Play eight more bars, then we'll give the cat on table a solo."

"*Let me have some of the same stuff you just sold my man.*"

"Hell, actually I should be acknowledged leader of the sub-
terraneans. I was beat long before Kerouac."

"*Dig that crazy music stand.*"

"Man, even the kids here speak French."

"Like to be or not to be."

"Just drive melody, man. Just drive melody."

"*Dig these new pay toilets.*"

Part 3

COMIC RADICALISM

6

COMIC RADICALISM

The New York *Citizen-Call* was a short-lived Black newspaper running from May 1960 to February 1961. "Our initial hypothesis was simple," explained an editorial in the inaugural issue, "a need exists for another Negro newspaper in New York City—surely America's largest Negro community of one million Negroes should be able to support at least two newspapers." The paper "expects to play its role fully in the universal struggle for equal rights." It advocated for Black business development and trumpeted Black achievement. It took pains in that initial edition to warn the Black community "that this happy road of integration they trod is a two-way street," that the paper would "oppose black racial hatred as vigorously as it fights white bigotry."[1]

The *Citizen-Call* was founded by C. Sumner Stone, a Tuskegee Airman World War II veteran from Hartford, Connecticut. Chuck Stone, as he was known, had accomplished a great deal before publishing the *Citizen-Call*. He had a bachelor's degree in political science from Wesleyan and a master's in sociology from the University of Chicago. After college, he served as an aid worker in Ceylon, Egypt, and India with the humanitarian organization CARE before becoming public relations director for the *New York Age*.[2] From there he made an effort to create his own paper, the New York *Citizen-Call*.

On August 6, 1960, the *Citizen-Call* debuted a comic strip by a new local artist, announcing, "With this cartoon sequence, we are pleased to introduce Cecil Brathwaite. We think you will find him a wise and witty young man." In the paper's next edition, the editors again pushed his work on the front page, publicizing the "furiously funny cartoonist."[3]

The comic strip alternated each week using two principal characters, Congressman Carter and Beatnick Jackson, allowing Brath to specifically address both Black politics and civil rights with the former and racism and the state of the Black community with the latter. Sometimes he fired at actual targets; occasional cartoons featured later coloring book targets like John F. Kennedy, Malcolm X, and Sammy Davis Jr. Others took on racism and racial double standards more broadly. The strip clearly demonstrates the comic development that would find its full flower in the coloring book.

The comic strip was the closest that Brath would come to Hughes's Jesse B. Semple. As Arthur Davis has explained, Hughes created Semple to be "the very highly articulate spokesman of the untrained-worker group and himself the voice of the educated Negro liberal." It was a productive contrast: "Simple generally exemplifies the directness and single-mindedness of the untrained Negro and Hughes the sophisticated tolerance and broadmindedness of the Black intellectual. The clash and interplay of these attitudes furnish much of the humor in Simple, but they also serve a deeper purpose; they point up and accentuate the two-level type of thinking which segregation tends to produce."[4] Thus it was that Hughes's Jesse B. Semple stories enunciated an entertaining elaboration of Du Bois's double consciousness, and a similar enunciation takes place in Brath's Congressman Carter and Beatnick Jackson cartoons.

"You cannot dislike *all* white people for what the bad ones do," says Hughes's erudite narrator. Jesse B. Semple, however, makes the case that exceptions prove the rule. He describes watching a documentary about wildlife protection. "This film showed how they put aside a thousand acres out West where the buffaloes roam and nobody can shoot a single one of them. If they do, they get in jail." It was, he argued, decidedly "more than the government does for me or my kinfolks down South." He suggested creating "Game Preserves for Negroes," a "place where we can go and nobody can jump on us and beat us, neither lynch us nor Jim Crow us every day. Colored folks rate as much protection as buffalo."[5]

Similarly, Congressman Carter represents the sophisticated, high-minded approach of Hughes's narrator, while maintaining a racial awakening. In one of the cartoons, for example, Carter is asked by a reporter the difference between Eisenhower and Kennedy. "Well, Eisenhower plays golf in Georgia," he responds. "Kennedy plays golf in Florida." Meanwhile, Beatnick Jackson gets frustrated because newspaper accounts describe white men and Negroes differently. The ostensible term of respect does not allow Black men to be called "men" in accounts. "All these people put their motherland first, ydig? Now where's Negroland?"[6]

The Semple newspaper columns were a successful formula for Hughes, argues Phyllis Klotman, for four reasons in particular: "1) the sure-fire appeal of the skit technique, 2) an apparent artlessness and simplicity in the development of theme and character, 3) reader identification and 4) the intermittent sound of the blues in prose."[7] The same could be said for Brath's Carter and Jackson comics. Each contained a specific skit that unfolds in the simplicity of eight small panels, using tropes that readers understand, both sides of Du Bois's double consciousness, and in a language that mimics the music of the street, on one hand, and clever political rhetoric on the other.

"Simple is not in the least ashamed of being Black," Melvin Williams explains, and it is "common to find him indulging his fantasies in varied roles of Black political power." In one such fantasy, Simple imagines becoming New York mayor, wherein he would decree "that any colored man who wants to rent an apartment downtown can rent one and no landlord can tell him, 'We do not lease to colored.'"[8] In another, he dreams that he speaks in front of the United Nations, taking as his text the word "Mississippi." Each letter of the state's name represents a descriptive word. The "M," for example, represents murder, "which is what they have done there to Negroes for years just for being colored, with nobody sent to jail, let alone electrocuted." He moves through the letters until he gets toward the end, imagining that he is an angel flying over Mississippi. "I will P all over the state. After which I will double the P, as it is in the spelling," he says. "As I fly, I hope none of them Dixiecrats has time to get their umbrellas up."[9]

Beatnick Jackson shared his frustration. "I don't know if our prestige has declined in the eyes of the rest of the world," he argued, talking about white America writ large, "but it certainly has dropped here in Harlem!!!"[10]

Christopher Hall's "About the Author" section in *Color Us Cullud!* claims that Brath's comic for the *Citizen-Call* helped influence the paper's policy, making it too radical for mainstream survival. While there is no specific evidence to support that claim, it is clear that the paper did begin to change its focus during the tenure of Congressman Carter and Beatnick Jackson. The newspaper, in its initial incarnation, was traditional fare for the Black press. The front-page article of its first edition, for example, was about northern support for Martin Luther King. As time passed, the *Citizen-Call* became more and more focused on African independence movements with a decidedly nationalist perspective, ending its run with coverage of the Mobutu coup in Congo and the murder of Patrice Lumumba. Such coverage may or may not have made the paper influential enemies, but it was clear that its chief woes were financial. Its final edition made several pleas to its readers for an influx of funds. "We need money. $50,000 to be specific," the paper explained. "This is the way business often goes. Just as the mountain peak of success is visible, the climb becomes that much more difficult."[11]

The real reason for the paper's financial woes was that Chuck Stone had taken a job in January 1961 as editor and manager of the Washington *Afro-American*, where he corresponded with coloring book targets like Sammy Davis Jr., Martin Luther King, Adam Clayton Powell, and Jackie Robinson.[12] He would go on to edit the *Washington Star* and the *Chicago Daily Defender*. In 1963, as Brath was writing the coloring book, Stone would make news when he was denied membership in the National Press Club, ostensibly because of his race. From 1965–1967, he served as special assistant to Adam Clayton Powell and later became chairman of the National Conference on Black Power. Stone's correspondence was necessarily more radical at that point. Nikki Giovanni, Romare Bearden, and LeRoi Jones were all friends.[13] Though his original editorial effort would be short-lived, it would introduce Brath, his art, and his wit to New York, laying the groundwork for *Color Us Cullud!* and providing a biting critique of American racism.

The AJASS announced the publication of *Color Us Cullud! The American Negro Leadership Coloring Book* in January 1964. The *Amsterdam News* described it as a group of "astringent cartoons deriding a widely varied group of American Negroes." It was a critique "done up in the manner of a child's coloring book," but its substance was a serious critique decidedly for adults.[14] The book took on a variety of civil rights leaders and entertainers, criticizing what Brath saw as an inauthenticity among those deemed to be the arbiters of the movement's national message. The book "'rocked' our Black Bourgeoisie," remembered Askia Muhammad Touré.[15] The illustrations were strong. The commentary was unique. The book also included a satirical poem about the violent integration struggle at Ole Miss.

And it was popular. As of March 1964, only two months after its original publication, the African Jazz-Art Society announced that the book would go into its second printing. *Jet* magazine announced that it was "selling like a hit." The group never disclosed how many copies were in either of its print runs, but it was clear that the book was doing better than Brath expected.[16]

Its success could, by some, be perceived as a threat. It was perhaps no coincidence that later that year, in 1964, the NAACP published its own comic book, *Your Future Rests . . . In Your Hands*, drawn by Larry Lieber, a Marvel Comics artist and creator of Iron Man, Thor, and other superheroes. He was white, the younger brother of Marvel Comics legend Stan Lee, and the story he told was of Jim Crow segregation thwarted by Black voting. It was traditional, saccharine; it was everything that *Color Us Cullud!* was not, and much of what it sought to push back against.[17]

"The book caused quite a stir among the civil rights leadership," the *Amsterdam News* reported, referring to Brath's effort, "as it lambasted all of the top, best known persons on the integration front." It was even able to break news, as its cartoon dealing with the Nation of Islam depicted Raymond Sharieff conspiring with Elijah Muhammad against Malcolm X, a rift in the relationship that was not publicly acknowledged until Malcolm announced on March 8 his formal break with the organization.[18]

The *Chicago Defender*'s Lillian S. Calhoun found the coloring book as proving that Brath was "a clever albeit vicious wit and artist" who "clobbers" civil rights leaders: "African nationalist Brath thinks we should all head back to Africa to develop 12 million sq. miles of virgin territory." The *Defender* announced the book's publication in March 1964, with Brath admitting to the paper that *Color Us Cullud!* would "undoubtedly not be enjoyed by all, but this book is not really meant to be comical. As a matter of fact, it is the clownish performances of the majority of these so-called leaders, that cause one to laugh."[19]

The *Pittsburgh Courier*'s Phyl Garland was more critical of the effort: "At first glimpse, 'Color Us Cullud' might be taken as propaganda from the united White Citizens Councils, since integration and integrationists are its main targets," he wrote. "However, the book happens to come from the exact opposite camp." And while integrationists were the book's most frequent targets, "no major school of racial thought escapes Brath's wrath." If the author had his way, Garland wryly explained, all of the lampooned leaders "should pack their bags immediately and go back to Africa—where most of them have never been."[20]

The book's underlying ideology was Caribbean radicalism as presented by a virtuoso comic artist who played on the long history of Black satire, particularly the work of iconoclasts like Wallace Thurman and Richard Bruce Nugent. And, of course, though the direction of the coloring book went in a very different direction, there was also influence from authors like Langston Hughes. "Haunted by minstrelsy's specter, even African American comedic writers found themselves dancing on shingles as they tried to create Black comedic images that were hilarious but inoffensive," argues Beth Turner.[21] It was a disconnect reconciled by Hughes, and one completely exploded by Brath.

7

CONGRESSMAN CARTER AND BEATNICK JACKSON COMIC STRIPS, 1960–1961

The cartoons that follow debuted on August 6, 1960, and ran through February 18, 1961. They appear here in order, one appearing every seven days in each new weekly edition of the *Citizen-Call*.

BEAT NICK JACKSON
By Cecil Brathwaite
SAY NICK...THE LANDLORD IN THE BUILDING NOW. YOU STILL WANNA SEE 'IM?
YEAH SAM. SEND THAT CAT UP HERE!
THAT LANDLORD CAT IS ALWAYS 'ROUND READY TO COP THE RENT, BUT AINT NEVER 'ROUND WHEN YOU NEED HIM!
YOU WANT TO SEE ME, MR. JACKSON?
YESSIR MR. ASH I THINK I'VE GOT A LEGITIMATE COMPLAINT!
WHAT ABOUT?
I'VE BEEN SOUNDIN' SAM THE SUPER, 'BOUT THE RATS IN THIS PAD... HE SAYS I'VE GOT TO SEE YOU.. NOW I PAY CLOSE TO $90 A MONTH FOR THIS ROOM, AND THE RATS DON'T CONTRIBUTE A DIME, SO I WANT YOU TO GET THEM TO LEAVE!
DON'T WORRY.. DON'T WORRY! I GIVE YOU THIS TO SOLVE YOUR PROBLEM!
YOU MUST BE JIVING! REALLY!
AND WHAT MAY I ASK, AM I SUPPOSE TO DO WITH THIS?
YOU JUST PUT IT IN A DISH AND LEAVE IT OUT FOR THE RATS. IT'LL FIX THEM!
MR. ASH CAN I ASK YOU SOMETHIN'?
SURE MR. JACKSON! GO RIGHT AHEAD!
JUST HOW WOULD YOU LIKE YOURS SERVED???

Congressman Carter and Beatnick Jackson Comic Strips 99

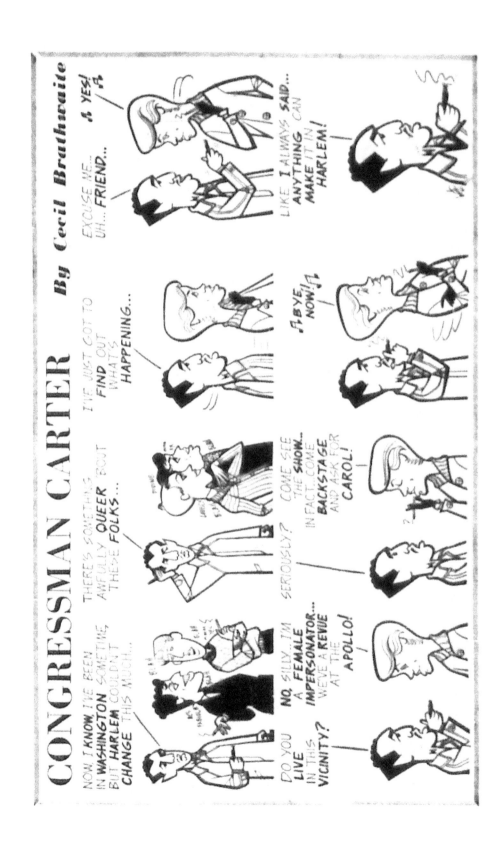

BEATNICK JACKSON

By Cecil Brathwaite

8

COLOR US CULLUD! THE AMERICAN NEGRO LEADERSHIP OFFICIAL COLORING BOOK, 1964

Color Us Cullud!
The American Negro Leadership Official Coloring Book

written and illustrated by
Cecil Elombe Brath

dedicated to the memories of
The Hon. Marcus A. Garvey
and
The Hon. Patrice Lumumba

as an educational document for
black people—at home and abroad

and to aid in promoting the program of the
African Nationalist Pioneer Movement
as administered by
The Hon. Carlos A. Cooks

Original cover illustration

Preface

This is not meant to be a comic book, for these are serious times. With the removal of the late John F. Kennedy from the scene, we can readily look forward to a reorganization of America's domestic policies. I wouldn't care how many times President Johnson invites the family cook to Congress, he is not going to put himself into a position to get assassinated over the civil rights issue.[1]

Civil rights (or is it "civil rites") demonstrations, had brought America almost to the brink of civil war when its "champion" was suddenly cut down. The death of JFK was no more violent than the death of Medgar Evers and the six children of Birmingham. But due to his race, and his high position in government, it shocked the nation into mass hysteria and touched off a series of theatrical, commercial and hypocritical ventures.[2]

There will most likely be a cooling off period, then a withdrawal of these tactics. For if certain elements will not stop at political assassination of white men (including the chief executive), then we may be sure that demonstrations featuring black people may well end like the ones that occurred in Sharpeville, South Africa, a few years ago.[3]

I believe that the direction that the new internal policies will take is definitely to the right, with a purge of all programs identified with "leftism," especially integration and civil rights. The honeymoon that many of the so-called-negro leaders have enjoyed with the New Frontier is all but over, and a divorce is in the making.[4] You can try to be as optimistic as you wish, but the idea of these "civil rites" leaders going in and out of the nation's penal institutions unscathed is as "dead as Oswald!"

Although dignitaries from all over the world attended the Kennedy funeral, I don't recall seeing the "Big Six," who were supposed to be so close to the administration. I doubt, no matter how cordial the relationship between them and the new administration may seem at first, [any] intelligent white man in public office is going to risk his life again by trying to educate overnight dumb peckerwoods, rednecks, and other types of crackers.[5]

The masses of black people will never be successfully integrated into the mainstream of America. Abraham Lincoln knew this and stated his position clearly on several different occasions. He said that, "Nature, habit and opinion have drawn indelible lines, that will forever restrict the two races from living equally free in the same society."[6] Lincoln was also in favor of sending the Africans back to their native clime, Africa, and was working towards that goal at the time of his untimely death.[7]

Integration is a sociological farce, invented by white carpet-baggers and scalawags, to use the black masses as a political football. The American Indian who was the original owner of this land, and who was much closer racially to white people than even the average mulatto, was never integrated into America. Since this is an indisputable fact, how can black people, whose forebears were brought here as slaves, actually look forward to such an illogical dream?

A fact that too many people try to ignore is that today we have "two different groups" living in the same race. You have the caste (negroes) who are "fighting" for civil rites, integration, miscegenation and assimilation. And you have Black men and women who understand the reality of the situation and are willing to work and build Africa for the general betterment of Black mankind.

And even though there has been pro-integration publicity throughout the mass media for a number of years, today we still find that the masses of black people are not fighting for integration, and the majority of white folks don't want it. If orthodox nationalism (self-determination) had half of the amount of publicity (with accurate reporting) that the "civil riters" have been given, we would celebrate those members of the race who honestly desire a solution for our common problems, who look in terms of making Africa into a natural base of eternal black security.

This is a changing world, where in the near future a few handpicked caste leaders will not be allowed to voice the aspirations of black people, for whom they themselves have little or no affinity at all. All of this hogwash about, "We've got a stake here in America" is ridiculous. You don't even have a "hamhock" or "meatball" relationship here. It's true that our foreparents put 300 years of labor in America, but our ancestors before them put over 3000 years of civilization, culture and majesty in Africa—the richest continent in the world!

This book, COLOR US CULLUD—The American Negro Leadership Official Coloring Book, is a sincere critical analysis of twenty of the most publicized individuals or groups, who are often designated to speak for over twenty million black people, who reside in the United States. When the "leadership abilities" of these present day public figures are closely examined, it is easy to understand why the black masses are confused and frustrated as they search for a program that is designed to combat their economic plight, inferiority complex and lack of initiative.

Marcus Garvey brought us such a program over forty years ago, but due to racial traitors, colored bourgeoisie, handkerchief heads,[8] miscegenationists, and other enemies of black opportunity, his movement was stalled. Garvey called for race pride, historical knowledge, self-determination and repatriation of the black masses to Africa, their true homeland![9] Yet today as millions of black people claim to be out of work, 12 million square miles of rich African continent waits to be developed. Black people, who hate their own physical image enough to actually spend millions of dollars annually trying to change it, and who can't stand the company of their own kind, are begging alien people to appreciate, accept and integrate them. While throughout the world all ethnic groups are busy gathering together in blocs and cliques to do for themselves, our people refute the idea of self-determination.

When Theodor Herzl tried to warn his people, who were living a successful life in Germany, about self-determination and nationhood, he was ignored, mocked and ridiculed. But when the Nazis suddenly came to power, they knew then that Herzl was a special visionary.[10]

We do not enjoy the same lucrative position as the Jews did in Germany.[11] Nor are we from the same racial stock as the political hierarchy, or the majority of the population. And nazism is blooming all over America. Sometimes it is called the Klan, sometimes the White Citizens Council, John Birch Society or even the Magnolia Rifles.[12]

Before all these different groups appeared, we had already furnished white racists over 7000 victims for their lynch mobs. A recent nationwide poll shows that the majority of white people do not like the company of black, negro, colored or caste people. And I would go as far as to say without fear of successful contradiction that judging from their statements, concepts of beauty, marriage and philosophies, that many of these so-called-negro leaders feel the same way about their caste brethren.

Patrice Lumumba came to the United States a few years ago and told black people that, "The Blackman built America ... In the building of America, one Blackman was worth five Indians ... If you could build America which was not yours, then you can surely build Africa, which is yours."[13]

For this, he was tortured and abused daily (remember the photographs in the newspapers, and the newsreels) and finally became the victim of an international crucifixion, organized by bands of conspirators whose point of origin, the world claimed, was 1600 Pennsylvania Avenue. The brutal and heinous assassination of the Premier of the Congo remains to this day as the most tragic event to befall black people universally in more than a decade.[14]

Jomo Kenyatta, who was tutored by Marcus Garvey in London, left "integration" in England to return to Africa to lead his people in their fight for freedom, which was far from non-violent. As a result of his realistic approach, today after "only" 40 years of fighting (including over 7 years sentence of hard labor for managing Mau Mau) he is the Prime Minister of Kenya—a land that white people called "God's own paradise"![15]

At the same time, his young black wife (a Gikuyu tribal girl) with a shaven head is "First Lady of the Land," while bleached caste women wearing $200 wigs continue a 100 year old chase after "equality" in America.[16]

Whether you believe it or not, or you like it or not, the United States will never be shared equally with anyone else but other white people. A White man can even become mayor in certain areas of the country without becoming a citizen. If you don't believe that, ask the citizens of Jersey City, New Jersey.[17]

It is time, therefore, that the black masses re-examine their so-called leaders and their respective (personal or organization) doctrines. "COLOR US CULLUD" is a satirical analysis of these familiar leaders, but its contents should be studied in all seriousness!

—C. E. Brath

MARCH ON WASHINGTON
Protest Job Discrimination... Jobs For All - Freedom Now!

Randolph˙ the Red Cap Porter was a protégé of W. E. B. Du Bois (who fought against Booker T. Washington's insistence that black people get a technical education) . . . Today, Randolph is searching for enough black workers who are technically prepared for the small quota of jobs that he can dig up . . . He fought against the philosophy and opinions of Marcus Garvey, who even the Japanese had a high respect for . . . When the U.S. sent Randolph to Tokyo to lecture the Japanese on "Government" (a people who have had continuous government since 660 B.C.), they ran him off the stage! . . . He's the head of the sleeping porters . . . Are you a sleeping porter? He also heads some "negro" labor council, who believe in black and white uniting for "freedom now, jobs for all" . . . Beware of black and white labor groups dealing in freedom . . . Color his cap red . . . Color him pink or maroon!

Rev. King,[†] I presume . . . We ought to call him King Sadim (that's Midas spelled backwards) because everything this king touches turns to failure for his followers, but enriches him. He moves into a town, starts a lot of demonstrations, and moves out quickly, leaving the black residents confused, frustrated and at the mercy of the crackers . . . Maybe we should call him King Sadist! He sends children out to try and soothe the savage beasts, but the cracker beasts must be deaf, because they blew up the children, songs and prayers, along with the church too. King still says to love the cracker, turn the other cheek, and, "If any blood must be spilled, let it be our blood and not the blood of our white brothers!" He tried to commit suicide twice in his youth, but even this ended in failure. Now he's dealing in dreams . . . Color him a nightmare!

Color Us Cullud! The American Negro Leadership Official Coloring Book   127

Old Uncle Roy,[‡] the NAACP's figure head leader . . . He represents "cullud people." He believes in Santa Claus, as he couldn't go along with the Xmas boycott. He also believes that we may be able to have a cullud president in the next fifty years . . . It's over fifty-four years, and even the NAACP hasn't had its first cullud president! A few years back, on television, in answer to a question implying that integration might lead to intermarriage, he said in effect that he believed that, in the future, we wouldn't be black and white, but we'd all be brown! I think he's finally jumped the gun . . . Color him cullud!

Whitney[¶] is hoping that black people will get preferential treatment in obtaining jobs. Can you imagine unemployed white people surrendering their seniority to help us catch up? The late President Kennedy was asking for an expansion of the European immigration quota, white Cuban immigrants have replaced black migrant workers in the South, and millions more destitute white folks shaken by the tides of nationalism in Africa and Asia will be landing soon on these shores. Since we're always the last hired and first fired, how does Whitney hope to avoid this dilemma? . . . Color him hopeless!

This farmer[§] plants seeds of miscegenation . . . He leads sit-ins, kneel-ins, dive-ins, crawl-ins, wash-ins, pray-ins, and all kind of ins, even chain-ins. If he really wants to help, why doesn't he open up "his own chain of inns," with all the respective facilities! I wonder why he doesn't take his white wife on some of his crusades . . . His group should be called CORN . . . the Congress of Racial Nincompoops! He's the right man for CORE, though . . . Because all he seems to want is the cores, pits, rinds, shells and the rest of the leavings . . . Color him garbage collect-in'!

Forman[#] and Lewis sounds like a comedy team . . . Representing "Snick-er" (that's a laugh) . . . a group similar to CORE, they're supposed to be more "militant" in the "non-violence" movement! They campaign directly in the field among the masses they're trying to convert, but fighting a losing battle for a lost cause without any weapons! Forman, the quiet straight man plays it cool, while his vociferous partner often lands in jail . . . Lewis like a young diddy-bop shouts dramatic but comical lines like, "We'll march through Dixie like Sherman!" He wrote a tough speech for the D.C. prayer meeting, but then let a white bishop persuade him to water it down . . . Color Forman mysterious . . . Color Lewis irresponsible!

Thurgood** used to be legal head of the NAACP, until he got
kicked upstairs to become a federal judge . . . He had to wait
almost a year to get the cracker's approval, and might wait longer
to get a case. He didn't marry a white woman; I think his wife
is Polynesian! He once wrote that "Negroes want the right to
have everything the white man has, including syphilis" . . . I'm
glad I'm not a negro . . . I think somebody kicked him upstairs
before . . . like during his childhood . . . Color him like crazy!

BIENBENIDO
A MI IGLESIA
RELIGIÓN Y POLITICA
SE JUNTA AQUI

This is Adam[††] . . . excuse me . . . Senhor Powellito! He loves a fiesta . . . See his wavy hair . . . It falls over his face when he preaches . . . Cullud women adore him . . . He looks just like a white man . . . In fact, he is white . . . He's been passing for black for years . . . He shook up his large female congregation when he married his Puerto Rican secretary . . . He went to Puerto Rico and told the people to "speak English"; they ran him home. Now he's back to lead the so-called "Black Revolution." He always manages to know which way the winds of change are blowing . . . Color him opportunist!

Here's Dr. Bunche[‡‡] . . . He always says the wrong thing all the time . . . He said the wrong thing in Suez and Nasser sent him home. He said the wrong thing in the Congo and Lumumba sent him home. He said the wrong thing in Harlem and the masses sent him home. He said the wrong thing at the white man's tennis club, and Whitey sent him home . . . Why doesn't he stay home? . . . Color him homeless!

This is James[¶] the writer . . . He just came back from Europe to help lead you . . . to Giovanni's pad! Isn't that wonderful? He told some black children, at his old alma mater, that they should be proud of slavery and forget about their African past . . . Is that supposed to be inspiring? That's so ridiculous that he sounds funny. Don't you think he's funny? . . . I think he's funny! . . . Color him funny, for days!

Belafoney,§§ the One Worlder entertainer . . . He believes in mixing everything up . . . He sings mixed-up calypsoes, mixed-up blues, mixed-up jazz, and mixed-up folk music . . . In fact, everything he does seems to be mixed-up . . . Right now, he seems to be trying to make a talented South African singer sing mixed-up material instead of her own original, authentic repertoire. His wife is white, but some folks try and say she's cullud and others claim she's Indian . . . Color them mixed-up!

We had forgotten about Miss Horn,## when she suddenly announced she was retiring in order to join the integration struggle . . . Now! She married a white composer who composed . . . uh . . . uh . . . Off hand, I can't remember any tunes he composed, but I remember he was busy composing himself in the rest room while his wife was fighting two white men who had insulted her a few years back! They used to tell us that Miss Horn was the "most beautiful woman in the race" . . . The race away from our racial standard, maybe! Her daughter followed in her footsteps and married a white man too. I sure hope nobody else follows this kind of leadership . . . Color her no comment!

Miss Katt*** now claims she wants to do her part in the civil rights fight too. Sometime ago, she was asked by a leading caste magazine to name the "Ten Most Handsome Men!" . . . You guessed it, she named ten white men! She also made headlines in Europe and much of white society . . . She married a white man and had a cullud baby with white skin, blonde hair, and blue eyes!! After 3 years her marriage broke up. In another caste magazine she stated her reasons when she described the kind of man she married . . ." I find American men, adorable as they are, are just babies, and I am tired of being a mother. They know how to make money and carry out big deals, but they seem to have forgotten how to love!" In her autobiography, she claims she was "high yellow," but I don't think she's that light . . . Color her low brown!

This is Stereotype Sammy.[†††] He's for the race too . . . The race after white women, white friends and white society! His Hollywood escapades could even scare a producer to death . . . just "as-Kim" about his romances! Sometime ago when some white chorus girls were doing a benefit minstrel show, he encouraged them to use old "blackface" routines, which they had neglected . . . Another time, he and his "friends" (Frank and Dean, etc.) gave a benefit called "Tribute To The Rev. Dr. King" at Carnegie Hall. When asked what type of show he was going to present, Sammy said, "We're trying to match with a little dignity the great dignity of the good Dr. King." If you saw the show, as I did, then you'll have to agree it was offensive, with most of the white TV comedians who participated resorting to obscene jokes and gestures . . . Dean called Sammy "my little cullud fag friend," and Frank corrected it with "my little cullud Jewish fag friend." By the way, Sammy once stated that he became a Jew because he wanted to belong to a people with a history . . . Didn't he know Moses was born and educated in Egypt, Africa? . . . Color him simple!

Jackie[+++] is a real blockbuster . . . He looks like a Zulu, is listed as a tan ballplayer, and talks like a cracker. He was the "1st Negro" to play baseball with white men in the Major Leagues . . . He was overshadowed by other black men in the black baseball leagues, but he stood out fabulously among the white ballplayers! He moved into lily-white St. Albans, and his white friends moved out . . . When more black people moved into St. Albans, Jackie moved out . . . all the way to Connecticut . . . Now he's some kind of straw boss in charge of the black workers of a big coffee company . . . From his home in Connecticut, he tries to tell the masses in Harlem how happy they should be with their economic status quo . . . He's not too popular in Harlem, because he's far out of touch with the black masses . . . Color him far out!

Floyd[IIII] was being tutored to be another Jackie. He was supposed to be an "introspective fighter" . . . I think it was because
he used to sleep in subways when he was a crazy mixed-up kid!
Floyd went to Egypt on a tour as a honored guest of the Cairo
government. Nasser, to show his sincerity, even extended cordial hospitality to Floyd's Jewish lawyer, who accompanied him
. . . Floyd showed his gratitude upon his return to the states by
publicly stating, in effect, if negroes could see the conditions
of Egypt, they would realize how well off they are here! And
didn't he try and sue a white beauty parlor when they refused
to straighten his wife's hair? An advocate of King's policies, he
tried that non-violence nonsense on Liston twice, and it failed
both times . . . Color him introspectively blue!

Dick[§§§] is helping to lead the race too . . . He's a comedian. Isn't that a joke? Can you think of any other group of people in the world led by a comedian? They call him "The Conscience Of America," but everybody knows that America doesn't have a conscience! He went down to Mississippi and told the crackers, "You dirty dogs, let me drink coffee with you . . . You dirty dogs, let us go to your schools . . . C'mon we want to be with you . . . You dirty dogs!" . . . Now really, isn't that a joke? . . . Ha ha ha ha ha ha . . . Color him a joke!

Isn't it queer how suddenly Bayard### came on the scene? They claim he was working in the background for years, but since he was a prime instigator for the March On . . . I mean the "March In Washington," his importance should be realized . . . He is obviously a man of moral convictions, but doesn't he know that the direction he's helping to lead us isn't moral? Although he is credited for masterminding the biggest gimmick of the sixties, the "March On Washington," he came out three months later and said, "Gimmicks will not bring the Negroes closer to their goal and will only defeat them in the end." . . . Color him a gimmick!

Lomax**** came into prominence by helping a white television reporter spy on the Muslims, and trap a black borough president! How's that for credentials for leadership? . . . Huh? The white people continue to try to build him up, but he always goofs . . . With everyone Africa conscious, he writes a book on his reluctance to be African . . . He goofed again when he came to African Nationalist conscious Harlem, and told the people that they "weren't going back to Africa." He barely escaped in one piece! He's supposed to be against nationalism, but his biggest "idea" to date was a Xmas boycott, something the African Nationalists have been doing for over twenty years! By the way, didn't that Xmas boycott turn out to be a goof? . . . Color him goofy!

Malcolm brings us a message from Elijah,†††† who got a message from Fard (who was whiter than Powell), who got a message from Allah, who had also given a message earlier to the original Mohammed. The white man never worries about us when we have messenger's jobs! That's why he always has got the Muslims featured on TV, radio, and in all his publications. They say that the white man is the devil, which may come as a shock to the millions of followers of Islam throughout the world. Anyway, wouldn't that make us inferior, since the devil is supposed to be a supreme being? And what's this foolishness about keeping your hair cut close, because "our hair is cursed?" I wouldn't argue with them about The Bible being a poisoned book, but why then do they always quote from it? They scoffed when the non-violence folks' church got blown up by the southern cracker, but the west coast crackers shot up their temple, killed the head "minister," paralyzed a young member, and then locked them all up! They also say our original language was Arabic, but if that was true, we must have been speaking a different dialect than the Arab slave traders who helped get us into our "original predicament." They want the white man to give us a few states here, but everybody knows he wouldn't even let us have Harlem. Right now they're having a power struggle, which might end up with Malcolm back as a newsboy. But then who would speak for them, since Elijah is as incoherent as Malcolm is articulate? . . . Color them divided and misinformed!

All movements have to have spiritual guidance,†††† and the "civil riters" sure have theirs . . . It's a general stereotype cliché that "cullud" folks believe in ghosts. As a matter of fact, that's the reason the ku klux klan wear white sheets and hoods . . . as a terrorizing symbol. The "liberal" white people always manage to provide us with a spiritual image of one of their deceased. There's the Holy Ghost, Log Cabin Ghost, New Deal Ghost, Great Lady Ghost, and now they're offering you the New Frontier Ghost! . . . Don't color them, because they're transparent . . . Everybody knows you can see through a ghost!!!

THE SAGA OF OLE MISS'''''
by Cecil Elombe Brath

In the deep south, the part most backwards,
    lies the state of Mississippi.
So poor, some whites farm in backyards,
    but still claim superiority.

And in this primitive, huge plantation,
    racial feelings are pretty tense.
In fact, the worst in all this nation
    that claims itself to be immense.

They have a university, they call "Ole Miss,"
    it's nothin' to brag about at all.
After viewing all the subjects on its list,
    you know its major is football.

Big simple, oafish, rowdies go there,
    the type I doubt you'd want to be with.
But one casteman longed to go here;
    titled, "Negro James Meredith!"

Veteran who'd gone to a foreign land
    to defend this same U.S.A.
Where white sent black to slay the yellow man,
    to make for them a brighter day.

He could've gone to a better school
    where color would not have held him back.
Yale, Princeton, M.I.T. as a rule
    will not bar you because you're black.

But to be the first known of his race
    to register, at dear Ole Miss,
To accelerate the integration pace,
    he chose not to pass up this.

But thinking just with common sense,
    if they claim that they're superior;
Yet, on them you force your presence—
    does that not show you feel inferior?

And in the north, groups were conniving,
    how Ole Miss would integrate.
They'd show the crackers, they weren't jiving
    by gambling with this casteman's fate.

In Governor's Mansion, in Mississippi
    Old Ross planned to show defiance.
Told his aid[e]s and every trustee,
    "Supreme Court laws need no compliance!"

Governor Patterson of Alabama
    wired Barnett his support.
Adding to the scheduled drama;
    Ole Miss, now a southern fort.

Attorney General Kennedy
    who had made a deal with Ross,
As a sort of remedy,
    was caught now in a doublecross.

From Texas came ex-General Walker
    who once commanded NATO forces.
But now a rabble rousing talker,
    summoned klansmen "to their horses."

At Little Rock, he'd led his troops
　　to stand off hordes of council white.
Now at Ole Miss, he told these same groups,
　　"I was wrong then, now I'm right!"

Racists converged on Mississippi
　　at Walker's call, throughout the land.
Kicked off his post in West Germany,
　　he chose the campus to make his stand.

Now the pieces are all assembled,
　　for the setting of the stage.
The crowd with seething anger trembled,
　　then exploded in all its rage.

The world screamed at the indignation,
　　"Could this be democracy?"
The President told the troubled nation,
　　"We'll march on Mississippi."

Having trouble with Fidel Castro,
　　Ole Miss served as a distraction,
To stall the Cuban fiasco
　　he took long delayed action.

Marshalls [sic], troops and National Guardsmen
　　rushed to Ole Miss, as he willed.
Riots, instigated by klansmen;
　　seventy injured, two men killed.

Walker's brick-bat rebs defeated,
　　he himself in custody.
What punishment shall be meeted [sic]
　　to his pale page in history?

And shall the Governor go un-punished
    for his most contemptuous crime?
His was the pattern that was brandished,
    yet will he serve any time?

And they hanged on the campus,
    Meredith in effigy.
It stirred up quite a rumpus,
    mobs danced around in glee.

Soldiers came, the crowd fled
    cursing, and singing the Ole Miss song.
A sign across the dummy read,
    "Go back to Africa where you belong!"

There was a method to their madness,
    there is a message for all to see.
If the race weren't led by blindness—
    King, CORE and NAACP.

Who are the ones who are behind us
    in these much repeated schemes?
The same ones whose cunning blinds us
    to pursue these wild and hopeless dreams.

Heed what the un-thinking cracker told you.
    Beware his genocidal trend.
Return to the land, from whence he stole you;
    his next outburst, may be your end!

About the Author . . .

Cecil Elombe Brath, who compiled the research, illustrated and wrote this satirical analysis of the present crop of so-called leaders, is probably the least published artist dealing with social comment. This is due to the fact that although his artwork is of high calibre, he is unwilling to tone down his viewpoint to meet the demands of mass commercialism. To this accusation, he says, "Should a doctor tell a cancer patient that he has a common cold?"

I first met Cecil while we were both studying at the School of Visual Arts, which was known then as Cartoonists & Illustrators School. I was attending on the G.I. bill, and he was attending on a three year scholarship.

I can remember many of the students gathering around his desk to watch him work, especially on his caricatures of famous people and various students around the classroom. Even in school, I can remember most of his work having strong racial undertones.

Graduating from Thomas Knowlton J.H.S. in the Bronx, he passed admittance tests to attend the High School of Industrial Art (now the High School of Art and Design). He finished with honors, and won a three year tuition free scholarship to study at C&I in Manhattan. While he was still in school, he illustrated a Down Beat jazz review book, with caricatures of many of the top musicians.

He completed SVA, winning prizes and honorable mentions during the exhibitions held there, and illustrated the yearbook with caricatures of many of the instructors. It was a good thing he had officially finished, too, because some of his impressions were grotesquely accurate. However, after combating much discrimination in the art field, he was given a three month scholarship grant to return to SVA and study layout and design.

He also attended the "School of Higher Learning" in Harlem, studying African Fundamentalism under the Administrator, Carlos Cooks, and Nationalist Argumentation under Professor Rayfus Williams. This course and his association with his philosophical mentors ha[ve] influenced his interpretation of international and national incidents greatly.

Only 27 years old now, Cecil has been in the art field for almost seven years. His experienced include graphics for television, designing promotional films for several top firms, a film to promote a TV network, posters, brochures and book illustrations.

He also had a strip in the now defunct N.Y. Citizen Call newspaper, which literally "shook up" the Harlem community. The strip featured two characters that he originated: Beatnick Jackson and Congressman Carter. When these two outspoken characters began to sway the paper's editorial viewpoint, "the Call" suddenly shut down. The mystery clouding the disappearance of the Citizen-Call has never really been defined.

Cecil, along with his photographer brother, and another commercial artist associate, were largely responsible for the birth eight years ago of the Jazz-Art Society, which today is the African Jazz-Art Society & Studios, Inc. AJASS is an African organization of artists and photographers who also promote concerts, dances and shows. Its most famous production has been "Naturally '62" and "Naturally '63," which is an African coiffure and fashion extravaganza designed to restore and dignify our racial image. The show features the fabulous and world renowned Grandassa Models, a group of beautiful black women who model natural hair styles and African garments from home and abroad. Incidentally, this series of natural black beauty shows, and the Grandassa Models, were also originated by Cecil.

This book, "COLOR US CULLUD!... The American Negro Leadership Official Coloring Book," is the result of the same type of nationalistic thinking. If you have read it with an open mind, then it may enlighten ... pardon me, I mean "darken your mind with knowledge!"

Cecil, like myself, is a Blackman by birth and conviction. We hope that as a result of this book, COLOR US CULLUD, those of you who are still aligned with the rank and file of "castedom" will soon join us who are proud to be black!

—Christopher N. Hall

9

ANNOTATIONS TO THE COLORING BOOK

*A. PHILIP RANDOLPH

A. Philip Randolph was a product of the Great Migration, coming north from Jacksonville, Florida, to New York in 1911. Brath is right that Randolph's devotion to classical civil rights was shaped in large measure under the influence of W. E. B. Du Bois, his decision to devote himself to that cause coming after his encounter with Du Bois's *The Souls of Black Folk*. And Brath's enmity for Du Bois stemmed from both his integrationism and his long-standing feud with Booker Washington. Though Garvey never met Washington in person, arriving in the United States after his death in 1915, he carried on an extended correspondence with Washington and devoted himself to Tuskegee's model of industrial education.[1]

Randolph's devotion to socialism, however, came largely in consultation with his friend and ally Chandler Owen, with whom, in 1917, he founded *The Messenger*, a socialist monthly that combined its economic analysis with civil rights advocacy and opposition to World War I. He was also in opposition to the nationalism of Marcus Garvey, understandably so following the split in Caribbean radicalism between socialist and nationalist thinkers. Randolph and Garvey were openly derisive of one another. "Though the dispute between Garvey and the editors of the *Messenger* would flare most acrimoniously around incidental issues," explains historian Jervis Anderson, "it had its source in fundamental differences of political and economic belief."[2]

Randolph's relationship with Japan had always been strained. As early as the immediate post–World War I period, Randolph had argued that the Japanese were not to be trusted to support African American civil rights. The country was "reactionary," "imperialistic," and "autocratic." As explained by historian David Wright, "According to Randolph only one and a half million people were allowed to vote in Japan out of a total of fifty million and he reasoned that if Japan had no problems oppressing its own people it would not be unreasonable to assume that Japan would oppress foreigners as well."[3]

While such thinking on foreign policy clearly shaped his tenuous relationships with countries like Japan, Randolph's most lasting successes came as a labor leader. In 1925 he helped organize the Brotherhood of Sleeping Car Porters and became the group's president. Despite Brath's seeming contempt, the union was the first led by African Americans to become part of the American Federation of Labor, and after some early struggles was legitimately successful during the 1930s in protecting its workers. The Pullman Company, the nation's largest railroad car manufacturer, agreed to negotiate with the Brotherhood in 1935. A generation later, in 1959 Randolph would help organize the Negro American Labor Council, which began operations in 1960 with the stated goal of developing a Black labor organization that would work for integrationist civil rights.[4]

†MARTIN LUTHER KING JR.

Frustration with Martin Luther King among younger civil rights leaders was common and took much the tone of Brath's criticism. The charge that King was most concerned with his own image and well-being was a common complaint, beginning in earnest in 1961, three years prior to publication of the coloring book. When SNCC leaders, who had already made a series of Freedom Rides down the East Coast, through Georgia and into Alabama, tried to convince King to participate by accompanying them into Mississippi, feared to be the most dangerous proposition yet in a journey that had produced beatings, arrests, and a firebombing in Anniston, Alabama, King demurred. When faced with a charge that it was his moral obligation to accompany them, he responded by telling the SNCC protesters, "I think I should choose the time and place of my Golgotha." Such hubris rankled just as much as his refusal, and many in the organization began referring to him from that point on as "De Lawd."[5]

It was a reputation that earned no improvements the following year in Albany, Georgia. The Albany Movement had originally been a 1961 project of SNCC activists and had burgeoned into a wide-ranging campaign of local groups struggling on a variety of fronts. Hundreds had been arrested in a broad-based people's movement, but King was asked to come in December 1961 over the protests of many who assumed his presence would shift the Albany focus to King himself over and against those on the ground who had been suffering for the cause. King predictably became the story when he was arrested by police chief Laurie Pritchett, promised to stay in jail, then found himself out on bail. Arrested twice more in Albany in 1962, Pritchett refused to keep King in jail, outmaneuvering the leader and watching as he left the southwest Georgia city that summer in failure.[6]

The following year, in Birmingham, King, in the words of Brath, sent "children out to try and soothe the savage beasts." As part of the SCLC's campaign in that city, an attempt to provoke Public Safety Commissioner Eugene "Bull" Connor in a way that it could not provoke Pritchett, the "Children's Crusade" used children as young as eight as protesters in a controversial strategy to gain the moral and strategic upper hand. While the effort was generally successful, it was greeted by many in Birmingham as more evidence that the grandstanding King should not be stirring up more strife for locals in the city. It was an assumption only exacerbated when on September 15, 1963, members of the Ku Klux Klan bombed the Sixteenth Street Baptist Church, killing four young girls.[7]

His work in Birmingham, however, did prove successful, culminating in the March on Washington and King's "I Have a Dream" speech on August 28, which Brath also references. That success led *Time* magazine to name King its "Man of the Year" for 1963. In the article that accompanied that honor, the periodical claimed of the civil rights leader that "twice, before he was 13, he tried to commit suicide," the first incident responding to his assumption that his grandmother had died, the second to her actual death. That article appeared in early January 1964, just as Brath was completing work on the coloring book, and convinced him to include it in his commentary.[8]

‡ROY WILKINS

Roy Wilkins became executive secretary of the NAACP in 1955, and in 1964, the year of the publication of *Color Us Cullud!*, he became the organization's executive director. The year prior to Wilkins's final promotion, in September 1963 a Committee of Artists and Writers that featured Louis Lomax, James Baldwin, John O. Killens, and Ruby Dee held a press conference at New

York's Astor Hotel and announced a boycott of Christmas shopping to protest the violent events in Birmingham. The group argued that Americans "have no right to celebrate Christmas this year" and said that they had contacted major civil rights organizations asking for their participation. "On Christmas morning," said Dee, "mothers and fathers will say to their children, Santa Claus didn't come because bombers came to Birmingham." The group predicted that a successful boycott could reduce holiday revenues by up to two billion dollars.[9]

Not all saw the benefit of such a move. The *Pittsburgh Courier*'s Claude Hall saw the effort as futile, as "Negroes, alone, cannot wage a successful nationwide boycott, due to economic factors apparent, glaringly, to anyone who has taken the time to examine them. Secondly, it is unlikely that any substantial percentage of Negroes would follow such a national plan." Thus it was that the Council for United Civil Rights Leadership—representing SCLC, SNCC, CORE, NAACP, the Urban League, and the National Council of Negro Women—announced that the country's major civil rights organizations would not be participating in the boycott. Wilkins made much the same point as Hall, justifying his organization's abstention and adding that it would be unfair to Black children and would have no real impact on Birmingham. "That rotund bundle of joy, Santa Claus, just might wriggle down the nation's chimneys after all," reported the *Defender*.[10]

Brath does not mention that Martin Luther King broke with the Council for United Civil Rights Leadership and supported the boycott, nor that the boycott was undeniably unsuccessful, never achieving any national momentum. Christmas sales were up nationally and in major markets across the country.[11]

Wilkins's optimism about a Black president was something he would maintain for the rest of his life, repeating the claim in 1970.[12] And, of course, that optimism proved prescient. In addition, the NAACP leadership had been Black since 1920. John

Shillady had taken over as executive secretary of the NAACP in 1917 after a career in public service that had led him, most recently, to head the Mayor's Committee on Unemployment in New York. Shillady's tenure with the association would be comparatively short. He was white, which, it was assumed, would give him a measure of protection when venturing south. But when he traveled to Austin, Texas, in August 1919, he was attacked by a mob that included a county judge and a constable and was endorsed by the Texas governor. Shillady never fully recovered from the assault and resigned the following year, the last white leader of the NAACP. He was succeeded by the more notable tenure of James Weldon Johnson, who would in turn be succeeded by Walter White, then Wilkins.[13]

While Wilkins was an uncompromising integrationist, in 1965 he was asked at a symposium at Vanderbilt University, "Wouldn't intermarriage ultimately help your movement?" Wilkins responded, "Young lady, I would never advocate marriage for a cause, no matter how just." He remained an active integrationist proponent and leader of the NAACP until his retirement in 1977.[14]

¶WHITNEY YOUNG

Whitney Young began his career as an academic, serving perhaps most notably as the inaugural dean of Atlanta University's school of social work beginning in 1954. That leadership background would aid him when in 1960 he became executive director of the National Urban League. In that role, Young would make the Urban League a vital part of the civil rights movement, expanding its reach, its budget, and its mission. Part of that new mission was a fight to end employment discrimination, and Brath wasn't the only critic of the effort. In an effort to generate the hiring of more Black workers, Young developed relationships with corporate leaders. When combined with the substantial white membership of the Urban League and its pre-Young history of general conservatism, it led to charges that Young had sold out to white corporate masters for the pittance of a few extra working-class jobs.[15]

Brath's criticism of Young's employment effort is slightly different. He leaves the sell-out charge unstated, instead making the case that the immigration of white foreign nationals will lead employers to prefer them to domestic Black workers. There was precedent for this assumption. The early birth pangs of what would become the Great Migration began in the last decade of the nineteenth century and the first decade of the twentieth, a phenomenon that only exacerbated northern white racism. White industrialists focused their hiring practices on European immigrants because they could pay new arrivals the same low wage as Black workers and could keep their products associated with whiteness. Black workers, then, were relegated to jobs outside of industry like janitorial work, only finding opportunity for industrial work when brought in as scab labor during strikes, making them even less popular in a racist North. The first major example of this happened in 1904, when 28,000 meatpacking workers in Chicago went on strike and Black scabs controversially took their place.[16]

More recent to Brath's account, the transfer from the use of impoverished Black labor in farming to the use of immigrant labor happened after World War II with the consolidation of agriculture in factory farms and modern agribusiness. As Victor Olivera has demonstrated, from 1945 to 1987, the size of American farms more than doubled while the total number of farms dropped by roughly four million. It was during that transition that the move to Latin American farm labor occurred. While it is clear that anticolonial movements in Africa and Asia did create a new white population willing to emigrate, and while that willingness did drive a new white population to the United

States, it paled in comparison to the broader Latin American immigration, as well as that of indigenous peoples in those postcolonial states.[17]

§JAMES FARMER

James Farmer was born in Texas in 1920, and after earning degrees at Wiley College and Howard University, he helped found the Congress of Racial Equality (CORE) in 1942 in Chicago. A biracial organization dedicated to peaceful protest against segregation, it looked much like the NAACP, except that it focused more on public protests than legal action. There was also a less hierarchical leadership, CORE allowing its members to pursue action on their own terms, whether it be for integration or peace. Farmer not only led the organization since its inception but also put its focus on nonviolent direct action in the style and theory of Mohandas K. Gandhi, with whom he became enamored while studying theology at Howard.[18]

While there had been a variety of "sit-in" efforts at segregated public spaces in the early twentieth century, the sit-in movement began on February 1, 1960, when Black students at North Carolina A&T College in Greensboro sat down at a Woolworth's lunch counter and asked for service. It would grow from there as students across the South began engaging in similar nonviolent integrationist protest, those actions taking place principally in cities with a high concentration of Black college students and clusters of HBCUs like Atlanta and Nashville. They were successful, and while they led to the creation of the Student Nonviolent Coordinating Committee, Farmer's CORE was a vital part of the sit-in effort.[19]

From there, the effort spread to buses in an effort to force federal action. Farmer had (unsuccessfully) attempted a version of freedom riding in 1947, but in 1961 he helped plan the Freedom

Rides throughout the South.[20] All such action was part of his broader strategy of Gandhian nonviolent integrationist direct action that would never meet the favor of activists like Brath. Nor would Farmer's marriage to Lula A. Peterson, his second wife and a white woman, seen by Brath as a racial sellout and a version of the sit-ins applied to marriage.[21]

#JAMES FORMAN AND JOHN LEWIS

Brath's criticism of Forman and Lewis is similar to that of Farmer—that nonviolent integrationist protest was a futile effort. James Forman was older than most of his colleagues in SNCC. Born in 1928 and raised in Chicago (while also spending time in Mississippi), Forman served as executive secretary of SNCC from 1961 to 1966. Because he was in his thirties while the majority of SNCC activists were in their twenties, Forman tended to work at organizing, often staying behind the scenes and keeping himself "mysterious" in the eyes of Brath.[22]

Lewis served more as a public face of the movement. Born in 1940 and getting his first real civil rights experience in the Freedom Rides in 1961, Lewis became chairman of SNCC in 1963, working closely with Forman to guide the organization. A fiery orator, Lewis was the youngest speaker at the August 1963 March on Washington. The original draft of his speech criticized the Kennedy administration and the older generation of civil rights activists for their slow caution. It said, "We will march through the South, through the heart of Dixie, the way Sherman did. We shall pursue our own 'scorched earth' policy and burn Jim Crow to the ground—nonviolently." When the draft of his speech circulated before the event, many of the old guard objected to its language, including Attorney General Robert Kennedy and Patrick O'Boyle, Archbishop of Washington, DC. O'Boyle in particular threatened to pull out of the event if the speech was not changed. In a last-minute compromise, Lewis and SNCC leadership agreed to soften the tone of the speech to appease the older rights leaders and the white leadership contingent.[23]

**THURGOOD MARSHALL

Thurgood Marshall attended Howard Law School in the early 1930s, where he came under the influence of the school's dean, Charles Hamilton Houston. He began a relationship with the NAACP in 1934 when he represented the organization in *Murray v. Pearson* (1934), a case that successfully desegregated the University of Maryland Law School. The year after that, his mentor Houston left Howard to lead the NAACP's legal department, and Marshall's role with the group only increased. In 1936 he became part of the organization's national staff, and in 1940 he founded and led the NAACP's Legal Defense and Education Fund, which would carry on the legal effort to overturn *Plessy v. Ferguson* (1896), largely through cases establishing precedent in school desegregation litigation.[24]

In recognition for the work he did throughout the 1940s and 1950s, John F. Kennedy appointed him to a judgeship on the Second Circuit of the US Court of Appeals in May 1961. As Brath intimates, however, a group of southern senators led by Mississippi's James Eastland worked to block the nomination. Marshall served for most of 1961 as a recess appointee until finally confirmed. Though it had yet to happen at the time of *Color Us Cullud!*'s appearance, Marshall would be appointed Solicitor General in 1965 and Associate Justice of the Supreme Court in 1967.[25]

The quote Brath attributes to Marshall about syphilis might at first glance seem to be a commentary on the Tuskegee Syphilis Experiment, which ran from the 1930s to the 1970s, but the first vocal protest against the racialized ethics of that episode did not begin until 1965, the year following the coloring book's publication. Instead, the quote represents Marshall's wide-ranging approval of integrationist civil rights.[26]

Finally, Marshall originally married Vivian "Buster" Burey in 1929, who was active in the civil rights movement alongside her husband until her death in 1955. Later that same year, Marshall married Cecilia Suyat, a Hawaiian of Filipino descent. Suyat had originally worked as a stenographer for the NAACP before becoming a secretary for the group's leader, Gloster B. Current. As he demonstrates several times in the coloring book, marrying outside of the race tended to insult Brath.[27]

††ADAM CLAYTON POWELL

Adam Clayton Powell represented Harlem in the House of Representatives from 1945 to 1971, the first Black representative to be elected from New York—or, perhaps, the first person of African descent. Though Powell was a controversial political figure who at various times in his career was dogged by charges of corruption, and though he was a devoted integrationist who helped shepherd several pieces of civil rights legislation through Congress, Brath keeps away from such targets in his takedown, excepting his comment that "cullud women love him." The statement plays on the broad approval he received from Black integrationists as well as his reputation as a ladies' man.[28]

Brath also claims that Powell is white, that he has been "passing for black for years." Powell was the son of two parents of mixed race, one from Virginia and one from West Virginia, who both were listed as mulatto in census records for those states. His father was a successful pastor in Harlem, and Powell thus grew up wealthy and able to pass for white when necessary. He did have "wavy hair" and other white features, but he also identified as a Black leader for the entirety of his run as a congressional leader.[29]

Brath's other principal criticism of Powell is his relationship with Puerto Rico and his marriage to a Puerto Rican woman. Yvette Flores Diago was Powell's third wife, a twenty-seven-year-old hotel employee in San Juan when Powell met her, while he was still married to entertainer Hazel Scott. Two years later, in 1960 Powell divorced Scott and married Flores Diago. The two would divorce the year after the publication of the coloring book, but their marriage produced a child and another troubling political scandal. Flores Diago was, in 1961, placed on Powell's congressional payroll despite the fact that she did not work for his office and spent almost all of her time in Puerto Rico. That controversy, however, was not exposed until 1967, three years after the coloring book's publication. It was Powell's ability to survive such scandals that proved his ability to "know which way the winds of change are blowing."[30]

⚕RALPH BUNCHE

From 1928–1950, Ralph Bunche served as the chair of Howard University's department of political science. While serving in that role, Bunche was a researcher for Gunnar Myrdal's *An American Dilemma*. He helped plan and organize the United Nations and helped write the Universal Declaration of Human Rights and shepherd its adoption. He then worked for peace in the Israel-Palestine conflict, winning the Nobel Peace Prize in 1950. In 1968, years after *Color Us Cullud!*, Bunche was appointed Under-Secretary-General of the United Nations.[31]

As part of the United Nations in 1956, he supervised the deployment of 6,000 troops after Great Britain, France, and Israel attacked Egypt. The defense of Gamal Abdel Nasser's Egypt in what became known as the Suez Crisis was successful, strengthening Nasser and driving colonial powers from the nation. In 1960 Bunche was part of the UN peacekeeping mission in the Congo. Originally, prime minister Patrice Lumumba welcomed the aid of the United Nations, assuming that they would help quell secessionist movements in the newly independent nation. The UN troops, however, instead pursued a strategy of maintaining law and order over and against aiding the central government against rebellion. Lumumba, in response, felt that he had no choice but to turn to the Soviet Union.[32]

Bunche's domestic popularity in places like Harlem was obviously compromised by his work with the United Nations, as it was interpreted to be siding with colonial oppressors. His broader, more general popularity remained relatively solid, but even that could be compromised. In 1959 he was denied membership in the West Side Tennis Club in Forest Hills, Queens. The leader of the club ultimately resigned after national publicity of the incident, but Bunche refused a later offer of membership as it was based solely on bad publicity rather than a spirit of equality.[33]

¶¶JAMES BALDWIN

James Baldwin was one of the most influential voices in Black literature and civil rights, but he was no stranger to criticism in the Black press and from critics like Brath. Frustrated with the racism in the United States, Baldwin left the country to live as an expatriate in France in 1948 and remained there for much of the remainder of his life. He began returning to his home country in 1957, moved by the direction and results of the civil rights movement. He wrote a series of essays during the next decades detailing his own observations and experiences during the fight for equality, aligning himself most closely with the integrationist positions of the Congress of Racial Equality. When combined with his unapologetic homosexuality, he made a ripe target for Brath and other Black commentators.[34]

"Next Time, The Fire In Giovanni's Room" is a conflation of two of Baldwin's works: *Giovanni's Room*, his second novel published in 1957, and *The Fire Next Time*, a collection of two essays published in 1963. *Giovanni's Room* tells the story of an American gay man living in Paris. While it deals empathetically with homosexuality at mid-century, it is largely devoid of racial politics. Still, it provided fodder for many Black journalists and critics whose conception of Black masculinity had no room for homosexuality. As Rachel Corbman has noted, "funny" as used by Brath is a homophobic euphemism for homosexuality.[35]

The first essay in *The Fire Next Time*, however, takes on racial politics directly. "My Dungeon Shook—Letter to My Nephew on the One Hundredth Anniversary of Emancipation" argues that integration necessitates the Black population coming to terms with its past and accepting whites (as opposed to earning the acceptance of whites). It was not, as Brath portrays, a pride in slavery or a forgetting of Africa, but it is easy to see why a nationalist might interpret it as such, particularly when African nationalist masculinity came attendant with overt heterosexuality, making any breach of that norm a de facto rejection of Africa.[36]

§§HARRY BELAFONTE

Harry Belafonte's real breakthrough as a performer came with the release of his 1956 album *Calypso*, which sold more than a million copies and made the singer a household name. While he continued his music career, he also began starring in motion pictures, only further raising his profile. And he used that profile for civil rights activism. Like Brath, Belafonte was the child of Caribbean immigrants, his Jamaican ancestry influencing much of the *Calypso* album and also his eagerness to fight against colonial oppression. He participated in the civil rights movement by raising money and helping bankroll much of its activities. He was close to Martin Luther King and participated in the Freedom Rides, the March on Washington, and Mississippi Freedom Summer.[37]

His broader anticolonialism also caused him concern for places like South Africa. The talented singer whom Brath references was Miriam Makeba, whose career began at much the same time as Belafonte's. In 1959 her success in South Africa took her to London, where she met Belafonte, who took her under his wing and partially guided her career. Later that year, she moved to New York with Belafonte's help. While Makeba did sing popular Western music, she never abandoned traditional South African fare. Brath makes the assumption that any deviation away from that traditional music was the result of Belafonte's influence, but Makeba had always included nontraditional songs in her act. Of course, that assumption was much easier to make because Belafonte himself played in so many genres, as Brath notes. He moved from calypso to jazz and blues to folk music to pop relatively seamlessly, giving his songs, to the ears of nationalists like Brath, a lack of authenticity.[38]

It was an inauthenticity only exacerbated for Brath by Belafonte's white wife. The singer was originally married to Black actress Marguerite Byrd. In 1957 they divorced, and Belafonte had an affair with Joan Collins. Quickly on the heels of that seeming turmoil, still in 1957, he married Julie Robinson, a white Jewish dancer and actress with whom he would stay until their divorce in 2004. It was a path of which the founder of the Grandassa fashion shows and the Black Is Beautiful campaign would obviously disapprove. Still, in the decades that followed publication of the coloring book, Belafonte would become a prominent and uncompromising voice in the anti-apartheid movement for his protégé Makeba's home country.[39]

##LENA HORNE

Lena Horne was born to an upper-middle-class, mixed-race family in Brooklyn. In 1933 she began working at the Cotton Club in Harlem and rode her success as a singer and dancer to a career in Hollywood. As Brath intimates in his commentary, she became disenchanted with the movie industry in the 1950s and left Hollywood to focus both on music and civil rights efforts. She lobbied for anti-lynch laws, performed to raise money for a variety of civil rights groups, attended the March on Washington, and helped where she could to aid the cause.[40]

Though Horne's first husband was a Black political worker, her second was Lennie Hayton, the white music director at MGM, where he arranged music for a long line of movies, winning the Academy Award in 1950. While his compositions were not well known independently of the films of which they were a part, that music was vital to many important movies. Judy Garland's *The Harvey Girls, On the Town, Singin' In the Rain*, and many others featured Hayton's scores. He would win another Academy Award after publication of the coloring book for his work on *Hello, Dolly!*[41]

Hayton was, however, white, and his race comprises the bulk of Brath's criticism of Horne. The attack incident to which he refers took place in 1960. Horne and Hayton were having dinner in a Beverly Hills restaurant when Hayton left to make a phone call. When he did, Horne heard two men at nearby table make ugly racist remarks and responded by throwing a lamp and ashtrays at the men. She hit one in the face, cutting his eye, but he declined to press charges.[42]

***EARTHA KITT

Eartha Kitt was originally from South Carolina and became part of the Great Migration after the death of her mother, arriving in Harlem as a teenager. She joined the Katherine Dunham dance troupe during World War II before beginning a singing and acting career. Like so many other Black entertainers during the 1950s and 1960s, she spent much of her time and cultural capital engaged in the civil rights movement. Brath's criticism of Kitt centers not on her specific activities in relation to civil rights, but rather her claim that her father was an unknown white man (that she was "high yellow"), a claim from which she never backed away, and her romantic predilection for white men, an interest that ruined her racial credibility in the mind of Brath.[43]

It was certainly true that Kitt preferred white men, conducting a relationship with Charles Revson, the founder of Revlon cosmetics, before ultimately marrying real estate mogul John William McDonald in 1960. The two had a daughter together, but even though their official divorce did not take effect until 1965, the couple did not last long. Kitt explained in the October 1963 edition of *Jet* magazine why she was filing for divorce, citing a variety of marital issues including wealth inequity between the two, jealousy on the part of McDonald, and her busy travel schedule. "Cultural backgrounds must count, too," she argued, but wasn't referring to the couple's mixed racial status. McDonald had grown up with wealth and education while she was a child of "the school of hard knocks and responsibilities." Her husband was "a successful man but just not worldly enough for me." It was in that same article that Kitt made her statement about American men being babies.[44]

Brath's image of Kitt was based on the cover of *Ebony* magazine in January 1963, which featured Kitt playing with her child, who did appear decidedly white. In the article accompanying that cover photo, Kitt explained that she took her daughter with her on her travels throughout the world. The feature included a variety of pictures of Kitt and her daughter, as well as a family photo that included McDonald.[45]

The story of Kitt's unknown white father gained public attention in her first autobiography, *Thursday's Child*, published in 1956, and her search for who he might be remained a preoccupation for her throughout the remainder of her life. She also told her life story two more times after the appearance of the coloring book, publishing *Alone with Me* in 1976 and *I'm Still Here: Confessions of a Sex Kitten* in 1989, both of which continued the theme of the first and surely earned Brath's approbation.[46]

††† SAMMY DAVIS JR.

Sammy Davis Jr. was a dancer, musician, and actor who got his start as a child in the 1930s with his vaudevillian parents. After World War II he began recording his own albums and starring in movies. He became part of Frank Sinatra's Rat Pack in 1959. Like other Black entertainers, he used his fame and earnings to support civil rights causes. One of those efforts was the Tribute to Martin Luther King Jr., held at Carnegie Hall on January 27, 1961, which raised more than $50,000. King was overjoyed. "When I solicited your help for our struggle almost two months ago, I did not expect so creative and fulsome a response," he wrote Davis. "I hope I can convey our appreciation to you with the warmth which we feel it." The homophobic jokes that Brath claims occurred at the fundraiser were not recorded, but they are the kinds of jokes that would have been common of the Rat Pack.[47]

While there isn't any corroborating evidence that Davis ever encouraged white chorus girls to perform minstrel shows, he did star in the filmed version of *Porgy and Bess* in 1959, and was scheduled to star in a musical called *The Minstrel Man* that was based on the original minstrelsy circuit. That movie fell through—it would later be filmed as a television movie in 1977, without Davis—but Davis was clearly willing to engage with minstrelsy, at least on its periphery.[48]

Brath's two dominant problems with Davis, however, were Davis's preference for white women and his conversion to Judaism. The opening of Brath's commentary describing Davis's escapades that would "scare a producer to death . . . just 'as-Kim' about his romances," is a reference to Davis's 1957 relationship with Hollywood actress Kim Novak. Fearing a backlash from the interracial relationship, the head of Columbia Pictures contracted with Mafia hitmen to warn Davis off of the relationship and convince him to conduct a brief sham marriage with a Black dancer to salvage the studio's reputation. In 1960 Davis, now more popular and thus more powerful, married Swedish actress May Britt. While his employers never threatened him in the early 1960s, he was still inundated with threats and hate mail from those across the country who disapproved of interracial marriage. As a result of the wedding, Davis's invitation to perform at John F. Kennedy's inauguration was rescinded for fear of a political backlash.[49]

When they married, the ceremony was officiated by a rabbi because Davis had converted to Judaism. After a car crash that took his left eye, Davis was convinced of Judaism's benefit largely through the encouragement of Jewish comedian Eddie Cantor. It is true that Judaism's history and the resilience of its people did appeal to Davis, but he never denied the rich history of the Black population by comparison.[50]

Brath was not hostile to Jews in any sustained way, but he was consistently frustrated with Zionism and Israel's willingness to do business with apartheid regimes like that of South Africa.[51] That put Israel's interests at odds with "the worldwide African liberation struggle." And that, in turn, made groups like the

Jewish Defense League "neo-fascist" organizations that were diametrically opposed to Black interests. "To many of us who have basic problems trying to distinguish between the concept of a 'Chosen People' and the theory of a 'Master Race,'" he wrote in the *Amsterdam News*, "we find both the Zionist entity in Palestine and the neo-Nazi regime in Azania [South Africa] equally rooted in a false assumption of a selective white supremacy."[52]

⊞JACKIE ROBINSON

Jackie Robinson was a four-sport star as a collegian at UCLA. After brief stints with semi-professional football teams and as an athletic director for a small Texas HBCU, Robinson joined the Kansas City Monarchs Negro league baseball team in 1945. In 1946 he was signed by Brooklyn Dodgers general manager Branch Rickey, playing that season for the Montreal Royals. The next year, on April 15, 1947, Robinson desegregated the major leagues when he made his debut for the Dodgers. Brath is absolutely correct that Robinson was not in the highest echelon of Negro leagues players. He was chosen largely because he was college educated (or, in Brath's parlance, "talks like a cracker") and was willing to suffer the inevitable abuse he would experience without confrontation.[53]

Robinson retired from baseball prior to the 1957 season, and later that year he became vice president for personnel at Chock Full o' Nuts coffee company, where he would stay until 1964, just months after the coloring book's publication. He also joined the board of the NAACP and began a weekly syndicated column in the Black press where he discussed political issues. While he supported the nonviolent, integrationist version of civil rights, Robinson was surprisingly conservative on other issues. As Brath's caricature intimates, for example, corporate personnel directors like Robinson were inherently opposed to union gains.[54]

It was also true that Robinson's family had moved to the Addisleigh Park section of St. Albans, Queens, and then to Connecticut, but the racial motivations of those moves as told by Brath did not exist. When Robinson moved to St. Albans in 1949 it was a predominantly white neighborhood, but Count Basie, Ella Fitzgerald, and other entertainers had purchased homes there in the 1930s. Though those early purchases were challenged in courts because of racially restrictive housing covenants in Addisleigh Park, those challenges failed. The Robinson family stayed in the neighborhood until 1955, when the Dodgers finally won the World Series. After that season, the Robinsons moved to the New York suburbs just outside Stamford, Connecticut. Because it was from there that his newspaper column emanated, and because he was an economic conservative, it was "from his home in Connecticut" that "he tries to tell the masses in Harlem, how happy they should be with their economic status quo."[55]

¶¶¶FLOYD PATTERSON

Floyd Patterson was born poor in North Carolina, then moved north to Brooklyn with his family as part of the Great Migration. As Brath indicates, Patterson was a troubled child, engaging in a variety of petty crimes that eventually landed him at an upstate reform school. After that experience, Patterson began to excel at high school sports in New Paltz, New York. Boxing was his strongest game, and while still a teenager he won a middleweight gold medal at the 1952 Olympics. Four years later he became the world heavyweight champion. After losing the title to Ingemar Johansson, he regained it in 1960. He lost the title for a second time in 1962 when Sonny Liston knocked him out in the first round. Liston again knocked out Patterson in 1963, as Brath mentions ("he tried that non-violence nonsense on Liston twice, and it failed both times").[56]

Patterson made a trip to Egypt in March 1962, months prior to losing his title to Liston in September. His lawyer also attended, as did his brother Raymond. They met with Gamal Abdel Nasser while on the trip, but the leader's total control of the country, what W. K. Stratton called "the dictatorial gaze of Nasser," combined with the poverty of the citizens, left a bad taste in Patterson's mouth. While in Egypt, Patterson attended a United Arab Republic Boxing Federation amateur tournament. He was mobbed by fans at all of his stops, but particularly at the boxing matches. His criticism of Egypt upon his return was intended to be sympathetic to the Egyptian people, but criticism of a pan-African thinker like Nasser would always be anathema to Brath.[57]

Patterson expressed frustration with a beauty salon in Rockville Centre, New York, that made it virtually impossible for his wife to get an appointment, while a white woman friend of the family was easily able to get an appointment. Patterson didn't sue the salon, and there is no evidence of what kind of service his wife was seeking from its stylists, but he did talk publicly about the incident to demonstrate the prejudices that existed in the country, even in the North and even for the rich and famous.[58]

§§§DICK GREGORY

Dick Gregory was originally from St. Louis, Missouri, and was shaped in large measure by the racism he experienced there as a child. He began his career in comedy while serving in the military in the mid-1950s. Like all Black comics at the time, he initially performed his stand-up at African American venues, but in the early 1960s made the transition to mainstream white venues. It was a transition made all the more unlikely because Gregory's material, unlike that of "safer" comics like Bill Cosby, directly engaged discrimination. While a variety of leaders and entertainers over the years have been referred to as the "conscience of America," Gregory was seen as a "conscience" because his act demonstrated the absurdities of segregation and discrimination.[59]

That being the case, Gregory actively supported the integrationist civil rights movement in the early 1960s, traveling south to help in a variety of activist efforts. After the coloring book's publication, he would be part of Mississippi's Freedom Summer in 1964. He would go on to support a variety of causes throughout a career that became known as much for its efforts in aid of the dispossessed as it was for its comedy.[60]

Unlike many of his other caricatures, Brath's criticism of Gregory is built almost solely on the comedian's advocacy of integration. He also mocks the notion of a comedian being a civil rights leader, an ironic claim coming from someone using comedy to criticize civil rights leaders, and who was a different kind of civil rights leader in his own right.

###BAYARD RUSTIN

Bayard Rustin was a Pennsylvania Quaker who came to Harlem in 1937 after college. He had associations with the Communist Party during the 1930s, but eventually became disillusioned and joined the socialists under the influence of A. Philip Randolph. Rustin fought for civil rights causes throughout his life and was a leader of the Journey of Reconciliation in 1947, the first effort at what would later become known as the Freedom Rides. He originally joined the southern civil rights movement during the Montgomery Bus Boycott, helping with the organization of the Montgomery Improvement Association and teaching the protesters Gandhian methods of submission and nonviolence. After the boycott, he helped Martin Luther King organize the Southern Christian Leadership Conference.[61]

Because of his former communist affiliations and because he was gay ("Isn't it queer?" Brath asks, in a clear homophobic reference), Rustin remained in the background of the movement, as Brath intimates, worrying that a more public role would tarnish the broader movement. At the urging of Randolph, however, Rustin's role became more public when organizing the March on Washington. He had been part of Randolph's first attempt at a March on Washington in January 1941 and was tasked with spearheading its reprise. In response, South Carolina Senator Strom Thurmond made public a 1953 conviction for "sexual perversion" in an effort to discredit Rustin. The morals charge and its publicity a decade later are the reason Brath repeats the word "moral" in his commentary.[62]

Brath was no friend of the March on Washington, and his description of the event as a gimmick echoed language used by Rustin. But Rustin's description of a gimmick was not in reference to the March on Washington. "A demonstration should have an immediately achievable target, or it should have—it should throw up a position which if those in power or those who own the thing or whatever it is, can at least in part come through with some demand that you are making," he told Robert Penn Warren. "Now, when a demonstration is just against being a black man in America, this is not a demonstration to me, it is a gimmick. This is not real, it is unreal, and sooner or later even one's own group will not tolerate this, because they have to have victories in order to keep in the movement, and those victories must be clearly interpreted to them, so that they know truly what they have won."[63]

****LOUIS LOMAX

Louis Lomax was born in Valdosta, Georgia, the deepest of the Deep South, and grew up in a middle-class household in a hyper-segregated area to a family that valued education. Despite his family's standing in the community, Lomax was no stranger to racism in Jim Crow south Georgia, but he thrived through segregated education. After college, he became a journalist. He covered a series of desegregation fights in Kentucky and Tennessee and did foreign correspondent work in Haiti. He also profiled influential television journalist Mike Wallace, who then hired Lomax as a writer and interviewer for his program *Newsbeat*, on New York's WNTA. The program featured news stories that included exposés on borough presidents and other city officials.[64]

After a series of efforts goading Malcolm X and Elijah Muhammad, convincing them of the benefit of a working relationship, Lomax pitched his big scoop to Wallace, convincing him that the Nation of Islam would make a worthy subject for the show. Thus it was that in 1959 "The Hate That Hate Produced" debuted on *Newsbeat*, introducing the Nation of Islam to the country. Lomax interviewed the subjects and produced the show, but the incendiary title and commentary were Wallace's. While the Nation of Islam railed against Wallace, the group was pleased with its national exposure, and its leaders stayed close to Lomax. Later that year, for example, Lomax helped Malcolm produce the first issues of the group's newspaper, *Muhammad Speaks*.[65]

Lomax parlayed his success with Wallace into a book deal with Harper for a monograph about the modern political situation in Africa, ultimately published as *The Reluctant African*. The book took a decidedly integrationist stance, criticized what he saw as a stubborn unwillingness to compromise with whites by many anticolonial movements on the continent, and demonstrated a novice's understanding of the political issues facing the countries he visited. It was precisely the kind of treatment that would offend an African nationalist like Brath.[66]

It is also true that Lomax promoted integration to nationalist audiences, partly out of a sincere belief in the cause and partly as an effort in provocation. Just months after the publication of the coloring book, for example, Lomax would be the opening act for Malcolm X's "The Ballot or the Bullet" speech, pushing nonviolent integration to rile up the crowd and provide a foil for his friend.[67] Finally, Lomax was one of the founders of the Christmas Boycott, which is described in greater detail in the Roy Wilkins annotation above.

††††ELIJAH MUHAMMAD AND MALCOLM X

Wallace Fard migrated to Detroit likely from Afghanistan in 1930. There he worked a variety of odd jobs until forming a new religion, the Nation of Islam (NOI), loosely based on the Muslim faith. He argued, as Brath mentions, that Arabic was the original language of Africa, that Christianity was imposed on the Black population by slaveholders, and that a religion that rejected white hegemony could unify the African American population. Brath is correct, of course, that Arabic itself was actually an imposed language for West Africans. And members of Fard's new faith did often reference the Bible, but such was considered a necessity when preaching to those who were most familiar with Christianity.[68]

Fard's most devoted follower was Elijah Muhammad, the former Elijah Poole, who took over the faith in 1934 after Fard's mysterious disappearance. Muhammad continued the teachings of Fard while propping up the now-absent leader as a Christ figure. One of those teachings was that the Tribe of Shabazz was the original progenitor of all nonwhite peoples. They were Black, but their hair was silky and smooth. It only became kinky after the tribe migrated into central Africa and experienced the harsh climate of the region.[69]

Muhammad's most important pupil was Malcolm X, the former Malcolm Little, who converted to the Nation of Islam while in prison on a burglary charge. When he was released in

1952, he began working for the faith. In 1954 he took over the group's Mosque #7 in Harlem, where his influence grew largely as a commentator on civil rights issues around the country. Malcolm often called white people "devils," as did Muhammad. He criticized the civil rights movement's efforts in Birmingham in 1963, which culminated in September with the bombing of the Sixteenth Street Baptist Church.[70]

He also denounced violence against members of the Nation of Islam. The shooting incident Brath refers to in his commentary took place in the Watts section of Los Angeles in 1962. The Los Angeles Police Department targeted the NOI, claiming that the violence was the result of a shootout, despite the fact that the Black Muslims did not own or carry weapons. As Malcolm X explained to WBAI radio after the attack, "In the shooting that took place, seven men were shot. Seven Muslims were shot. None of them were armed. None of them were struggling. None of them were fighting. None of them were trying to defend themselves at all. And after being taken to the police station, they were held for 48 hours and weren't even given hospitalization. We have one now who is completely paralyzed. We just got all of them free last night."[71]

The power struggle to which Brath refers was also real. In March 1964, as the coloring book was going into its second printing, Malcolm split with the Nation of Islam. He was frustrated with Muhammad's infidelity, among other things, and Muhammad was frustrated with Malcolm's popularity and influence. The cartoon itself depicts Raymond Sharieff, national captain of the paramilitary Fruit of Islam group and Muhammad's son-in-law, conspiring with Elijah Muhammad against Malcolm X, a rift in the relationship that was not publicly acknowledged until Malcolm announced on March 8 his formal break with the organization.[72]

Brath was close to Malcolm. "I had observed Malcolm from the late 1950s, particularly in the old Temple No. 7," he explained, "and exhibited my artwork in his African-Asian Bazaars." The two first met early in 1961, "ironically because of a criticism of the Nation of Islam that I had made from a Black Nationalist position, which he thought 'interesting.'" Malcolm respected the African Nationalist Pioneer Movement, Carlos Cooks, and his followers, as "the authentic or orthodox 'Garveyite nationalists.' I had different occasions to talk with him about our mutual differences with the civil 'rites' movement until just before his assassination." Brath argued that Malcolm had been "a magnificent model for Black manhood and morality." On the twenty-fifth anniversary of Malcolm's assassination in 1990, Brath's Patrice Lumumba Coalition held a Black History Month series to honor the fallen leader and his work. In 1994 he helped spearhead the Save the Audubon Ballroom Coalition in an unsuccessful effort to preserve the legendary venue where Malcolm was killed.[73]

⸬JESUS, ABRAHAM LINCOLN, FRANKLIN AND ELEANOR ROOSEVELT, AND JOHN F. KENNEDY

The final caricature in the series depicts a group of white liberal saviors held up as paragons of virtue in relation to Black rights. The historically inaccurate white depiction of Jesus is the "Holy Ghost." Lincoln, commonly portrayed as the Great Emancipator, but someone who ended slavery largely as a means to an end, is the "Log Cabin Ghost." Franklin Roosevelt, whose New Deal did not directly target the Black population for fear of losing white southern votes, is the "New Deal Ghost," and his wife Eleanor, who served on the board of the NAACP and helped craft the Universal Declaration of Human Rights, is the "Great Lady Ghost." Kennedy, assassinated less than two months prior to the publication of the coloring book, is depicted standing, the newest arrival being propped up as the "New Frontier Ghost."

¶¶¶¶THE SAGA OF OLE MISS

In January 1961, James Meredith applied for admission to the University of Mississippi. Meredith was not a traditional student. After high school, he served in the Air Force for several years, then attended Jackson State College. But he wanted to integrate Ole Miss. "I am familiar with the probable difficulties involved in such a move as I am undertaking," he said, "and I am fully prepared to pursue it all the way to a degree from the University of Mississippi." Of course, he was swiftly denied admission, and in May, with the help of the NAACP's Legal Defense Fund, he filed suit.

The case went to court the following year, and the judge rejected Meredith's claim, arguing that he didn't prove his rejection was racially motivated. But after a series of legal battles between judges of the Fifth Circuit Court of Appeals, the courts ordered him admitted. The governor of Mississippi, Ross Barnett, adamantly opposed the ruling. A staunch segregationist, he knew the symbol that Ole Miss served for white Mississippians. He responded with an address on statewide television and radio. "We will not surrender to the evil and illegal forces of tyranny," he claimed. His administration tried everything it could to keep Meredith out of Ole Miss. Because Meredith had once been convicted on a charge of voter fraud after registering to vote in the wrong county, the state even passed a law that barred convicted criminals from attending a state school.

As Brath suggests, John F. Kennedy was no adamant proponent of the civil rights movement, despite having campaigned on the issue. He was an anti-communist first and foremost, a foreign policy president who wanted more than anything to win the Cold War. At the same time, however, like previous presidents he opposed the effort at interposition when governors interfered with federal orders. Thus Kennedy intervened, talking to Barnett and negotiating Meredith's entry into the school. On October 1, 1962, Meredith became the first Black student at Ole Miss.

The white students at Ole Miss and the white population that saw the school as a symbol of the state, however, were perfectly willing to fight back. There were riots on and around campus, forcing Kennedy to send in the National Guard and US marshals, sparking what became known as the "Ole Miss War." Forty-eight soldiers were injured and twenty-eight federal marshals were wounded by gunfire. Two people were killed, one of whom was a French journalist covering the story for the international news. Despite the initial upheaval, however, Meredith stayed, survived, and in 1963 graduated with a degree in political science.[74]

Part 4

MISCELLANEOUS ART AND ESSAYS

THE AFRICAN JAZZ-ART SOCIETY & STUDIOS, INC.
proudly presents

caste-life
REVUE

**a satirical & dramatic theatrical presentation
concerned with the lives of black people!**

starring the

AJASS Repertory Theatre Company

featuring

**FRANK ADU/DAVID WARD/LEROY GILES
SMOKEY MARTIN/ERNEST BAXTER/HORACE FOSTER**

and the

Grandassa Models

**Saturday Night / Curtain 8:30PM
MAY 22nd, 1965
at the
KING SOLOMON
GRAND LODGE
(formerly the RKO Alhambra)
7th Avenue Between 125th & 126th Streets**

Advance Tickets/ $2.50 & $3.00

For Tickets and additional information:
Harlem/AJASS 243 W. 125th St. suite 12 RI 9-6880

JAZZTONE RECORD SHOP
157th St. & Amsterdam Ave.
Brooklyn/Mr. C. HALL
GL 3-5595

WIL'S RECORD SHOP
147 W. 125th St.
Bronx/MELLO-TONE MUSIC SHOP
1299 Boston Rd. (near 169th St.)

poster design & artwork / Cecil Elombe Brathwaite

10

MISCELLANEOUS ACTIVIST ART, 1963–1970

Activists who are also artists find those two elements of their lives intersecting in a variety of ways that are not necessarily part of a uniform or continuous project. This poster for the African Jazz-Art Society's "Caste-Life Review" features some characters from the coloring book, like Martin Luther King, Sammy Davis Jr., and James Baldwin, but also tells the larger story of the southern civil rights movement, complete with abusive southern cops, George Wallace, and Lyndon Johnson. Original housed in the Grandassa Models Collection, 1963–1968, Sc MG 822, Schomburg Center for Research in Black Culture, New York.

The fashion shows staged by the AJASS came attendant with programs touting natural Black beauty standards. Essays by Brath and others staked out a theoretical position on African American self-worth tied directly to rejecting a mainstream white modeling of beauty. One year, along with such essays, Brath included a cartoon in the style of his *Citizen-Call* work. Original in *Naturally '63 Portfolio*, Grandassa Models Collection, 1963–1968, Sc MG 822, Schomburg Center for Research in Black Culture, New York.

Marcus Garvey
on prejudice

YOU CAN NEVER
CURB THE PREJUDICE
OF THE ONE RACE
OR NATION AGAINST
THE OTHER BY LAW.
IT MUST BE REGULATED
BY ONE'S OWN FEEL-
ING, ONE'S OWN WILL.
AND IF ONE'S FEELING
AND WILL REBEL A-
GAINST YOU NO LAW
IN THE WORLD CAN
CURB IT.

More than forty years ago, Marcus Garvey initiated
into the minds of Blackmen throughout the world, the idea
of self determination.
Today, the African jazz-art society is proud to an-
nounce the birth of the African jazz-art studio; a commercial art-photography....African dance and jazz promotional
agency......right in the heart of Harlem.
We cordially invite you to inquire about using our
various services........................RIverside 9-6880

the African jazz-art society
& studios
243 W. 125th Street   Harlem, 27, New York City

artist: cecil brathwaite

The veneration of Marcus Garvey and his ideology was part and parcel of everything Brath did, particularly in the AJASS. This flyer for the African Jazz-Art Studio features a portrait of Garvey drawn by Brath. Original in Grandassa Models Collection, 1963–1968, Sc MG 822, Schomburg Center for Research in Black Culture, New York.

"Of Land, Lunatics & the Cosmos" first appeared in the *Journal of Black Poetry* in its first Pan-African issue in 1970, a volume edited by Askia Muhammad Touré. Touré, born Roland Snellings, was a New York migrant from Raleigh, North Carolina, whose poetry and essays led him to become one of the leading figures of the Black Arts Movement. While Touré's political philosophy underwent a series of changes throughout his life, his Pan-Africanism remained relatively unquestioned. He took his name, for example, from the greatest of the Songhai emperors, who ruled the West African empire in the early sixteenth century.

The *Journal of Black Poetry* was a short-lived publication founded and edited by Joe Goncalves in San Francisco. Contributing editors included Imamu Amiri Baraka, Marvin X, Larry Neal, Touré, Ed Spriggs, and others. It was one of the principal outlets for Black poetry and essays in the Black Power era, one of the core bodies of Black Arts Movement work. Brath's poem, "Of Land, Lunatics & the Cosmos" fits perfectly into the Black Arts Movement style and trajectory and demonstrates a sophistication not normally shown by those for whom poetry is only a hobby or side project.[1]

OF LAND, LUNATICS & THE COSMOS

AFRICA

Black Star, guiding light
Of a new Underground Railroad
Land ho! AFRICA, the New World
O so proudly we *long* to hail
The Red, Black & Green
Wavering over *the real* Reclamation Site #1

AFRICA
Garvey *told* Kwame Nkrumah
"AFRICA Must Be Free"
FREE AFRICA
        And you will
        Free all the Hueys
        & all the Panthers, too
        Can you dig it?
Even in the old diddy-boppin' *gang-bustin'* days
It was always a question of turf
            Of territory
            Of Land
    See where I'm coming from?
A Vietnam Tombstone read:
            Here lies a Blackman
            Who thought he was a Brownman
            Sent here by the Whiteman
            To protect interest on land
            Stolen from the Redman
            And was killed by a Yellowman
            Who was *defending his land* . . .
            (The Vietnamese couldn't dig
            Where the Brother was coming from
            And sent him back to the *cosmos*)
            Oooooo cap!
Jomo Kenyatta
When he *really was* Jomo KENYATTA
Leader of the Kenya Land & Peace Freedom Army
(Whom the Whiteman called *Mau Mau*)
Sifted a handful of soil
Through his fingers &
Let it fall to the ground
Saying

"This Earth, this land (AFRICA)
This very dust is generations of my ancestors"
Can you understand that, Brothers?
I mean
Can you *really* dig it?
The Black woman (Naturally)
Is the most Beautiful Woman in the *Universe*
She is the Mother of the Black World
The Original People of Earth
Only she can *reproduce*
The Africanoid Black Species

       Of Mankind

       Of Our Kind

       Of me You   Us   We are

       As old as the Sun & Moon & Stars

Hear me, Sisters
Only a *lunatic* would fail to see that You are more heavenly
       Than any *celestial* body
Once upon a time
The Whiteman told us that

       "The cow jumped over the moon"

       Understand now . . .

       Mother Goose was *also* the Whiteman

       Did you ever dig that?

       Now he/she tells us that Armstrong

       (Jack Armstrong? The All-American boy?)

       Danced on the Moon

       Litterbug Jitterbug

       I know you all dug that . . .

And Tricky Dick telephoned
From the White House to the Man in/on the Moon
Out House
   And got through as clear as a bell
While on Earth

        My phone is clogged with static

        Because our lines are crossed & jammed & bugged

        Now you get to that

But the Nation

Became moonstruck

Lunatics

Of thee I sing

        Caught

        With your eyeballs focused on heaven again

While your pockets & your bellies still are

Caught short or *empty*

Double-Crossed by neglected priorities

After waiting so long

        For the Second Coming

        Of Christ

Come down to Earth, folks

'Cause *Earth is what's really happening*

And you had better *deal with it*

Stop getting *so high*

Brother, Sister

Talkin' bout You *trippin'* into outer space

Upon your re-entry

Into Earth *orbit*

You will find that Mother Goose

Has tricked You out of space

Out of Land & Air & Water

Out of AFRICA

Remember that he/she tricked you

Out of AFRICA *before*

Although you saw that *The Cross*

Was in his/her hand

Can you read me clear?

"We come in peace for All Mankind"

They proclaimed

While *jooging* their conquering symbols
Into the glassy crust of the Moon
For *All* Mankind? For All *Whose* Kind?
Not for All *My* Kind
"We come in peace for All Mankind"
    America
        The Indian fought & died
        The Black man *uncle tommed* & multiplied
        And the Whiteman took *the land*
"We come in peace for All Mankind"
    Australia
        But the Aboriginal Blackman
        Wouldn't *slave*
        The Whiteman sent him to an
        Early grave
        So that he could *inherit* the land
"We come in peace for All Mankind"
    Asia
        And in People's parks in China
        Signs started to appear
        Stating
        No dogs or Chinese allowed in here
        The Whiteman had to have *all* land
"We come in peace for All Mankind"
    AFRICA
        Then the Whiteman *introduced* his "Holy Bible"
        Ending all peace in the African's paradisiac Lands
        With the Blackman *buried* in The Bible
        Whites seized all *pieces* of Black highlands
        The early predators still roam
        This jungled planet/world/land
But there arose from the People
A cry for LAND
    "Give Us Back Our Land"

Let Europe *be* for Europeans &
Asia for Asians
      But Above All
      Let AFRICA *Be For* AFRICANS
      Those at Home & those abroad
      Roared the *Winds of Change*
      Hurricane containing the *cosmic force*
      Of Garvey's Ghost
For Immortal Garvey can never die
Death being *but a return* to the cosmos
Energy spent & transmitted into an unknown form
Organic   gaseous   liquid   dust-like
But none-the-less
      A cosmic force
      Can you feel the psychic vibrations?
Acemendese
First charted the sun, moon & stars
Evolving a perfect calendar
Of thirteen months
      Each containing 28 days
      & Cosmic harmony
      Until the Whiteman
      Juggled the *Black Studies of Calculus*
      Producing "Leap Year" & daily confusion
Beware Whiteman tampering with *the moon*
Enchantress of the menstrual cycle
And controller of the tides &
All of the Earth's waters
      That brings flood & rains & mass upheaval
      Of Nature's balance
      Ah, but could that be *too deep?*
Now dig this
This is Man's World
And Men the World over

Today will assert themselves
Over the question of LAND
                Their Lands
                Lands of their Ancestors &
                Land of/and/is their Ancestors
                BLACKMAN
                Come down to Earth
                To the Real Down-To-Earth Space Race
                For AFRICA
                My AFRICA   Your AFRICA   Our AFRICA
                We are the Sons & Daughters
                Of Mother AFRICA
                Fathered by The Sun
                First born Children of Earth
                Far scattered *long lost*
                Heirs of this planet's richest real estate
                AFRICA
Kidnapped & brought
Out of space in AFRICA
Like new found specimens displayed to an alien world
and quarantined
        For over 350 years
        Transplanted questioned   studied experimented upon
        Released for *propaganda* purposes
        But always under
        Constant surveillance &
                Maximum *security*
        Promised a projected landing
        In The Sea of Tranquility
        Miscalculation
        We touch down among the *rugged craters*
        Of the Sea of Crises
But now, amoeboid
We stir & replenish ourselves & grow

As satellites we
      Retrace our *orbital* path
      Guided by our distant Star of Destiny
      AFRICA
         Terrestrial compass
         Of a wandering *people*
         No longer *lost in the stars*
            Finding our way back *home*
In Body & Mind & Spirit
We search for LAND
Yearning to set unshackled feet
On the Good Earth
Our Good Earth
Land ho! AFRICA, the New World

Wanting To Desert...

written by
The Hon. Marcus A. Garvey

illustrated by
Cecil Elombe Brath

A Casteman who got rich did stray
   And claimed he was not of the race.
But all the world could only say
   He was a fool and sore disgrace.

You cannot change your skin my man
   For Nature made you as you are.
Your wish to break your fathers clan,
   Is ignorance that goes too far.

The woman of another race
   You choose to share your fortune with,
And have her take your mother's place
   May slay you yet, as in siren's myth.

And when you find the deed unwise
   It will be late, too late to mend.
And then the race you did despise
   Will count you out with traitor's end.

"Dedicated especially to the caste partners of interracial couples.

In this cartoon, Brath illustrates a poem by Marcus Garvey about Black men trying to get white using the imagery of Sammy Davis Jr., continuing the critique that he began in the coloring book.

11

ESSAYS, 1979–1990s

Included here is a small selection of Brath's written work to demonstrate the formal argumentation for ideas presented in the coloring book and comic strip, all of it coming after that earlier artwork. The first describes the outgrowths of American Pan-Africanist thinking in the late 1970s. The second criticizes American leadership in 1980 and historically, reminding readers of the racism of the "founding fathers" and the reality that they are not the founding fathers of the Black population. The third essay is a paean to Marcus Garvey and Garveyism, describing both Garvey's intellectual heirs in the United States and analyzing the nationalist-communist divide described in the introduction. The final essay criticizes American political opportunists on the occasion of Nelson Mandela's release from prison in February 1990 and his planned visit to the United States. In particular, Brath takes issue with civil rights activist Jesse Jackson and New York mayor David Dinkins, giving them a more fulsome version of the criticism he leveled at earlier Black leaders in the coloring book, particularly in relation to their relationships to the South African government and international banks who do business with it. Thus the included essays serve in microcosm as a representative combination of Brath's domestic and foreign work.

BLACK SOLIDARITY DAY DENOUNCES RIGHTS RECORD[1]

In one of the most militant and impressive displays of international Black solidarity involving contingents of African people from over ten cities, at least nine states, five boroughs and the suburbs, the Caribbean and Africa, several thousand demonstrators marched nearly four miles from Harlem down to the United Nations, by-passed police barricades and scaled the fence to the General Assembly building to raise Garvey's red, black and green banner of African "self-determination" and charge the US government with "genocide"!

Utilizing the ten year old annual Black Solidarity Day celebration as a dramatic catalyst for denouncing Carter's "human rights" campaign, as well as recent racist attacks in the US (including everything from hospital cutbacks to KKK cross-burnings and "mass murder"), the National Black Human Rights Coalition (NBHRC), a year old umbrella group that enlisted over a hundred organizations and countless individuals for the mammoth effort, was successful in getting thousands of people to participate in what amounted, for many, to be a general strike and a boycott of major businesses (considered exploitive) and schools (considered non-functioning).

General Consensus

It was a general consensus among all involved that the Carter Administration's "human rights" campaign was a brazen and hypocritical political ploy directed at embarrassing revolutionary regimes that have found that they are sometimes forced to use what many call "heavy manners" to restrain the destructive activities of local fifth column elements trying to stabilize their respective governments in the service of western imperialism.

However, in this case, the tables were reversed as many representatives of progressive countries and movements were pleasantly surprised to see the self-righteous government of the "home of democracy, the free and the brave" shamefully exposed as a historic violator of the human rights of Black people in this country.

A brief synopsis of the United Nations in relationship to the concept of universal human rights shows that the world body is the proper arena to raise the contradictions of US violations against its Black populace—a strategy that originated with the Honorable Marcus Garvey's initiative at the former League of Nations (the UN's immediate predecessor) and was continued later with the work of Paul Robeson, William Patterson, and El Hajj Malik El Shabazz (Malcolm X), among others of less renown.

Article 55 in the United Nations Charter calls for the "promotion of universal respect for, and observance of, human rights and fundamental freedom for all people, without distinction as to race, sex, language, or religion."

This theme is considered a basic tenet of the UN, and the United States is not only a founding member of the UN (June 26, 1945) but an original signatory to its Charter, of which it constantly boasts of its concern for human rights.

When the UN Economic and Social Council's (ECOSOC) Commission on Human Rights prepared its Universal Declaration of Human Rights, which was adopted on December 10, 1948 by a then 56-member General Assembly that was dominated by the imperialist and colonialist powers, there were only three regional economic commissions to report to the Council: one for Europe, whose priority was Jewish refugees; one for Asia and the Far East; and one for Latin America.

There was neither a regional commission for Africa nor one for North America. And at that time only three African states and Haiti were listed among the so-called "independent" nations, while the rest of Africa remained under a brutal colonial oppression.

Zionist Terrorists

Concurrently, Zionist terrorists (as they were considered at the time) were in the process of dispossessing the Palestinian people of their homeland to satisfy Jewish aspirations for a "homeland" for the refugees of Nazi genocide, going as far as to assassinate the UN Mediator, Count Folke Bernadotte of Sweden—an act that it is said, by many authoritative sources, to have been ordered by the now present prime minister of Israel, Menachem Begin.

At this same time in history the Caribbean was viewed as a British, French, Dutch and American colonial paradise, while Latin America, while formally drawn into a US controlled Organization of American States, was derisively looked upon as a string of "banana republics."

More "close to home," Black veterans, who had been inducted into the US armed forces to go to Europe to keep that continent "safe for democracy" and shed their blood fighting fascism, returned to the land of their birth, ironically, to rejoin their brethren still under an American apartheid system, subject to the sadistic whims of white racist lynch mobs which often overlooked their service uniforms in lieu of the uniformity of their racial characteristics.

Thus, when the UN Secretary-General, the late Trygve Lie of Norway, and a special ECOSOC committee presented its Convention on Genocide to the General Assembly in 1948, and it was accepted and hailed by its members, Africans—and other oppressed nationalities and/or ethnic groups—in the US rejoiced. But when the Convention finally came into force in January of 1951, and by the middle of 1957 fifty-five nations had promised to adhere to this Convention (although, strangely, some did so "with special reservations"), Africans in this country became highly suspicious when the US was not among those to ratify the Anti-Genocide Pact!

Our concern is justified because Africans, along with the indigenous population of this country, are the only national, racial or ethnic group upon which a policy of deliberate destruction, in whole or in part, has been practiced within the United States.

And the thought that to this very day the US has still not ratified the Convention on Genocide, while our people are constantly coming under savage and barbaric Klan and Nazi racist attacks, inadequate health services are being cut back further while life-threatening diseases are reaching epidemic proportions in the Black communities, while police harassment incidents have grown more vicious and victims have become younger (ironically, in the International Year of the Child!), while sterilization is being "legally" forced on our mothers, wives, sisters, etc., while frustration is driving more and more of our youth to narcotics, alcoholism, abnormal sexual behavior and increasing suicides, are enough reasons to understand why thousands of us were assembled on this November 5 on Black Solidarity Day—not because of any paranoia but because of the gross violations of the human rights of the African people of the United States of America!

The Universal—and universal is a very all encompassing term—Declaration of Human Rights states that among the rights of man specified in its 30 articles are the right to life, liberty and security of person—of which millions of our people have been systematically deprived, from prior to 1619 until 360 years later.

The right not to be held in slavery is made a mockery when we realize that, both down-south and up-south, migrant workers are many times held in virtual bondage through intimidation, threats of beatings, deportations, contrived debts to work-crew leaders, and forced labor among those the system manipulates into its prisons is a major industry in this country that thrives on such cheap labor.

Guarantees against physical torture are cynically violated when scores of our Brothers are forced to undergo brain lobotomies in diabolical experiments to alter militant behavior patterns, and other insidious controlled behavior modification programs, like the infamous Tuskegee case, where Black men are actually given diseases—which are allowed to go untreated—so that Nazi-like authorities can study the effects.

Obvious Contradiction

Equality in the eyes of the law has become such an obvious contradiction in regards to Black people in search of justice in this society that it has become a sad and tragic joke, and the vile insults and castigations that have been visited upon Judge Bruce Wright for his attempts to follow the above listed proper procedure only goes to show how much the so-called "law enforcement officers" view this right with utter contempt.

Protection of rights before the courts, including assurance of a fair trial—the notorious Black Panther inquisition trials make a caricature of this particular right, and as Angela Davis is credited with saying, concerning her own trumped-up trial, "the only fair trial would be no trial at all!"

The right to nationality is a fundamental right of freedom that Black people have been denied since their kidnapping from Africa and enslavement in the western hemisphere. That is why we say that "self-determination for African people is a basic human right!"

The freedom to marry and to found a family is made almost impossible by a system that manipulates socio-economic conditions in such a way that, in a great many cases, forces mothers to reluctantly separate from their spouses in order to subsist on some welfare pittance.

Freedom of Thought

Freedom of thought, conscience, religion, opinion, and peaceful assembly and association is also hailed . . . providing that your thoughts don't become too ideological, your conscience too demanding for social justice and reparations, your religion too eastern-oriented or away from the familiar "western" dominated Judeo-Christian ethic, your opinion too critical of the capitalist system, your peaceful assembly too devoid of the "non-violent" principle, and your association too close to radical internationalist-oriented camaraderie in general and the African liberation struggle in particular.

THE US AT 205[2]

On Saturday, July 5th, 1980, the United States of America entered the 205th year of its Declaration of Independence from the tyranny of British imperialism—an imperialism, I must add, that the former colonized have long ago surpassed.

The hypocrisy contained within the original declaration is no less a contradiction than the activities of some Black folks over the holiday weekend, particularly the parts played by some personalities and groups with considerable followings.

In Miami the NAACP, the anachronism of the civil "rites" movement, was summing up its 71st annual convention amidst the garish trappings of the Fontainebleau Hotel while outside, behind police barricades, their more victimized brethren were denouncing them for causing millions of dollars to be spent in a city where outrageous racist inequities had recently driven thousands of them to brave police and national guard bullets to demand their "inalienable rights" to life, liberty and the pursuit of happiness.

Black Masses

Ignoring the cries of the Black masses, the National Association for the Advancement of Colored People went on about their business as usual—once again "endorsing" Jimmy Carter for President and the US capitalist system for perpetuity, pausing only in an obscene gesture to assuage their guilt by sending several busloads of delegates on a sightseeing tour—at $6 a head—to view ravaged Liberty City and see the natives in their native habitat.

Harlem produced a scene equally as gross when remnants of an organization that many had considered to be the antithesis—and nemesis—of the NAACP were seen parading through the streets, waving the flag and loudly proclaiming their "patriotism," ostensibly to "project unyielding solidarity in support of the American Constitution and its true meaning and objectives as envisioned by our forefathers."

Further, a spokesman for the obnoxious festivities announced, the event was to also herald their mission to "continue the struggle towards the real American Dream"—the nightmarish situation confronting the broad masses of our people in this country today notwithstanding!

Now, while it may still be possible for many to subscribe to the idealistic words inscribed within the US Constitution, one cannot understand "its true meaning and objectives as envisioned by our forefathers" unless first one deals with the Declaration of Independence (written 13 years before the Constitution) and places both documents in the context of their time and defines whose "forefathers" envisioned what.

The fact remains that the forefathers of the African and/or Black people in the US (called Negroes, Colored People, Moorish- and Afro-Americans by some, Bilalians by others) were indigenous Africans who had been enslaved by the forefathers of the Europeans currently making up most of both the American ruling and working class!

This being the case, we should have a different historical perspective of events than our oppressors. If not, then surely something is dreadfully wrong—and wrong enough to guarantee that our sense of appreciation for genuine liberation and self-determination will forever be detoured into illusionary dreams of political, economic and social equality.

Very Inception

Whether a member of the NAACP, the American Muslim Mission, or any other organization, we should never forget that from its very inception the United States was fraught with irreconcilable contradictions: a slave-holding society espousing the freedom and equality of man. And no wonder. Its "founding fathers" were bonafide racists, many of whom even owned slaves themselves.

General George Washington, the so-called "father of the country" whose military rank reflected his reputation of leading repressive annihilation activities against the indigenes of this continent, kept slaves at his plantation in Mount Vernon, Virginia. In fact, Washington once bragged that on his vast estate, "I have more working negroes by a full moiety, then can be employed to any advantage in the farming system, and I shall never turn Planter (i.e., tobacco) thereon."

To add further insult, Washington also is said to have traded African slaves between his Mount Vernon abode and the Caribbean for kegs of molasses and rum (for which ole George had more than a fond taste!)

Thomas Jefferson, the universally acknowledged author of the Declaration, had about 250 Africans held as chattel at his Monticello, Virginia plantation while he was expounding those indelible words which claim: "We hold these truths to be self-evident, that all men are created equal and are endowed with certain inalienable rights, among these are life, liberty and the pursuit of happiness."

If Jefferson's hypocrisy was not yet self-evident, given the fact that half a million human beings (one-fifth the population at the time) were maintained in bondage, his *Notes on Virginia* clearly revealed both his agonizing over the question of slavery and his own personal contempt for Black people, which was still further compromised by his continuous intimate relationship with his slave mistress Sallie Hemmings.

On another occasion, however, Jefferson did deal factually with how he and his cohorts actually felt about the presence of the African in their society. "Nothing is more certainly written in the book of fate than that these people (Black folks) are to be free," he wrote, "nor is it less certain that the two races equally free cannot live in the same government. There are two alternatives for the future: The Negroes and Whites must either wholly part or wholly mingle."

Fearing Latter

Perhaps fearing the latter, James Madison added: "If the purity of the two Races is to be maintained they cannot continue to live side by side, and this is a problem from which there can be no escape."

There can be no escape from Ole Benjamin Franklin's position either. The "Renaissance man" of the founding fathers is recorded as having taxed his alleged genius to find ways to keep the United States untarnished of "the Sons of Africa" by not only "excluding all Blacks and Tawneys" but to prohibit most non-Anglo-Saxon Europeans from further entry. (Spaniards, Italians, French, Russians, and even Swedes and Germans were considered "two swarthy"!)

No doubt the horror of all these revelations moved Frederick Douglass to point out, in a historic 1852 address denouncing 4th of July celebrations, that since Black people had not yet attained full freedom, the Independence festivities "only reveals the immeasurable distance between us (and the white citizenry)."

In admonishing his white audience Douglass also gave the African still in search of social justice in America something to seriously think about. Said Douglass, "The blessings in which you this day rejoice, life, liberty, prosperity and independence bequeathed by your fathers is shared by you, not by me . . . What then to the American Black slave is your fourth of July? I answer.

"A day that reveals to him more than all of the days of the year the gross injustice to which he is a constant victim. To him, your celebration is a sham. Your boasted liberty—unholy license. Your national greatness—swelling vanity. Your sounds of rejoicing are empty and heartless. Your shouts of liberty and equality—hollow mockery. Your prayers and hymns, your sermons and thanksgivings with all your religious parade, their solemnity are to him mere bombast, fraud, impiety, deception and hypocrisy, a thin veil to cover up crimes which would disgrace a nation of savages. There is not a nation on the face of the earth guilty of practices more shocking and bloody then the people of the United States at this very hour."

Status of Africans

While those words were spoken 128 years ago, and the status of Africans in the US has risen from chattel to wage slave (with bourgeoise aspirations), the substance of Douglass's observations are just as relevant today—especially when the recent upsurge of "patriotism" is engulfing the country, ushering in a white backlash of reaction, and a Boraxo cowboy/actor is waiting in the wings to carry the banner to really "project unyielding solidarity in support of the American Constitution and its true meaning and objectives as envisioned by his forefathers!"

FROM 1900 TO 2000: THE PAN-AFRICAN CENTURY: A VINDICATION AND VICTORY FOR THE VISION OF MARCUS GARVEY[3]

As we enter the 21st century many people are looking back on the last hundred years in various attempts to review how this important period impacted on either general or specific issues confronting the struggle of Africa and her peoples. In this regard I would like to have you briefly reflect upon the phenomena of the philosophical and ideological program we have come to know as Pan-Africanism. I believe that to do this is of tremendous importance to us as a people because from the dawning of the 20th century, both in a literal and/or figurative sense, the concept of Pan-Africanism has manifested itself as the most consistent key ingredient in the movement involving the unification and liberation of black people worldwide.

Pan-Africanism is an idea that is both simple to understand yet complex in trying to bring about its successful application. The term itself tells it all. First, the prefix *pan* is Greek in origin and means "all." Its usage has regularly been seen in such formations as Pan-Hellenic (all Greek), Pan-American (all countries in the Americas—South, Central and North America, stemming from the 1889–90 First International Conference of American Pan-States that were popularly known as Pan-American Conferences), and Pan-Slavic, Pan-Germanic, Pan-Arabic, etc.

The term Pan-Africanism is similar in its origin. As previous examples show, it makes use of the prefix *pan*, applying it to African people. The word African, whatever its origin, is the accepted identification of the indigenous people of Africa (also known in antiquity as Ethiopians, Nubians, Nguni/a Bantu, Twa, KhoiSan, etc.), as well as their descendants and kinsmen in the Diaspora and the Pacific Islands. And the suffix, *ism*, is a Latin word meaning "philosophy." Therefore, the term Pan-Africanism, in effect, is a philosophy that embraces all African people, wherever they are on this planet.

This definition is basic, yet simplistic. The complexity is dramatized when we remember that Pan-Africanism is largely a concept initiated and developed by Africans born outside of Africa, particularly those in the western hemisphere. Thus in most instances they have been shorn of any fundamental single ethnic (read "tribalistic") subjective prejudices that would make them biased to any individual African group, but envision and embrace the whole continent of Africa as the epicenter of our people.

But having said that, I must add that Pan-Africanism, in my view, cannot simply just be successful as an umbrella mobilization tactic where every Black person is assumed to have a monolithic position on the liberation of African people worldwide without taking into account the class distinctions which exist among us.

Perhaps a brief retrospective timeline is in order to lay the basis of why I believe that the recently concluded 20th century should be viewed as the centerpiece of Pan-Africanism. Incidentally, the term Pan-African was coined in 1899 by Henry Sylvester Williams, a Trinidadian barrister who was the first Black man to practice law in pre-apartheid (but still racist) South Africa during 1898 and issued the call for the first self-professed Pan-African Conference in 1900.

The next time we find the use of the term was when Dr. William Edward Burghardt Du Bois, a participant in Williams's Pan-African Conference, initiated a series of Pan-African Congresses that would establish the development of the organizing of Black people under that theme. W. E. B. Du Bois, who had stated, "The problem of the 20th century [would be] the problem of the color line," is widely regarded by academics and Marxists as the "father of Pan-Africanism." However, while he would actively organize Pan-African Congresses in 1919, 1921, 1923 and 1929 (each in Europe), Du Bois was a full-time leading member of the National Association for the Advancement of Colored People.

The NAACP, with its program of social integration to resolve the problem of the color line in the US, was diametrically opposed to the organizing efforts of the Universal Negro Improvement Association and African Communities League, a Black nationalist organization founded and led by Marcus Garvey. The UNIA & ACL, while it did not necessarily define itself as Pan-Africanist, was the embodiment of an all African organization grounded in a philosophy and ideological line to unite Africans throughout the world towards the redemption and liberation of Africa for the Africans.

Therefore, it was a tragic but nevertheless historical fact that Du Bois and the NAACP found themselves in a relentless struggle to not promote Pan-Africanism on a daily basis but collaborate with other members of the early 20th century Black leadership and the US Government in trying to discredit the efforts of Marcus Garvey and the UNIA & ACL, the largest and most strategically placed organization ever developed by African people before its founding in 1914. Neither has there been such an organization that would mobilize Black people under the political, social and economic guidelines of Pan-Africanism since John Edgar Hoover and his Bureau of Investigation (the forerunner of the FBI), prompted by groups led by the NAACP and the threat that the early American transnational corporations and their Western European allies felt from Garvey's mass movement against colonial exploitation, was able to frame the Jamaican-born leader on a bogus mail fraud case in 1924, incarcerate him in a federal penitentiary for nearly three years and later deport him in 1927.

Thus the first quarter of the 20th century was marked by the historic struggle led by the two titans identified as leaders in the Pan-African movement. Even today, the visions of these two men still dominate the thinking of those who consider themselves Pan-Africanist—Du Bois for his theoretical positions on Pan-Africanism, Garvey for his organizing of the critical mass of working and peasant class members of Africans throughout the world to struggle to wrest Africa from foreign control and bring the world's wealthiest continent under a program self-determination of its indigenous people and their brethren (and "sistren") in the Diaspora.

Ironically, in spite of Du Bois playing a key role in ruining Garvey and the UNIA from carrying out their program of African redemption, the academically endowed professor would later have a falling out with many of his own former allies, and have some misgivings about his early denunciations of his Jamaican rival, ending up in effect repatriating to Ghana where, in another irony, he died on the eve of the 1963 March on Washington, the largest civil rights mobilization of the period.

While it is true that Du Bois joined the US Communist Party shortly before he died, it is equally true that he also showed remorse for his role in helping to lead the "Garvey must go" campaign that was instrumental in having his nemesis deported.

Another leading Black detractor of Garvey who also was a member of the Communist Party was George Padmore, the author of *Pan-Africanism or Communism* and the highest-ranked Black communist member, heading up the Negro Bureau of the Red International of Labor Unions (Profintern) in Moscow. A communist since 1937, after becoming disenchanted with his comrades after they abandoned their support of the Black Belt South, the Trinidadian-born Malcolm Nurse [Padmore's original name] later had a change of heart. Reflecting upon his earlier ridiculing of Garvey and his movement, Padmore recanted in 1957, stating, "Marcus Garvey was undoubtedly one of the greatest Black men since Emancipation, a visionary who inspired his race in its upward struggle from the degradation of slavery."

Padmore also repatriated to Ghana, where both he and Du Bois are buried, and libraries have been named in their honor.

Tragically, because of their work against Garvey, the UNIA leader never got a chance to get to Africa, let alone Ghana, whose first leader, Osagyefo Dr. Kwame Nkrumah, led the former Gold Coast colony to independence on March 6, 1957. Nkrumah, however, had been heavily influenced by Garvey. In retrospect, Nkrumah paid the UNIA leader the highest respect. "I had read Engels, Hegel and Marx," the Ghanaian leader wrote, "but of all the books that I have read, the one that fired my enthusiasm the most was *The Philosophy and Opinions of Marcus Garvey*."

At Nkrumah's funeral in Guinea, during May 1972, President Ahmed Sekou Toure reiterated that thought when he said, "It was Marcus Garvey and his philosophy of 'Africa for the Africans' that inspired him most."

Sekou Toure was a revolutionary Muslim, ardent Pan-Africanist who believed in scientific socialism and who had made the Ghanaian president his co-president after he was overthrown by a US-CIA-engineered coup in February 1966. Toure's admiration for Nkrumah was based on a shared commitment to Pan-Africanism. He had become endeared to the Ghanaian leader as a true comrade-in-arms when Nkrumah came to Guinea's assistance after Toure defied France's President Charles De Gaulle and opted for independence rather than become a neocolonialist member of the French Community.

In the US the two most preeminent personalities of the 1960s, the Rev. Dr. Martin Luther King, Jr., representing the civil rights movement, and Minister Malcolm X (El-Hajj Malik El-Shabazz), who after representing the Program of the Nation of Islam for a decade became a spokesperson for Black Nationalism both recognized their debt to Garvey's Pan-Africanism in 1964. Malcolm pointed out that, "Every time you see another nation on the African continent become independent, you know that Marcus Garvey is alive."

Continuing, Malcolm credited all contemporary efforts at racial redemption and unification to the UNIA leader. "It was

Marcus Garvey's philosophy of Pan-Africanism that initiated the entire freedom movement, which brought about the independence of African nations. And had it not been for Marcus Garvey, and the foundations laid by him, you would find no independent nation in the Caribbean today," stated Malcolm. "All the freedom movements that are taking place right here in America were initiated by the work and teachings of Marcus Garvey. The entire Black Muslim philosophy here in America is feeding upon the seeds that were planted by Marcus Garvey."

The following year, when King visited Jamaica, he confessed something that he had never said publicly in the US. "Garvey was the first man of color in the history of the United States to lead and develop a mass movement. He was the first man on a scale and level to give millions of Black people a sense of dignity and destiny, and make the Black man feel that he was somebody."

Even Eldridge Cleaver, one of the most world renowned leaders of the Black Panther Party for Self-Defense, speaking in Algeria in 1970, admitted that "Marcus Garvey gave the ultimate statement of Black identity. He went directly to its root, and in doing so he gave Black people a firm foundation on which to build."

These praises came long after Garvey had died from asthma, stress frustration and—as Amilcar Cabral said at Kwame Nkrumah's funeral—the "cancer of treason." A note should also be made that Garvey's name and reputation might have remained besmirched if not for the intervention of a Garveyite whose father was the head of one of the five branches of the UNIA in the Dominican Republic: Carlos Cooks.

It was Carlos Cooks who became a member of the UNIA's Juvenile Division, youngest member of the Universal African Legion, head of the Advanced Division of the UNIA & ACL, and founder of the African Nationalist Pioneer Movement (ANPM) one year after Mr. Garvey's death. Although little known, he was both a predecessor as well as a contemporary of both Dr.

King and Malcolm (who adopted his Black nationalist positions from Mr. Cooks).

In fact, from abrogating the word "Negro" and replacing it with African, flying the red, black and green colors, wearing one's hair natural and promoting the "Black is Beautiful" movement, "Buy Black" campaigns, black paramilitary uniforms, teaching of African history in the schools from kindergarten to the university and from the days of African antiquity on through today's support of African liberation struggles, all were part and parcel of Cooks's arsenal against white supremacy.

Another link of mutual acquaintances that tied Malcolm and Cooks to the theory and practice of internationalizing Black nationalism was Robert Williams. A Korean War veteran who returned from the war to become the Monroe County, North Carolina NAACP President, Williams—who would become the nemesis of both Senator Jesse Helms, today's head of the US Senate foreign relations committee, and his father, who was the county police and fire chief—was forced to flee into exile when the veterans he had organized to match the Ku Klux Klan's racist gunfire with retaliatory shootouts started to get the best of the conflict.

Living first in Cuba where some of his fiery nationalistic rhetoric unsettled a few of the communist leadership but was allowed by Fidel Castro, Williams would later find residency in the People's Republic of China. While in China he was able to convince Chairman Mao Tse-tung to issue a public statement similar to China's position supporting national liberation in Africa's decolonization struggle, indicating that the then 600 million Chinese people were equally supportive of the struggle of Black people in the US. To both Williams and Mao's surprise, the statement was immediately denounced by the NAACP's Roy Wilkins, CORE's James Farmer and the Urban League's Whitney Young.

Williams also spent time in then-North Vietnam, where Ho Chi Minh informed him of how much he felt influenced by Marcus Garvey and his creed of "Europe for the Europeans, Asia for the Asiatics and Africa for the Africans" when he heard the UNIA & ACL leader speak at a rally he attended in New York. It was the sum of these experiences that Williams was able to relate to the nascent revolutionary movement in the US.

It was the militancy of activists like Robert Williams and the grasp of a Black-oriented sense of internationalism that would later influence groups like the Black Panther Party for Self-Defense beginning in the mid-1960s, and such formations as the African Liberation Day Coordinating Committee (ALDCCI) in 1972, which later evolved into the African Liberation Support Committee (ALSC) in 1973 and mobilized tens of thousands of Blacks in the US, Canada and the Caribbean in massive demonstrations that generated hundreds of thousands of dollars to African national liberation movements engaged in armed struggle to free themselves from racist colonial exploitation.

Unfortunately, the ALSC had a short shelf-life when a controversy arose between those disposed towards emphasizing a program of Black nationalism and those demanding Marxist-Leninism. This was similar to the raging conflict between the Garvey movement and the self-professed communists 50 years earlier. But to make matters worse, in the 1970s the argument was further complicated on the left by the Soviet-Sino schism which had caused divisions within the international communist movement.

Thus, within the left-forces were those who were guided by Marxist-Leninist Mao Tse-tung who reviled Moscow as "Soviet social imperialist," and those who still admired the communist old guard as not genuine socialist comrades. And yet the consensus among the leadership, as I remember from both quarters, was that what Marcus Garvey had accomplished during his time was a mighty work. However, not too many of the leadership had learned from the mistakes that had been made in the movement 50 years ago. The wisdom of Jimmy Abu, a contemporary African nationalist, that "advice is free, you have to pay for experience," was lost on the leadership of what was potentially one the broadest based grassroots organizations echoing Pan-Africanism since the Garveyites held sway during the 1920s.

From the 1970s and into the 1980s and today, Pan-Africanism that based the centrality of Africa's liberation, unification and repatriation as the ultimate act of reparation was manifested by the All-African People's Revolutionary Party and the Patrice Lumumba Coalition. The AAPRP is very active in work study, calling for an African United Front and mobilizing around annual African Liberation Day celebrations; and the PLC is working closely with African national liberation movements and progressive states, as well as raising the consciousness of ordinary Black people by providing them with historical and updated information pertaining to Africa and Africans all over the globe.

Towards the late 1980s and continuing through today, Pan-Africanism was also promoted by articulating the concept of nationhood for Africans within the geographical configuration of what is currently the United States, joining those that struggled for the achieving of a republic of the Black belt in the South, following the lead of such well established nationalist organizations as the Republic of New Afrika, National African Liberation Front and others, as well as supporting the total liberation and unification of Africa.

Whereas one cannot foretell the future of Pan-Africanism, many of us can agree with the late Dr. John Henrik Clarke who warned us that we must understand that the choice is, "Pan-Africanism or perish." To understand the significance of such a choice is to appreciate why many of us believe that the past century was indeed the century of Pan-Africanism, vindicating Garvey's vision. And since our goal is still not completely accomplished, it seems that we will have to continue our struggle either through—or throughout—the 21st century to vindicate our own visions or be forced to admit to our lack of commitment and/or fortitude.

BLACK POLITICAL OPPORTUNISTS: DIS THE ANTI-APARTHEID MOVEMENT[4]

In all of the current political scrambling to establish favorable positions in anticipation of Nelson Mandela's trip to the United States, two of the most prominent names mentioned to receive the African National Congress leader are the Rev. Jesse Jackson and the Mayor of New York City, David N. Dinkins. Indeed Jesse, who was one of, if not the first African-American to reach Victor Verster Prison upon Mandela's February 11th release, extended an invitation to visit New York to the world's most prominent political prisoner on behalf of His Honor, The Mayor.

Since then Jackson has been busy making himself a public nuisance with transatlantic flights ostensibly, he claims, to confer with Mandela about the future of South Africa. Others view Jackson's claims with skepticism. Some even use blunt language, questioning the popular civil rights activist/leader's persistence and timing, dismissing it as "constant buggin" of the ANC deputy president.

At a time when the ANC is busy trying to concentrate all of its efforts at strategizing against the apartheid regime's devious and manipulative "reformist" campaign and intra-African internecine political warfare orchestrated by elements of the militaristic National Security Management System, renown public seeking personalities need to back off.

Whether he realizes it or not, Jesse's interests have become suspect. But worse, his intervention is also bothersome. This is especially true when his main interest seems apparently to be a thinly disguised self-aggrandizing, photo-opportunity session aimed at positioning himself for a 1992 presidential campaign run.

Jackson's attempt to accurately interpret the current events in South Africa present another problem. As a civil rights leader identified prominently with the nonviolence movement of the late Dr. Martin Luther King, Jr., a movement which advocated

Black people relying on moral suasion and loving "thine enemy," Rev. Jackson is hardly the one to articulate Mandela's defense of his organization's armed struggle against the violence of the fascistic, apartheid regime. As a matter of fact, on the matter of principle, it would seem that Jackson's history is, at least to a certain extent, diametrically opposed to the ANC's equally principled position on this key question.

We clearly remember that when many of our people wanted to develop a more militant response to the brutal murder of the four little Black girls killed in a racist bombing in Birmingham, Alabama in 1963, Dr. King admonished them not to respond in kind. "If any blood must be spilled," he advised, "let it be our blood and not the blood of our white brothers."

It should be evident that this type of reasoning would be difficult for the survival of the leadership of a serious national liberation movement. But it would also be masochistic for the group's membership and suicidal for the organization's objectives on the whole. Most African-Americans are neither truly united nor secure with the concept of being nonviolent in the face of relentless and systematic attacks—whether by the state, a mob or an individual, or whether the assailant is Black, white or other.

By the same reasoning, this discredited line of thinking should not be offered as advice to Mandela or the ANC. Guinea-Bissau, Mozambique, Angola, Zimbabwe and recently Namibia all gained their independence because their respective armed combatants replied to imperialist aggression and settler colonialist continuous brutal repression with enough firepower to convince their oppressors that the negotiating table was safer than the battlefield. Other countries were granted their independence because their rulers wanted to avoid similar experiences. In a sense, the shedding of blood does have its redeeming values, providing the bloodshed is equally or, at least, proportionately shed.

Thus to truly appreciate the courage and commitment of those revolutionary forces that have chosen to fight rather than submit to the whims and caprices of their ruthless oppressors is to respect their choice of options. And the fact remains that the majority of the youth in South Africa (i.e., young African men and women, and many so-called Coloured and Indians) do not subscribe to the concept of mere passive resistance either. This is not in spite of but because of the tremendous sacrifices that Black youth have had to endure, particularly since the Soweto uprising of 1976.

To ignore this reality is to play into the hands of the opponents of the African democratic and revolutionary process that has just taken state power in Namibia and is now poised to repeat in South Africa itself. Ironically, as the enemies and rivals of the ANC try to present the Congress as either some antiquated "communist terrorists" on one hand or an integrationist-oriented civil rights movement on the other, Jackson can offer little help in negating these false perceptions. His own veiled anti-communism and pro-capitalist past history prevents him from presenting an accurate response to constant red-baiting attacks against the ANC.

Equally disturbing are Jackson's frequent attempts to portray the Congress as a counterpart to the NAACP or SCLC, which aid in promoting the impression that ANC critics in South Africa like to project. When Jackson returned to the US after his first meeting with Mandela and told a New York audience that the ANC leader's message to African-Americans was that he had spent 27 years in prison simply for the right to vote, Jesse seemed more to be speaking for himself. Nevertheless, this subjective characterization subliminally undermined both Mandela's reputation and the ANC's mandate as representative of a national liberation movement.

This type of self-serving rhetoric in an alleged defense of the ANC casts further suspicion on Jackson's sudden media-propelled image as the leading force in the anti-apartheid movement in the US. Consistently acting as a maverick, unaccountable to other activists in the southern African support network, Jesse eschews any collaboration with longtime grassroots activists. In fact, it seems that his trips to South Africa are coordinated more with his personal availability and Pretoria's mood at the moment rather than any respect for the anti-apartheid movement's plans to completely isolate the racist republic. Jackson not only chooses if and when he will go to South Africa, but he also encourages others to go, sowing confusion in the movement as to what is the proper policy to pursue regarding the total isolation of the regime.

The case of David Dinkins is just as sad. Consider his dilemma. About a week ago the mayor was caught in an embarrassing situation when it was revealed that he and his wife had accounts in Manufacturers Hanover Trust, a bank that has been under siege by anti-apartheid activists for over the last year. What has drawn the wrath of the protesters is the fact that Manufacturers Hanover's loan arrangement with South Africa allowed the apartheid state off the hook with its recent debt crisis.

Manny Hanny, as the bank is often called, has rolled over at least $25 million in outstanding debt, converting short term loans into long term, thereby extending South Africa's repayment schedule an additional ten years. It is this kind of breathing space that Pretoria desperately needs in order to break the increasing stranglehold that the international sanctions campaign has placed on the financial support of the apartheid system.

When it was revealed in *Newsday* (Thurs. April 19) that the mayor and first lady had "tens of thousands of dollars," in the contested bank, Dinkins professed that he didn't realize that he had a conflict of interest, although Manufacturers Hanover has long been the primary focus of an intense "Boycott Apartheid's Bankers" campaign.

Even though Dinkins immediately withdrew most of his deposits the day after the revelation, it was not without stirring up further controversy. His spokesperson, Leland T. Jones, claimed that the money was in Manufacturers' to build up towards the Mayor's retirement fund. The fact that Dinkins was just finishing the first "100 days" of his first term and a committee had been initiated to solicit funds for his re-election campaign, yet he was already thinking about a retirement fund, was not lost on many activists.

Furthermore it was pointed out that the expected yield on the deposits in Manufacturers was not considered a good investment. According to Jones, Dinkins's accountant had advised him for some time "that he could obtain a better return if he invested his money elsewhere and that he had intended to move it" anyway. Therefore, in reality, the Mayor saw his withdrawal action compromised as he came out of the episode as less interested in the principle of upholding the issue of enforcing economic sanctions against apartheid and more concerned with the principle of how much his bank interest yielded in the future!

If that isn't bad enough, it seems that Mr. Dinkins has not learned his lesson in the hanky-panky at Manny Hanny. He's about to get himself in another banking contradiction that will really damage his reputation as a creditable voice in the anti-apartheid movement. The conflict is as follows: The word on the financial hotline is that Dinkins is planning to support an application by CS First Boston to become "senior bookrunning manager" for New York City, wherein every time the city wants to sell bonds First Boston would be the senior banker. Since New York does over $7 billion in bonds a year, the contracts would be worth about $5–10 million annually for the city's "lead banker." Underwriting bonds is a little known but lucrative market. For instance, because New York State has not yet passed its budget, the City has notified the financial community that it intends "to sell $900 million in bonds this week." According to the *New York Daily News* (Tuesday April 17, 1990), letters were sent out notifying brokerage firms that New York intends to borrow between $400 million and $900 million for 49 days, "a move that will result in $3.6 million and $9.2 million in interest" being earned by the lenders.

If First Boston is successfully chosen as the major underwriter to "sell billions in city debt," they will reap millions of dollars each year. Among many other banks and investment firms, First Boston responded to the city's request for proposal (RFP) as a potential underwriter on Wednesday, May 2nd, And if they win approval, then Ron Gault, Dinkins's tennis partner and member of the mayor's transition team, who happens to be a director (i.e. a first vice president) at First Boston, it is rumored "will profit handsomely."

But this is not the major contradiction in what is an obvious conflict of interest. The conflict is with the mayor's public posture of being a leading force of the municipal government, a key player in the city's fight to close all loopholes in its anti-apartheid legislation. Given the embarrassing situation that his recent Manufacturers Hanover deposits caused him, it seems that he should have learned a lesson. But apparently he hasn't.

One of the conditions that potential underwriters were asked to address in the RFP issued by the city was to address in detail their connections with South Africa. The concern was how the city could "maintain South Africa-free relationships without jeopardizing the city's financial interests." According to Jeanne Nathan, spokeswoman for Deputy Mayor for Economic Development Sally Hernandez-Pinero, "This information will certainly be an important factor in tipping the scales between two equally qualified candidates."

It is difficult at the time of this writing to judge the merits or demerits of "two equally qualified candidates" of the 52 investment banking firms that cast their bids on Wednesday, May 2nd, regarding whether one or more are tainted by having collaborated with racist South Africa. But there is enough evidence to indicate that First Boston's apartheid connection is every bit as soiled as Manufacturers'. Perhaps even more so.

As of December 1988, First Boston was 44.4 percent owned by a Swiss holding company that is owned—and controlled—by Credit Suisse, a Swiss bank that does extensive business with the apartheid regime. In fact, Credit Suisse has an office in Johannesburg. And although CS First Boston claims that it was one of the first banks to break all direct ties to the regime, two Black mayors and their city councils have already come to the conclusion that contrary to the US bank's argument, the parent company does exercise control over the American branch.

In January of last year, Mayor Tom Bradley and the Los Angeles City Council nixed a proposed city contract with CS First Boston to underwrite bonds for an expansion project at the LA Convention Center. Bradley, ever mindful of the embarrassing situation that he found himself in a few years back, was not sleeping this time. He had become the subject of ridicule in 1982 when a photograph of him giving the key to the city to South Africa's counsel general appeared in the foreign media and was circulated by anti-apartheid activists from coast to coast. And he was not about to get caught in a similar situation.

"In my view," stated Bradley in a January 24, 1989 letter to the LA City Council, "a forty-four percent ownership stake by one company in another constitutes 'control' within the meaning of the city's ordinance. We simply should not award a city contract to a company that will in turn share a large portion of the profits from that contract with a company that does business in South Africa."

Denouncing First Boston's deceitful approach, Bradley "strongly urged the council to deny First Boston's request for an exemption to the city's anti-apartheid Contracting Ordinance." Disappointed but not defeated, First Boston then tried to become one of the firms hired to sell $125 million worth of bonds for the city of Oakland, California, in their billion dollar campaign to entice Los Angeles Raiders owner Al Davis to bring the NFL team back to the city it had left in 1982. But Oakland

Mayor Lionel Wilson took a "strong position against retaining First Boston" when documents filed with the Securities and Exchange Commission revealed the Credit Suisse-South Africa link. As an underwriter, First Boston stood to make "as much as $4 million" if they could have gotten approval and the bond issue deal came through. But request documents exposed that Credit Suisse was part of a banking consortium that had, according to the *Los Angeles Examiner* of Sunday, March 25, 1990, "extended at least $8 billion in loans to South Africa in recent years," and as a result they lost out. The fact that Archbishop Desmond Tutu had blasted Credit Suisse as a "collaborator with the evil system prevailing in South Africa" for deferring their repayment schedule didn't help First Boston's cause either.

If two African-American mayors and their respective city councils have already agreed not to allow First Boston to participate in their critical underwriting plans, how can a Black mayor who poses as being on the cutting edge of the anti-apartheid movement even entertain the thought of making that same financial institution his city's senior bookrunning manager?

He can't if he's serious. Is David Dinkins serious? One would hope so, but a growing number of his electoral constituents have been developing serious doubts and are becoming alienated because of his seeming disinterest to their respective concerns. And his assigning of a deputy mayor for intergovernmental affairs who treats the African community of New York City as a foreign nation only makes matters worse. Bill Lynch, said to be Dinkins's "closest staff member," was recently quoted as preparing for Mandela's forthcoming trip to New York by boasting, "We are going to give him the same treatment as a head of state would get."

Now that's just fine. But while that might impress the mayor and his cavalier former campaign manager, it is not Mandela's primary concern when he arrives here. Anyone familiar with his life should know that he would much rather simply be treated with mutual respect. This is especially true with those who claim that they are committed to the cause of African liberation and the dismantling of the oppressive apartheid system. And that can only be done by intensifying one's bond with the common people, the most disposed, and the activist cadres that dedicated themselves to be the shock troops of the people's movement.

In this Dinkins has been a total failure, especially in his pattern of behavior towards the broad masses of African people that elected him mayor. His election is the result of (1) Black and Latino citizens of New York becoming fed up with an administration that in a dozen years chalked up over 300 killings of their brethren by the city's police department; (2) the fear of a rising neofascist succeeding Koch and duplicating—and maybe even surpassing—his venal exploits; and (3) the brutal racist murder of young Yusuf Hawkins that unleashed the anger of the African community and shook up the powers-that-be with the prospect of a violent confrontation, particularly after thousands of demonstrators engaged the NYPD in a physical struggle on the Brooklyn Bridge last August 31st. All of these conditions are reflective of similar situations that still prevail in South Africa and have been successfully overcome in Namibia, when a dedicated leadership united with a fighting people who truly wanted to bring about a radical political, social and economic transformation of society. Dinkins, unfortunately, can see the horror of the oppressive conditions in Southern Africa and the need for dramatic and revolutionary changes there. He can pontificate upon inhumane brutality and uphold the rights of political prisoners everywhere else but in the United States in general and New York City in particular. He doesn't display the same concern and compassion for those who placed their trust, hopes and dreams in his hands when they voted for him as *their* mayor.

On what basis does Dinkins, or Jackson, et al., justify their public posturing with the likes of a Nelson Mandela or a Walter

Sisulu? The unabashed arrogance of African-American civil rights leaders and politicians stands in stark contrast to the humility and commitment of the two veteran South African leaders, as well as other lesser-known members of the Mass Democratic Movement.

The discipline, loyalty and accountability to one's organization and one's constituency (i.e., *your people*) has been an outstanding character trait of the Mandelas. Sisulu and others tower over Jackson's elitist relationship to the Rainbow Coalition membership and Dinkins's nonchalant disregard of the aspirations and well-being of Black people in New York. Consider Mandela's defiance of the racist, neo-Nazi Pretoria regime after emerging from nearly three decades of imprisonment by embracing Joe Slovo, the Lithuanian-born, Jewish leader in the South African Communist Party and a key strategist in Umkhonto we Sizwe, the military component of the ANC. Contrast that to Dinkins's denial and renouncing of Jitu Weusi and Sonny Carson, two Black activists who went against the grassroots community's conventional wisdom not to support the Manhattan Borough President's mayoralty race. Afterward, they came under a racist and scurrilous attack of bogus charges of "Anti-Semitism" and, in the case of Carson, being a kidnapper and, even more ridiculous, a "murderer."

Both Jitu and Sonny showed more principled reactions, traits identified with Mandela's kind of loyalty—while one need not necessarily totally agree with you don't dissolve relations suddenly and jettison former friends and/or allies in order to insulate yourself from some sort of political contamination based on guilt by association. Like in South Africa, Dinkins actually *banned* controversial activists from his campaign. And his tolerance of the slimy television commercial designed to exploit the controversy over Minister Louis Farrakhan and the Zionists was as infamous as George Bush's Willie Horton TV spots.

Wasn't Mandela's embrace of Yasser Arafat the same type of statement of solidarity and sympathy to a just cause as Rev. Jesse Jackson's earlier encounter with the Palestinian leader? However, Jesse's constant attempts to minimize—or even wish away—his photo opportunity with Arafat is both humiliating and embarrassing—to him and his people.

Taken at a time when it was politically expedient in the wake of Ambassador Andy Young's forced resignation because he met with an official of the PLO, Jackson's contrition stands in shameful contradiction to that of Mandela's response in a similar situation. When warned that his own warm embrace of and statement in support of the Palestinian leader might cause him some trouble with members of South Africa's affluent 120,000 Jewish settlers, Mandela's reply was that it was "too bad," in effect, if the truth hurts.

Furthermore, he went on to establish the analogous historical circumstances that the South African and Palestinian struggles shared. Neither Jackson nor Dinkins can afford to agree to that. Not because it isn't true, but because their opportunism to advance their political careers does not permit them to comment on such "sensitive" an issue.

A couple of months ago, Monday, February 12th to be exact, the day following Mandela's release, Mayor Dinkins had a hastily organized press conference with the Nelson Mandela Reception Committee. Standing on the steps of City Hall, the mayor threw his proverbial political hat into the ring, projecting himself as a bona fide fighter against any compromise with strengthening the isolation of the white minority government ruling South Africa. As he stood surrounded by scores of religious, union, elected officials and appointees, anti-apartheid activists (most of whom were placed as far away from the mayor as possible), Dinkins declared, "Now is the time to intensify the struggle on all fronts. The role of the international community in exerting the full weight of economic sanctions against Pretoria has never been more critical than now."

And indeed, this is true. After all, hadn't Mandela himself, the day before, said that "to relax our efforts now would be a mistake which generations to come will not be able to forgive." And they shouldn't, and we won't.

Dinkins's paraphrasing of Mandela's statement was correct, but his actual conduct hasn't measured up. The previous Manufacturers Hanover's boo boo, the present First Boston covert operation, and the possibility of another Manny Hanny plus contradiction all raise questions about the mayor's sincerity that he intends to close up all loopholes (e.g., Intro 1137) in anti-apartheid statues. On Friday, May 4th, it was reported that the New York City Banking Commission had authorized 28 banks—including Chemical, Chase Manhattan and, once again, Manufacturers Hanover—to hold approximately $200 million in city deposits for the year ending August 1991. Needless to say, Manufacturers was not the only bank listed that still had dealings with South Africa.

Notes

PREFACE

1. "Introduction," *Journal for the Study of Radicalism* 1 (Spring 2007): vii.

2. William L. Van Deburg, *New Day in Babylon: The Black Power Movement and American Culture, 1965–1975* (Chicago: University of Chicago Press, 1992), 25, 140, 171.

3. Peter Olisanwuche Esedebe, *Pan-Africanism: The Idea and Movement, 1776–1963* (Washington, DC: Howard University Press, 1982), 3.

4. Algernon Austin described racial essentialism as a way of thinking that sees certain groups "as possessing an essence—a natural, supernatural, or mystical characteristic—that makes them share a fundamental similarity with all members of the group and a fundamental difference from non-members." Austin quoted in Tunde Adeleke, *The Case Against Afrocentrism* (Jackson: University Press of Mississippi, 2009), 11. Gender policing serves to group individuals into "culturally sanctioned gendered categories, enactments, characteristics, and bodily practices." See "Policing Masculinities and Femininities," in *The SAGE Encyclopedia of LGBTQ Studies*, ed. Abbie E. Goldberg (Thousand Oaks, CA: SAGE Publications, 2016), 859–63, quote from 860.

1. THE CARIBBEAN ORIGINS OF ELOMBE BRATH'S RADICALISM

1. Don D. Marshall and Glenford D. Howe, eds., *The Empowering Impulse: The Nationalist Tradition of Barbados* (Kingston, Jamaica: Canoe Press, University of the West Indies, 2001), x.

2. Winston James, *Holding Aloft the Banner of Ethiopia: Caribbean Radicalism in Early Twentieth-Century America* (New York: Verso, 1999), 12; Franklin W. Knight, "Introduction," in *Caribbean Crusaders and the Harlem Renaissance*, by Joyce Moore Turner (Urbana: University of Illinois Press, 2005), xvi; and Joyce Moore Turner, *Caribbean Crusaders and the Harlem Renaissance* (Urbana: University of Illinois Press, 2005), 4.

3. James, *Holding Aloft the Banner of Ethiopia*, 22–24, 30, 32–40.

4. James, *Holding Aloft the Banner of Ethiopia*, 41–45; quotes from 48–49.

5. Glenford D. Howe, "De(Re) Constructing Identities: World War I and the Growth of Barbadian/West Indian Nationalism," in Don D. Marshall and Glenford D. Howe, eds., *The Empowering Impulse: The Nationalist Tradition of Barbados* (Kingston, Jamaica: Canoe Press, University of the West Indies, 2001), 110–27, quote from 127. See also C. L. R. James, *Beyond a Boundary* (London:

Hutchinson, 1963), 40; and James, *Holding Aloft the Banner of Ethiopia*, 52–53, 55–65.

6. Wickham even traveled to New York with Brathwaite in 1927, three years after the elder Cecil Brathwaite emigrated from Barbados. F. A. Hoyos, *Barbados: A History from the Amerindians to Independence* (London: Macmillan, 1978), 195–97; *Pittsburgh Courier*, May 21, 1927, 4, and November 12, 1938, 14; and Howe, "De(Re) Constructing Identities," 126–27. Quote from *Herald*, December 6, 1924. See also Keith Hunte, "The Struggle for Political Democracy: Charles Duncan O'Neal and the Democratic League," in *Emancipation XI: Aspects of the Post-Slavery Experience of Barbados*, ed. W.K. Marshall (Bridgetown, Barbados: National Cultural Foundation and Department of History, University of the West Indies, 1988), 20–38; and F. A. Hoyos, *Builders of Barbados* (London: Macmillan, 1972), 117–25.

7. Rodney Worrell, "Pan-Africanism in Barbados," in Don D. Marshall and Glenford D. Howe, eds., *The Empowering Impulse: The Nationalist Tradition of Barbados* (Kingston, Jamaica: Canoe Press, University of the West Indies, 2001), 200–204, quote from 203.

8. Harold Cruse, *The Crisis of the Negro Intellectual: A Historical Analysis of the Failure of Black Leadership* (1967; New York: New York Review of Books Classical, 2005), 12, 13.

9. See Jonathan Gill, *Harlem: The Four-Hundred Year History from Dutch Village to Capital of Black America* (New York: Grove Press, 2011).

10. Quoted in Gilbert Osofsky, *Harlem, The Making of a Ghetto: Negro New York, 1890–1930* (New York: Harper & Row, 1966), 71.

11. For more on early Harlem, see Brian D. Goldstein, *The Roots of Urban Renaissance: Gentrification and the Struggle Over Harlem* (Cambridge, MA: Harvard University Press, 2017); and Jervis Anderson, *This Was Harlem: A Cultural Portrait, 1900–1950* (New York: Farrar, Straus and Giroux, 1991).

12. Cruse, *The Crisis of the Negro Intellectual*, 19.

13. The AARC was a direct response to the Hudson Realty Company, a white group whose principal goal was to keep Black investors out of the area. But the AARC would win that contest. "The matter of better and still better housing for colored people in New York became the dominating idea of [Payton's] life, and he worked on it as long as he lived. When Negro New Yorkers evaluate their benefactors in their own race, they must find that not many have done more than Phil Payton; for much of what has made Harlem the intellectual and artistic capital of the Negro world is in good part due to this fundamental advantage." James Weldon Johnson, *Black Manhattan* (New York: Perseus Books, 1930), 147.

14. Alain Locke, *The New Negro: An Interpretation* (1925; New York: Simon & Schuster, 1992), 304; and Jervis Anderson, *This Was Harlem: A Cultural Portrait, 1900–1950* (New York: Farrar, Straus and Giroux, 1982), 49–56.

15. Nail would actually become the first president of the Negro Board of Trade in Harlem, the first African American elected to the Real Estate Board of New York, a member of the Mayor's Housing Committee, and vice-president of the Republican Business Men's Club of New York City, which was incredibly exclusive and almost entirely white. See Kevin McGruder, *Race and Real Estate: Conflict and Cooperation in Harlem, 1890–1920* (New York: Columbia University Press, 2015).

16. For more on Ali, see Ian Duffield, "Dusé Mohamed Ali and the Development of Pan-Africanism 1866–1945" (PhD diss., Edinburg University, 1971); and Mustafa Abdelwahid, *Dusé Mohamed Ali (1866–1945): The Autobiography of a Pioneer Pan African and Afro-Asian Activist* (Trenton, NJ: Red Sea Press, 2011). For more on Washington, see Thomas Aiello, *The Battle for the Souls of Black Folk: W. E. B. Du Bois, Booker T. Washington, and the Debate That Shaped the Course of Civil Rights* (Westport, CT: Praeger, 2016); and Louis R. Harlan, *Booker T. Washington: Wizard of Tuskegee, 1901–1915* (New York: Oxford University Press, 1986).

17. The paper would survive until 1933. The scholarship on Garvey is vast. The original standard biography is Edmund David Cronon, *Black Moses: The Story of Marcus Garvey and the Universal Negro*

Improvement Association (Madison: University of Wisconsin Press, 1955). Tony Martin took up the scholarship beginning in the 1970s with *Race First: The Ideological and Organizational Struggle of Marcus Garvey and the Universal Negro Improvement Association* (Westport, CT: Greenwood Press, 1976). More recently, Adam Ewing, *The Age of Garvey: How a Jamaican Activist Created a Mass Movement and Changed Global Black Politics* (Princeton, NJ: Princeton University Press, 2014), has taken up the mantle of monograph-length academic Garvey evaluations. Running concurrently to this work, the University of California Press, and later Duke University Press, under the editorship of Robert A. Hill, continued collecting and publishing archival material relating to Garvey in *The Marcus Garvey and Universal Negro Improvement Association Papers* (thirteen volumes to date).

18. Anderson, *This Was Harlem*, 185–91; and Irma Watkins-Owens, *Blood Relations: Caribbean Immigrants and the Harlem Community, 1900–1930* (Bloomington: Indiana University Press, 1996), 112–25. For more on Garvey's Pan-Africanist vision, see Robert A. Hill and Barbara Bair, eds., *Marcus Garvey, Life and Lessons: A Centennial Companion to the Marcus Garvey and Universal Negro Improvement Association Papers* (Berkeley: University of California Press, 1987); Amy Jacques-Garvey, ed., *Philosophy and Opinions of Marcus Garvey*, vol. 1 (New York: Universal Publishing House, 1923); and Amy Jacques-Garvey, ed., *Philosophy and Opinions of Marcus Garvey*, vol. 2 (New York: Universal Publishing House, 1925).

19. Marcus Garvey, *Message to the People: The Course of African Philosophy*, ed. Tony Martin (Dover, MA: Majority Press, 1986), 134–38, quote from 134. See also Marcus Garvey, "The Negro, Communism, and His Friend" and "Capitalism and the State," in *Philosophy and Opinions of Marcus Garvey*, vol. 2, ed. Amy Jacques-Garvey (New York: Universal Publishing House, 1925), 69–71, 72–73.

20. Watkins-Owens, *Blood Relations*, 103–4, 160–61. For more on the evolution of Black communism, see Theodore Kornweibel Jr., Seeing

Red: Fede*ral Campaigns Against Black Militancy, 1919–1925* (Bloomington: Indiana University Press, 1999); Ronald A. Kuykendall, "The African Blood Brotherhood: Independent Marxist During the Harlem Renaissance," *Western Journal of Black Studies* 26, no. 1 (2002): 16–21; J. A. Zumoff, "The African Blood Brotherhood: From Caribbean Nationalism to Communism," *Journal of Caribbean History* 41 (January 2007): 200–226; Mark I. Solomon, *The Cry Was Unity: Communists and African Americans, 1917–36* (Jackson: University Press of Mississippi, 1998); Minkah Makalani, *For the Liberation of Black People Everywhere: The African Blood Brotherhood, Black Radicalism, and Pan-African Liberation in the New Negro Movement, 1917–1936* (PhD diss., University of Illinois at Urbana-Champaign, 2004); and Theman Ray Taylor, *Cyril Briggs and the African Blood Brotherhood: Another Radical View of Race and Class in the 1920s* (PhD diss., University of California at Santa Barbara, 1981).

21. When Garvey was released from prison in 1927, he was immediately deported, but even then, the UNIA didn't die. It held conventions every year, and even after Garvey died in 1940 the organization continued. James, *Holding Aloft the Banner of Ethiopia*, 70–71; and *Pittsburgh Courier*, June 30, 1923, 1, 11. See also Marcus Garvey, File no. 190–1781–6, Federal Bureau of Investigation, FOIA, available online at https://vault.fbi.gov/marcus-garvey, accessed March 12, 2019.

22. James, *Holding Aloft the Banner of Ethiopia*, 123, 126. See also Jeffrey B. Perry, *Hubert Harrison: The Voice of Harlem Radicalism, 1883–1918* (New York: Columbia University Press, 2009); and Jeffrey B. Perry, *Hubert Harrison: The Struggle for Equality, 1918–1927* (New York: Columbia University Press, 2020).

23. For more on Rogers, see William L. Van Deburg, ed., *Modern Black Nationalism from Marcus Garvey to Louis Farrakhan* (New York: New York University Press, 1997), 64–72; Thabiti Asukile, "Joel Augustus Rogers' Race Vindication: A Chicago Pullman Porter and The Making of *From Superman to Man* (1917)," *Western Journal of Black Studies* 35 (Fall 2011): 281–93; Thabiti Asukile, "Joel

Augustus Rogers: Black International Journalism, Archival Research, and Black Print Culture," *Journal of African American History* 95 (Summer-Fall 2010): 322–47; *Atlanta Daily World*, February 10, 1991, 7; *Los Angeles Sentinel*, February 14, 1991, A8; and Aric Putnam, "Ethiopia Is Now: J. A. Rogers and the Rhetoric of Black Anticolonialism During the Great Depression," *Rhetoric and Public Affairs* 10 (Fall 2007): 419–44. Quote from the Garvey interview from New York *Amsterdam News*, November 17, 1926, 1, 7. See also *Pittsburgh Courier*, November 20, 1926, 1, 3. For Rogers's coverage of Garvey in Europe, see *Pittsburgh Courier*, October 27, 1928, A6, and November 3, 1928, 5.

24. *Pittsburgh Courier*, June 30, 1923, 1, 11; and Watkins-Owens, *Blood Relations*, 92–99, 107–8.

25. *Pittsburgh Courier*, June 30, 1923, 1, 11; and Joyce Moore Turner, "Richard B. Moore and His Works," in *Richard B. Moore, Caribbean Militant In Harlem: Collected Writings, 1920–1972*, ed. W. Burghardt Turner and Joyce Moore Turner (Bloomington: Indiana University Press, 1988), 38–39.

26. New York *Amsterdam News*, September 29, 1926, 1; October 6, 1926, 1; and September 23, 1978, B3; and *Chicago Defender*, October 20, 1928, 2. Moore would continue to suffer such arrests. See, for example, New York *Amsterdam News*, September 11, 1929, 20, and September 18, 1929, 3; and New York *Herald Tribune*, September 5, 1929, 3.

27. Moore's most influential book was *The Name "Negro": Its Origin and Evil Use*, published in 1960. New York *Amsterdam News*, September 18, 1943, 9; May 4, 1946, 11; March 25, 1950, 2; August 12, 1967, 15; and September 23, 1978, B3; and *Chicago Defender*, September 14, 1929, 11; September 25, 1943, 8; and November 5, 1960, 3. For more on Moore, see William L. Van Deburg, ed., *Modern Black Nationalism from Marcus Garvey to Louis Farrakhan* (New York: New York University Press, 1997), 78–83; Joyce Moore Turner and W. Burghart Turner, eds., *Richard B. Moore, Caribbean Militant in Harlem: Collected Writings, 1920–1972* (Bloomington: Indiana University Press, 1988); and Moore (Richard B.) Papers, 1902–1978, Sc MG 397,

Schomburg Center for Research in Black Culture, New York Public Library, New York.

28. Franklin W. Knight, "Introduction," in *Caribbean Crusaders and the Harlem Renaissance*, by Joyce Moore Turner (Urbana: University of Illinois Press, 2005), xvii–xviii; and James, *Holding Aloft the Banner of Ethiopia*, 76. See also Watkins-Owens, *Blood Relations*, 1–10, 126–35.

29. Two years later, Cooks invited Bilbo to speak at the UNIA's Garvey Day celebration, but protests by the NAACP and other groups kept him away. Cooks spoke in his place. Robert Harris, Nyota Harris, and Grandassa Harris, *Carlos Cooks and Black Nationalism from Garvey to Malcolm* (Dover, MA: Majority Press, 1992), xi–xiii; New York *Amsterdam News*, June 24, 1939, 1; and August 23, 1941, 12; *New York Times*, August 17, 1941, 41; and Michael W. Fitzgerald, "'We Have Found a Moses': Theodore Bilbo, Black Nationalism, and the Greater Liberia Bill of 1939," *Journal of Southern History* 63 (May 1997): 293–320. Robert Harris, whose account is used here and remains the most ubiquitous telling of Cooks's life, was a comrade of Brath and fellow follower of Cooks. See New York *Amsterdam News*, August 26, 1989, 8; and November 7, 1992, 30. For Rogers's dissent, see *Pittsburgh Courier*, August 30, 1941, 7; and May 28, 1955, A12. Finally, the most recent account of Cooks's life comes from historian Pedro Rivera. For a more in-depth accounting of Cooks's life, see Pedro R. Rivera, "Carlos Cooks and Garveyism: Bridging Two Eras of Black Nationalism" (PhD diss., Howard University, 2012). Rivera's work benefited directly from Brath's knowledge and mentorship, and the dissertation is, in fact, dedicated to Brath.

30. The owners of the restaurant swore out a warrant against Cooks, who had been holding anti-Fascist protest meetings there regularly. The owners claimed that they had paid Cooks $250 to move them elsewhere, but the meetings persisted. Cooks, unable to post $2,000 bail, remained in jail for weeks after the incident. The extortion charge ultimately went to court in September, but jurors were split as to Cooks's guilt, and the judge declared

a mistrial. New York *Amsterdam News*, July 18, 1936, 1, 4; July 25, 1936, 1; August 1, 1936, 1; August 8, 1936, 1; and September 26, 1936, 1; *New York Times*, July 14, 1936, 15; and July 18, 1936, 30; *Atlanta Daily World*, July 23, 1936, 1, 6; and Harris, *Carlos Cooks and Black Nationalism from Garvey to Malcolm*, xii–xiii.

31. New York *Amsterdam News*, July 25, 1936, 11.

32. Cooks was charged and convicted of disorderly conduct. Harris, *Carlos Cooks and Black Nationalism from Garvey to Malcolm*, xiv; *New York Times*, August 5, 1942, 8; and New York *Herald-Tribune*, July 31, 1942, 5. Quote in New York *Amsterdam News*, July 22, 1942, 6. This was not a universally accepted premise among Harlem Black nationalists. Cooks was joined by leaders like Harry Frederick, who argued that Hitler's disruption of European powers would weaken their ability to colonize Africa. Richard B. Moore, however, disagreed vehemently. He argued that "fascism is the most deadly enemy of the Negro peoples." New York *Amsterdam News*, November 1, 1941, 16.

33. Carlson's investigation was part of a broader study of fascist sympathy in the United States during World War II. In that context, he called Cooks "one of the more intelligent fascist leaders in Harlem." He was, for Copeland, one of "Harlem's own black fuehrers [*sic*]." Cooks had spent three years in the army after his praise of Hitler, spending much of his service in Italy. New York *Amsterdam News*, September 28, 1946, 8; and John Roy Carlson, *Under Cover: My Four Years in the Nazi Underworld of America* (New York: E. P. Dutton, 1943), 156, 158.

34. *Street Speaker* 1 (April 1940), Sc Micro RS-513, Schomburg Center for Research in Black Culture, New York, quote from 4.

35. The Universal African Nationalist Movement was founded in 1946 at the Eighth International Convention of African Peoples of the World. The "Buy Black" campaign was successful enough to worry local authorities. In 1950 Cooks was taken into police custody after distributing posters to Black-owned businesses in Harlem that notified potential customers of their status. Police argued that the posters would "cause a riot," that they would "arouse bad feeling in the community"—this despite the fact that the campaign had been active for years by 1950. Harris, *Carlos Cooks and Black Nationalism from Garvey to Malcolm*, xiv, xv–xx; Deburg, *Modern Black Nationalism from Marcus Garvey to Louis Farrakhan*, 84–92; and New York *Amsterdam News*, December 16, 1950, 1. The first edition of the new *Street Speaker* appeared in July 1955. That edition survives on microfilm at *Street Speaker* 1 (July 1955), Sc Micro RS-513, Schomburg Center for Research in Black Culture, New York.

36. More than 500 attended his funeral at Long Island National Cemetery, including Garveyites like Otley Brooks and Henry A. Kerr and allies like James Lawson. He would continue to be honored annually by his African Nationalist Pioneer Movement and followers like Brath. Peniel E. Joseph, "Malcolm X's Harlem and Early Black Power Activism," in *Neighborhood Rebels: Black Power at the Local Level*, ed. Peniel E. Joseph (New York: Palgrave Macmillan, 2010), 28, quote from Nkrumah included in Joseph's account, as well; New York *Amsterdam News*, July 19, 1958, 2; May 14, 1966, 1, 2; June 22, 1968, 19; May 4, 1991, 2; and May 1, 1993, 53; and Harris, *Carlos Cooks and Black Nationalism from Garvey to Malcolm*, xxi–xxiv. For more on Cooks's influence on Black national radicalism in Harlem, see *New York Times*, March 1, 1961, 1, 25; July 3, 1966, 1, 29; and March 12, 1968, 45.

37. New York *Amsterdam News*, July 11, 1964, 13; and *New York Times*, March 25, 1987, B1, B4. After his death, the ANPM created a new periodical, *Extra: African Nationalist Pioneer Movement News*. "The Chief is gone but he left the black race a superbly developed political doctrine," announced the first edition, "a solution, that will, if appreciated, bring life, liberty, and happiness to a race of people that have been reduced to the lowest status amongst men. That doctrine, African Nationalism, racial unity and racial action. May his will be done." A later edition in January 1967 speculated on potential government conspiracy in Cooks's death. *Extra* was a brief mimeographed newsletter rather than a

professionally designed publication. Two editions survive at *Extra: African Nationalist Pioneer Movement News*, Sc Micro RS-999, Schomburg Center for Research in Black Culture, New York; quote from "The Chief Is Gone," *Extra: African Nationalist Pioneer Movement News* 1 (May 1966): 1.

38. "African Nationalist Pioneer Movement," Box 1, Photographs [graphic]/Kwame Brathwaite, Sc Photo Portfolio (Brathwaite, K.), Schomburg Center for Research in Black Culture, New York. First quote from *Street Speaker* 1 (July 1955): 1, Sc Micro RS-513, Schomburg Center for Research in Black Culture, New York; second quote from New York *Amsterdam News*, December 10, 1988, 26; and April 29, 1989, 5.

39. R. Waldo Williams, "The Awakening Call," *The Black Challenge*, available online at https://www.freedomarchives.org/Documents/Finder/DOC32_scans/32.Various.BLM.The.Black.Challenge.pdf.

2. THE LIFE AND WORK OF ELOMBE BRATH

1. *New York Times*, June 26, 1971, 20.
2. Kweku Ampiah, *The Political and Moral Imperatives of the Bandung Conference of 1955: The Reactions of the US, UK and Japan* (Folkestone, UK: Global Oriental, 2007), 1–7, 29–38, 203–20; and Jason C. Parker, "Small Victory, Missed Chance: The Eisenhower Administration, the Bandung Conference, and the Turning of the Cold War," in *The Eisenhower Administration, the Third World, and the Globalization of the Cold War*, eds. Kathryn C. Statler and Andrew L. Johns (Lanham, MD: Rowman & Littlefield, 2006), 153–74. For more on the American presence at Bandung, particularly emphasizing the role of Richard Wright, see Brian Russell Roberts, *Artistic Ambassadors: Literary and International Representation of the New Negro Era* (Charlottesville: University of Virginia Press, 2013), 146–72.
3. King and X had more similarities than are often acknowledged. They were ministers who cared about the poor and fought against police brutality. Malcolm became more supportive of civil rights legislation after his break with the Nation of Islam and King became more focused on poverty and global politics in the last three years of his life. They were also connected through mutual friends like journalist Louis Lomax. See Manning Marable, *Malcolm X: A Life of Reinvention* (New York: Viking, 2011); Michael Eric Dyson, *Making Malcolm: The Myth and Meaning of Malcolm X* (Oxford: Oxford University Press, 1995); Peniel E. Joseph, *The Sword and the Shield: The Revolutionary Lives of Malcolm X and Martin Luther King Jr.* (New York: Basic Books, 2020); and Thomas Aiello, *The Life and Times of Louis Lomax: The Art of Deliberate Disunity* (Durham, NC: Duke University Press, 2021).

4. According to the *Amsterdam News*, it was Cecil who gave his children their artistic interests, and Etelka who gave them "a fierce sense of race pride." Jimbe Carroll, "Activist Elombe Brath Goes Home to the Ancestors," *New York Beacon* 21 (June 5–11, 2014): 5; New York *Amsterdam News*, January 31, 1970, 41; and April 5, 1980, 34; and "Who Was Elombe Brath?" Elombe Brath Foundation, https://www.elombebrathfoundation.org/legacy, accessed March 2, 2019.

5. Brath described the group's success to the *New York Times* by explaining that the group chose material that African Americans "are responsive to—they can become totally involved with what we do." *New York Times*, January 21, 1970, 35. Offices for the AJASS were on 125th Street in Harlem. "Interview Transcript Summary: Elombe Brath," Bronx African-American History Project, Grandassa Models Collection, 1963–1968, Sc MG 822, Schomburg Center for Research in Black Culture, New York.

6. New York *Amsterdam News*, January 16, 1982, 11; May 8, 1982, 15, 42; October 23, 1982, 15, 48; November 20, 1982, 2; April 26, 1986, 2; April 29, 1989, 5, 36; May 6, 1989, 2, 18; April 14, 1990, 2; and April 21, 1990, 63. Quote from May 8, 1982, 15.

7. "Who Was Elombe Brath?"; Carroll, "Activist Elombe Brath Goes Home to the Ancestors," 5; and "Elombe Brath," World African Diaspora Union,

Grandassa Models Collection, 1963–1968, Sc MG 822, Schomburg Center for Research in Black Culture, New York.

8. "To us, Biafra, as a nation, does not exist," said Brath. "All tribes must have security in any African state, but there must not be this Balkanization." *New York Times*, January 14, 1970, 17.

9. New York *Amsterdam News*, March 14, 1970, 31; April 4, 1970, 4; and November 16, 1974, A7; *New York Times*, December 12, 1970, 26; and "Miscellaneous Black Nationalist Events," Box 1, Photographs [graphic]/Kwame Brathwaite, Sc Photo Portfolio (Brathwaite, K.), Schomburg Center for Research in Black Culture, New York.

10. New York *Amsterdam News*, April 24, 1976, A2; January 1, 1977, C1; June 4, 1977, B1, B2; June 18, 1977, B8; July 9, 1977, A3; and November 20, 1982, 2; and *New York Times*, May 17, 1990, D1, D8; and June 24, 1990, E1.

11. New York *Amsterdam News*, July 2, 1966, 9.

12. New York *Amsterdam News*, December 21, 1991, 6.

13. "Patrice Lumumba Coalition Press Release," November 26, 1975; Patrice Lumumba Coalition, "Southern Africa Must Be Free! USA Subversion Must Be Exposed!" August 25, 1976; and Patrice Lumumba Coalition, "Resolution 268," August 26, 1976, Patrice Lumumba Coalition, African Activist Archive, Michigan State University Libraries, documents available online at http://africanactivist.msu.edu/browse_results.php?category=all&member=-Patrice%20Lumumba%20Coalition&org=Patrice%20Lumumba%20Coalition, accessed March 22, 2019. For more on the PLC, see "Patrice Lumumba Coalition, 1982," Anti-Apartheid Movements, Box 15, folder 597, ES Reddy Papers, MS1499, Manuscripts and Archives, Yale University Library, New Haven, CT; and "Pamphlet about the Patrice Lumumba Coalition," 2015.97.27.1, Collection of the Smithsonian National Museum of African American History and Culture, Washington, DC, available online at https://nmaahc.si.edu/object/nmaahc_2015.97.27.1, accessed March 31, 2019. For more on Lumumba, see Emmanuel Gerard and Bruce Kuklick, *Death in the*

Congo: Murdering Patrice Lumumba (Cambridge, MA: Harvard University Press, 2015).

14. Along with Brath, the founders of the AJASS were his brother, Kwame Brathwaite, Robert Gumbs, Chris "Acemendes" Hall, Frank Adu, and Jimmy Abu. First quote from New York *Amsterdam News*, August 21, 1965, 20; second from *New York Times*, June 26, 1971, 20; third from New York *Amsterdam News*, September 14, 1968, 7. See also "Who Was Elombe Brath?"; *Chicago Defender*, March 8, 1971, 18; and *Atlanta Daily World*, February 23, 1971, 2. The AJASS was actually founded in 1956, but began its productions in the early 1960s. New York *Amsterdam News*, December 29, 1962, 35; December 6, 1969, 18; December 5, 1970, 5; and December 7, 1991, 21.

15. Elombe Brath, "The Winds of Change—In Coiffure and Fashion," Naturally '63 Portfolio, Grandassa Models Collection, 1963–1968, Sc MG 822, Schomburg Center for Research in Black Culture, New York.

16. His belief in Garveyite separatism was complete, and his advocacy led to a close friendship with Garvey's widow, Jamaican author and activist Amy Jacques Garvey. In 1970, when Garvey protested attempts by several Black authors to secure her husband's correspondence with her while he served his prison sentence in Atlanta, she called upon Brath to act as her representative in the United States. On the twentieth anniversary of the founding of the AJASS in 1976, Brath helped organize a two-day symposium on "Marcus Garvey and Afrikan Liberation." *New York Times*, March 12, 1968, 45, 49; and New York *Amsterdam News*, August 21, 1976, D16; and October 9, 1976, D5.

17. New York *Amsterdam News*, August 21, 1965, 20; March 15, 1969, 5; and October 18, 1969, 26; and Dr. Noel Brathwaite, obituary, in possession of the author.

18. See www.elombebrathfoundation.org.

19. *New York Times*, December 21, 1986, A1; and New York *Amsterdam News*, December 21, 1991, 6.

20. New York *Amsterdam News*, August 22, 1987, 3, 35; October 31, 1987, 3; April 9, 1988, 3, 47;

November 26, 1988, 1, 38; March 18, 1989, 1, 38; September 30, 1989, 1, 38; December 9, 1989, 3; November 3, 1990, 15, 46, 60; and May 30, 1992, 5, 32; and *New York Times*, October 18, 1987, 1; and April 26, 1991, 1.

21. "Demonstrations—Tawana Brawley," Box 1, Photographs [graphic]/Kwame Brathwaite, Sc Photo Portfolio (Brathwaite, K.), Schomburg Center for Research in Black Culture, New York.

22. New York *Amsterdam News*, January 16, 1988, 2, 58; June 25, 1988, 3, 36; October 1, 1988, 1, 36; March 25, 1989, 3, 37; April 21, 1990, 1, 44; and January 19, 1991, 3, 49.

23. "I am forever grateful to Elombe," said Kevin Richardson, one of the Central Park Five, in response to his work on the case. Despite that work and the obvious innocence of the boys, however, they were convicted and served sentences of up to thirteen years in prison. In 2002 the actual rapist confessed, and DNA evidence proved he was telling the truth. After their release the defendants sued the city for discrimination and malicious prosecution. In 2014 New York settled the case for $41 million. Herb Boyd, "Elombe Brath 'Showing' Us the Way," New York *Amsterdam News*, May 10, 2017, http://amster damnews.com/news/2017/oct/05/elombe-brath -showing-us-way/?page=2, accessed March 15, 2019; Sarah Burns, *The Central Park Five: A Chronicle of a City Wilding* (New York: Knopf, 2011); Timothy Sullivan, *Unequal Verdicts: The Central Park Jogger Trials* (New York: Simon & Schuster, 1992); *New York Times*, April 24, 1989, B3; and New York *Amsterdam News*, April 29, 1989, 3, 36; May 6, 1989, 18, 49; August 5, 1989, 1, 10; December 2, 1989, 1, 41; April 7, 1990, 1, 53; July 28, 1990, 3; December 1, 1990, 1, 38; December 15, 1990, 3, 37; April 18, 1992, 5; quote in paragraph from April 29, 1989, 3; quote in note from Boyd, "Elombe Brath 'Showing' Us the Way."

24. New York *Amsterdam News*, June 15, 1991, 4.

25. Bob Reisner and Cecil Brathwaite, *Beat Jokes, Bop Humor, & Cool Cartoons* (New York: Citadel Press, 1960).

26. New York *Amsterdam News*, February 16, 1974, A5; October 26, 1974, A1, A2; October 15, 1975, D15; April 17, 1976, B3; October 29, 1977, D12; January 21; 1978, D12; November 10, 1979, 18; July 12, 1980, 15; August 16, 1980, 67; January 16, 1982, 11; May 8, 1982, 15; October 23, 1982, 15, 48; November 27, 1982, 15; July 18, 1987, 3, 10; December 5, 1987, 52; April 29, 1989, 5, 36; July 11, 1992, 2, 31; July 25, 1992, 8, 31; and November 28, 1992, 8.

27. The younger Garvey returned periodically to Harlem, and Brath was always part of the hosting retinue. New York *Amsterdam News*, April 14, 1973, 21; and July 6, 1974, B11.

28. Dr. Suzanne Ross of the NYC Free Mumia Coalition said, "Elombe was unflinching in his support of Mumia," referring to the political prisoner Mumia Abu-Jamal. Carroll, "Activist Elombe Brath Goes Home to the Ancestors," 5; Saaed Shabazz, "What is the Future of Pan African, Black Nationalist Movements?" *BlackPress USA*, July 8, 2014, https://www.blackpressusa.com/what-is-the-future -of-pan-african-black-nationalist-movements/, accessed March 15, 2019; Herb Boyd, "Elombe Brath 'Showing' Us the Way," New York *Amsterdam News*, May 10, 2017, http://amsterdamnews.com/news/ 2017/oct/05/elombe-brath-showing-us-way/?page =2, accessed March 15, 2019; and Sabamya Juangu, "A Tribute to Elombe Brath: Pan-African Revolutionary Teacher," unpublished reflection in possession of the author.

29. Charles B. Rangel, "In Honor of Elombe Brath," *Congressional Record*, May 13, 2013, E644–45.

30. It was an honor tinged with irony, as his sign rests at Adam Clayton Powell Plaza, so named for one of Brath's principal targets, both in the coloring book and in his Congressman Carter strip. Herb Boyd, "Elombe Brath 'Showing' Us the Way," New York *Amsterdam News*, May 10, 2017, http://amster damnews.com/news/2017/oct/05/elombe-brath -showing-us-way/?page=2, accessed March 15, 2019.

3. THE RHETORICAL ORIGINS OF ELOMBE BRATH'S SATIRE

1. Bambi Haggins, *Laughing Mad: The Black Comic Persona in Post-Soul America* (New

Brunswick, NJ: Rutgers University Press, 2007), 2, 4. See also Derek C. Maus and James J. Donahue, *Post-Soul Satire: Black Identity after Civil Rights* (Jackson: University Press of Mississippi, 2014); Dana A. Williams, ed., *African American Humor, Irony, and Satire* (Newcastle upon Tyne, UK: Cambridge Scholars, 2007); and Paul Beatty, ed., *Hokum: An Anthology of African-American Humor* (New York: Bloomsbury, 2006).

2. Terrence T. Tucker, *Furiously Funny: Comic Rage from Ralph Ellison to Chris Rock* (Gainesville: University Press of Florida, 2017), 2; and Glenda Carpio, *Laughing Fit to Kill: Black Humor in the Fictions of Slavery* (London: Oxford University Press, 2008), 5.

3. See Chesnutt's novels *The House Behind the Cedars* (New York: Houghton, Mifflin, 1900) and *The Marrow of Tradition* (New York: Houghton, Mifflin, 1901); and Darryl Dickson-Carr, *Spoofing the Modern: Satire in the Harlem Renaissance* (Columbia: University of South Carolina Press, 2014), 1–2. See also William Andrews, *The Literary Career of Charles W. Chesnutt* (Baton Rouge: Louisiana State University Press, 1980).

4. Pauline Hopkins, *Contending Forces: A Romance Illustrative of Negro Life North and South* (Boston: Colored Co-operative Publishing, 1900); and Pauline Hopkins, *Of One Blood: Or, the Hidden Self* in *The Colored American* (November 1902; December 1902; January 1903). See also Lois Brown, *Pauline Elizabeth Hopkins: Black Daughter of the Revolution* (Chapel Hill: University of North Carolina Press, 2008).

5. "Benjamin Banneker to Thomas Jefferson, 19 August 1791," in *The Papers of Thomas Jefferson*, vol. 22, *6 August 1791–31 December 1791*, ed. Charles T. Cullen (Princeton, NJ: Princeton University Press, 1986), 49–54; Chris Apap, "'Let no man of us budge one step': David Walker and the Rhetoric African American Emplacement," *Early American Literature* 46 (June 2011): 319–50; and Wilson Jeremiah Moses, *The Golden Age of Black Nationalism, 1850–1925* (1978; New York: Oxford University Press, 1988). See also Wilson Jeremiah Moses, ed., *Classical Black Nationalism: From the American Revolution to Marcus Garvey* (New York: New York University Press, 1996).

6. See Robert Steven Levine, *Martin Delany, Frederick Douglass, and the Politics of Representative Identity* (Chapel Hill: University of North Carolina Press, 1997). Delany's work was part of an early nineteenth-century legacy of Black publishing that would also presage what Brath was able to publish. William Wells Brown, an escaped slave from Kentucky, became the first African American novelist, publishing *Clotel, or the President's Daughter* in 1853. It used the Jefferson/Hemmings story to create a fictional account of slaveholder/slave relationships. There were also poets like George M. Horton and James M. Whitfield.

Black women published as well. Frances Ellen Watkins Harper and Harriet E. Wilson both published fiction and poetry. Wilson's *Our Nig: Or, Sketches from the Life of a Free Black, in a Two-Story White House, North* (1859) was the first novel published by a Black woman in the United States. It compared the lives of Black domestic workers in the North with those of southern slaves. But it received little attention, and even when it did people assumed it was a white writer. William Wells Brown, *Clotel, or the President's Daughter* (London: Partridge and Oakey, 1853); W. Edward Farrison, "William Wells Brown, Social Reformer," *Journal of Negro Education* 18 (Winter 1949): 29–39; George M. Horton, "Life of George M. Horton, the Colored Bard of North-Carolina," in *The Poetical Works of George M. Horton, the Colored Bard of North Carolina, to which Is Prefixed the Life of the Author, Written by Himself* (Hillsborough, NC: Heartt, 1845), iii–xx; Joan R. Sherman, "James Monroe Whitfield, Poet and Emigrationist: A Voice of Protest and Despair," *Journal of Negro History* 57 (April 1972): 169–76; Corinne T. Field, "Frances E. W. Harper and the Politics of Intellectual Maturity," in *Toward an Intellectual History of Black Women*, eds. Mia Bay, Farah J. Griffin, Martha S. Jones, and Barbara D. Savage (Chapel Hill: University of North Carolina Press, 2015), 110–26; Harriet E. Wilson, *Our Nig: Or, Sketches from the Life of a Free*

Black, in a Two-Story White House, North (Boston: George C. Rand and Avery, 1859); and Eric Gardner, "'This Attempt of Their Sister': Harriet Wilson's *Our Nig* from Printer to Readers," *New England Quarterly* 66 (June 1993): 226–46.

7. James Weldon Johnson, *Autobiography of an Ex-Colored Man* (Boston: Sherman, French, 1912).

8. Heather Russell, "Revising Critical Judgments of *The Autobiography of an Ex-Colored Man*," *African American Review* 40 (Summer 2006): 257–70. There were also white versions of this kind of satire, but that went over decidedly (and understandably) more poorly. T. Bowyer Campbell's novels *Black Sadie* (1928) and *White Nigger* (1932), for example, played with these same issues, but to an effect that came off as far more racially condescending. Campbell was an author, notes Sterling Brown, "whose preference is for the stereotype of the contented slave of the South," who "ironically accounts for the Harlem fad by the desire of jaded sophisticates for a new thrill." T. Bowyer Campbell, *Black Sadie* (Boston: Houghton Mifflin, 1928); T. Bowyer Campbell, *White Nigger* (London: W. Collins, 1932); and Sterling A. Brown, "Negro Character as Seen by White Authors," *Journal of Negro Education* 2 (April 1933): 199.

9. Renoir W. Gaither, "The Moment of Revision: A Reappraisal of Wallace Thurman's Aesthetics in *The Blacker the Berry* and *Infants of the Spring*," *CLA Journal* 37 (September 1993): 81, 84; and Nathan Irvin Huggins, *Harlem Renaissance* (New York: Columbia University Press, 1974), 239.

10. Gaither, "The Moment of Revision," 85; Dickson-Carr, *Spoofing the Modern*, 52–75; Wallace Thurman, *The Blacker the Berry* (New York: Macaulay, 1929); and Wallace Thurman, *Infants of the Spring* (New York: Macaulay, 1932).

11. Dickson-Carr, *Spoofing the Modern*, 75–86; Richard Bruce Nugent, *Gentleman Jigger* (New York: Da Capo Press, 2008); and Thomas H. Wirth, *Gay Rebel of the Harlem Renaissance: Selections from the Work of Richard Bruce Nugent* (Durham, NC: Duke University Press, 2002), 1–60.

12. Dorothy West, *The Living Is Easy* (1948; New York: Feminist Press at City University of New York,

2013); Lawrence R. Rodgers, "Dorothy West's *The Living Is Easy* and the Ideal of Southern Folk Community," *African American Review* 26 (Spring 1992): 161–72; and Pamela Peden Sanders, "The Feminism of Dorothy West's *The Living Is Easy*: A Critique of the Limitations of the Female Sphere through Performative Gender Roles," *African American Review* 36 (Autumn 2002): 435–46. See also Verner Mitchell and Cynthia Davis, *Literary Sisters: Dorothy West and Her Circle, A Biography of the Harlem Renaissance* (New Brunswick, NJ: Rutgers University Press, 2011).

13. Nella Larsen, *Passing* (New York: Alfred A. Knopf, 1929); and Mary Mabel Youman, "Nella Larsen's *Passing*: A Study in Irony," *CLA Journal* 18 (December 1974): 235–36.

14. Rudolph Fisher, *The Walls of Jericho* (New York: Alfred A. Knopf, 1928); Rudolph Fisher, "The City of Refuge," *Atlantic Monthly* (February 1925), reprinted in *The City of Refuge: The Collected Stories of Rudolph Fisher*, ed. John McCluskey (Columbia: University of Missouri Press, 1987), 3–16; and David Levering Lewis, *When Harlem Was in Vogue* (New York: Oxford University Press, 1989), 229–30.

15. Richard Wright, "Blueprint for Negro Writing," *New Challenge* 2 (Fall 1937), reprinted in *The Richard Wright Reader*, eds. Ellen Wright and Michel Fabre (New York: Harper and Row, 1978), 37–38.

16. Theodore Kornweibel, *No Crystal Stair: Black Life and* The Messenger, *1917–1928* (Westport, CT: Greenwood Press, 1975), 108; and Theophilus Lewis, "The Theater: The Souls of Black Folks," *The Messenger* (July 1926): 214–15.

17. For more on Schuyler, see Jeffrey Ferguson, *The Sage of Sugar Hill: George S. Schuyler and the Harlem Renaissance* (New Haven, CT: Yale University Press, 2005); and Oscar R. Williams, *George S. Schuyler: Portrait of a Black Conservative* (Knoxville: University of Tennessee Press, 2007).

18. George S. Schuyler, *Black No More* (New York: Macaulay, 1931). See also Jane Kuenz, "American Racial Discourse, 1900–1930: Schuyler's *Black No More*," *NOVEL: A Forum on Fiction* 30 (Winter 1997): 170–92; and Stacy Morgan, "'The Strange and

Wonderful Workings of Science': Race Science and Essentialism in George Schuyler's *Black No More*," *CLA Journal* 42 (March 1999): 331–52.

19. George S. Schuyler, "The Negro-Art Hokum," *Nation* 122 (June 16, 1926): 662–63.

20. Langston Hughes, "The Negro Artist and the Racial Mountain," *Nation* 122 (June 23, 1926): 692–94.

21. The biographical work on Hughes is voluminous, but for one of the foundational and easily accessible accounts, see Arnold Rampersad, *The Life of Langston Hughes*, vol. 1, *I, Too, Sing America* (New York: Oxford University Press, 1986); and Arnold Rampersad, *The Life of Langston Hughes*, vol. 2, *I Dream a World* (New York: Oxford University Press, 1988).

22. Donna Akiba Sullivan Harper, *Not So Simple: The "Simple" Stories by Langston Hughes* (Columbia: University of Missouri Press, 1995), 3. "Of course, he's not a real character in the sense that he's based on a single person," Hughes explained. "He's a composite. But he did grow out of a conversation that I had with a young man during the war." Quoted in James Presley, "The Birth of Jesse B. Semple," *Southwest Review* 58 (Summer 1973): 219.

23. Harper, *Not So Simple*, 3–5, quote from 5.

24. Harper, *Not So Simple*, 6–7. See also Sam G. Riley, "Langston Hughes's Jesse B. Semple Columns as Literary Journalism," *American Periodicals* 10 (2000): 63–78.

25. Harper, *Not So Simple*, 9; and Langston Hughes, *The Best of Simple* (New York: Hill and Wang, 1961), vii.

26. Blyden Jackson, "A Word about Simple," *CLA Journal* 11 (June 1968): 315.

27. Langston Hughes, "American Dilemma," in *The Return of Simple* (New York: Hill and Wang, 1994), 75.

28. Julian C. Carey, "Jesse B. Semple Revisited and Revised," *Phylon* 32 (2nd Qtr. 1971): 158–59.

29. Charles A. Watkins, "Simple: The Alter Ego of Langston Hughes," *Black Scholar* 2 (June 1971): 18–26.

30. Harper, *Not So Simple*, 7.

31. Tim Jackson, *Pioneering Cartoonists of Color* (Jackson: University Press of Mississippi, 2016), 11–26. Jackson's book provides the basis for this paragraph, carrying through in much greater depth the story of Black cartooning from the nineteenth century to Aaron McGruder's "Boondocks" and its contemporaries.

4. DOWN BEAT JAZZ RECORD REVIEWS ILLUSTRATIONS, 1957

1. Langston Hughes, *The First Book of Jazz* (New York: Franklin Watts, 1955); Langston Hughes, *The Weary Blues* (New York: Alfred A. Knopf, 1926); and Langston Hughes, *Not Without Laughter* (New York: Random House, 1930).

2. For more on Lawrence, see Patricia Hills, *Painting Harlem Modern: The Art of Jacob Lawrence* (Berkeley: University of California Press, 2009). For more on Douglas, see Amy Helene Kirschke, *Aaron Douglas: Art, Race, and the Harlem Renaissance* (Jackson: University Press of Mississippi, 1995).

3. F. Scott Fitzgerald, *Tales of the Jazz Age* (New York: Charles Scribner's Sons, 1922).

4. Cab Calloway, Bessie Smith, Fats Waller, Bill Robinson, and Louis Armstrong were all featured in "The Old Mill Pond." "The Old Mill Pond," Metro Goldwyn Mayer, 1936, available at https://www.youtube.com/watch?v=CQbbADi600g (accessed March 22, 2020); and "Little Ol' Bosko and the Pirates," Metro Goldwyn Mayer, 1937, available at https://www.youtube.com/watch?v=oVyvk_TshcI (accessed March 22, 2020).

5. *New York Times*, January 21, 1970, 35; and "Interview Transcript Summary: Elombe Brath," Bronx African-American History Project, Grandassa Models Collection, 1963–1968, Sc MG 822, Schomburg Center for Research in Black Culture, New York.

5. CARTOONS FROM *BEAT JOKES, BOP HUMOR, & COOL CARTOONS*

1. Bob Reisner and Cecil Brathwaite, *Beat Jokes, Bop Humor, & Cool Cartoons* (New York: The

Citadel Press, 1960); and *New York Times*, 22 February 1974, 36.

6. COMIC RADICALISM

1. New York *Citizen-Call*, May 21, 1960, 14; and *New York Times*, November 3, 1981, 14. The *Citizen-Call* survives on microfilm at Sc Micro RS-934, Schomburg Center for Research in Black Culture, New York Public Library, New York.

2. "World Politics Discussion Series to Open Thursday," March 25, 1953; "Hartford's Stone Gets Ceylon Post," April 8, 1956; and "Chuck Stone Joins Staff of New York Age," August 16, 1958, in About Stone, 1945 Mar. 22–1991 Nov., Clippings Series, Box 4; and "The Windsor Community Pays Homage to the Tuskegee Airmen," March 11, 2006, Correspondence, Box 66, Chuck Stone Papers, 1931–2007, RL.01259, David M. Rubenstein Rare Book and Manuscript Library, Duke University, Durham, North Carolina.

3. New York *Citizen-Call*, August 6, 1960, 1; and August 13, 1960, 1.

4. Arthur P. Davis, "Jesse B. Semple: Negro American," *Phylon* 15 (1st Qtr. 1954): 21–28.

5. Langston Hughes, *The Best of Simple* (New York: Hill and Wang, 1961), 61–62.

6. See comics below.

7. Phyllis R. Klotman, "Jesse B. Semple and the Narrative Art of Langston Hughes," *Journal of Narrative Technique* 3 (January 1973): 66–75.

8. Melvin G. Williams, "Langston Hughes's Jesse B. Semple: A Black Walter Mitty," *Negro American Literature Forum* 10 (Summer 1976): 68; and Langston Hughes, *Simple Speaks His Mind* (New York: Simon & Schuster, 1950), 174.

9. Langston Hughes, *Simple Stakes a Claim* (New York: Rinehart, 1950), 166.

10. See comics below.

11. New York *Citizen-Call*, May 21, 1960, 1; February 11, 1961, 1, 12; February 18, 1961, 1, 2, 10, 14.

12. "Chuck Stone Named Wash. AFRO editor," January 7, 1961, in About Stone, 1945 Mar. 22–1991 Nov., Clippings Series, Box 4; "Adam Clayton Powell to C. Sumner Stone," December 22, 1961; "Sammy Davis, Jr. to C. Sumner Stone," July 13, 1961; "Martin Luther King, Jr. to C. Sumner Stone," June 6, 1962; and "Jackie Robinson to C. Sumner Stone," October 25, 1962, General Correspondence, 1961–1969, Correspondence Series, Box 16, Chuck Stone Papers, 1931–2007, RL.01259, David M. Rubenstein Rare Book and Manuscript Library, Duke University, Durham, North Carolina.

13. *New York Times*, May 30, 1963, 32; August 7, 1963, 31; August 30, 1964, SM8; July 10, 1965, 23; December 4, 1965, 38; October 23, 1967, 33; August 30, 1968, 24; June 18, 1969, 54; March 28, 1972, 39; and November 3, 1981, 14; "Nikki Giovanni to Chuck Stone," May 16, 1969; and "Romare H. Bearden to Chuck Stone," August 30, 1968, General Correspondence, 1961–1969, Correspondence Series, Box 16; and "LeRoi Jones to Chuck Stone," April 24, 1968, General Correspondence, 1963–1987, Correspondence Series, Box 16, Chuck Stone Papers, 1931–2007, RL.01259, David M. Rubenstein Rare Book and Manuscript Library, Duke University, Durham, North Carolina.

14. Brath also vigorously opposed the term "Negro." "Negro is a Spanish word which means black in that language and was adopted by the white man to describe us so that he could rob us of our identity with Africa." New York *Amsterdam News*, January 18, 1964, 23; and *New York Times*, March 12, 1968, 45, 49.

15. Askia Muhammad Touré, "Brother Cecil Elombe Brath," *Journal of Black Poetry*, 1st Pan-African Issue 1 (Winter-Spring 1970): n.p.

16. New York *Amsterdam News*, March 14, 1964, 20; and "New York Beat," *Jet*, March 5, 1964, 63.

17. Larry Lieber, *Your Future Rests . . . In Your Hands* (New York: NAACP, 1964), GLC09640.160, Gilder Lehrman Collection, Gilder Lehrman Institute of American History, New York.

18. New York *Amsterdam News*, March 14, 1964, 20.

19. *Chicago Defender*, January 20, 1964, 9; and March 16, 1964, 5.

20. *Pittsburgh Courier*, February 8, 1964, 13.

21. Beth Turner, "Simplifyin': Langston Hughes and Alice Childress Re/member Jesse B. Semple," *Langston Hughes Review* 15 (Spring 1997): 37.

8. *COLOR US CULLUD! THE AMERICAN NEGRO LEADERSHIP OFFICIAL COLORING BOOK,* 1964

1. Writing in the immediate wake of Kennedy's assassination and published in January 1964, Brath here reflects the fears of many as a white southern Democrat ascended to the presidency to replace the slain leader. Johnson was one of three southern senators who had refused to sign the Southern Manifesto in 1956. Less than a week after taking over the presidency, he announced to a joint session of Congress that he wanted swift action on a civil rights bill—the bill that would become the Civil Rights Act of 1964. But while radical Black nationalists were particularly inclined to mistrust white leaders, particularly those from the South, early mistrust of the sincerity of Johnson's racial pronouncements was common among most African Americans. See, for example, Sylvia Ellis, *Freedom's Pragmatist: Lyndon Johnson and Civil Rights* (Gainesville: University Press of Florida, 2013); Nick Kotz, *Judgment Days: Lyndon Baines Johnson, Martin Luther King Jr., and the Laws That Changed America* (Boston: Houghton Mifflin, 2005); and Clay Risen, *The Bill of the Century: The Epic Battle for the Civil Rights Act* (New York: Bloomsbury, 2014).

2. Evers, field secretary of the Mississippi NAACP, was murdered in his Jackson, Mississippi, driveway on June 12, 1963. Three months later, on September 15, four girls were killed when members of the Ku Klux Klan bombed the Sixteenth Street Baptist Church in Birmingham, Alabama. Two teenage boys were killed in the aftermath of the bombing, one shot by police, the other by an angry white teenager. For the murder of Evers, see Maryanne Vollers, *Ghosts of Mississippi: The Murder of Medgar Evers, the Trials of Byron de la Beckwith, and the Haunting of the New South* (New York: Little, Brown, 1995); and Minrose Gwin,

Remembering Medgar Evers: Writing the Long Civil Rights Movement (Athens: University of Georgia Press, 2013). For the Sixteenth Street Baptist Church bombing, see Frank Sikora, *Until Justice Rolls Down: The Birmingham Church Bombing Case* (Tuscaloosa: University of Alabama Press, 1991); and Doug Jones, *Bending Toward Justice: The Birmingham Church Bombing That Changed the Course of Civil Rights* (New York: All Points Books, 2019).

3. Brath here refers to the Sharpeville Massacre, occurring in the Transvaal Province of South Africa on March 21, 1960. In response to South African pass laws designed to regulate internal movement for minority groups, thousands of protesters descended on the police station at Sharpeville. Police opened fire on the crowd, killing sixty-nine and wounding 180, many shot in the back while fleeing. The massacre led to a wave of protest in South Africa, as well as in the United Nations and countries around the world. It is also credited as one of the catalysts turning dissident groups in the Pan-Africanist Congress and the African National Congress to support for armed resistance. See Tom Lodge, *Sharpeville: An Apartheid Massacre and Its Consequences* (New York: Oxford University Press, 2011); and Philip Frankel, *An Ordinary Atrocity: Sharpeville and Its Massacre* (New Haven, CT: Yale University Press, 2001).

4. First enunciated by Kennedy at the Democratic National Convention in 1960, the slogan "New Frontier" became a label for his policy agenda. Civil rights was originally part of that proposal, but Kennedy's civil rights record prior to his assassination was disappointing. See Irving Bernstein, *Promises Kept: John F. Kennedy's New Frontier* (New York: Oxford University Press, 1991).

5. The "Big Six" civil rights leaders were labor leader Asa Philip Randolph, SCLC's Martin Luther King, CORE's James Farmer, SNCC's John Lewis, the National Urban League's Whitney Young, and the NAACP's Roy Wilkins, all of whom helped organize the August 1963 March on Washington, and all of whom are further ridiculed in the coloring book.

6. Brath here mistakes Lincoln for Thomas Jefferson, who wrote in 1821, "But it was found the

public mind would not yet bear the proposition [emancipation], nor will it bear it even at this day. Yet the day is not distant when it must bear and adopt it, or worse will follow. Nothing is more certainly written in the book of fate than that these people are to be free. Nor is it less certain that the two races, equally free, cannot live in the same government. Nature, habit, opinion has drawn indelible lines of distinction between them. It is still in our power to direct the process of emancipation and deportation peaceably and in such slow degree as that the evil will wear off insensibly, and their place be pari passu filled up by free white laborers. If on the contrary it is left to force itself on, human nature must shudder at the prospect held up." Thomas Jefferson, *The Autobiography of Thomas Jefferson, 1743–1790: Together with a Summary of the Chief Events in Jefferson's Life*, ed. Paul Leicester Ford (Philadelphia: University of Pennsylvania Press, 2005), 44.

7. Lincoln was not a consistent advocate of colonization, but he did see it as a tangible benefit to both races. When a delegation of Black leaders met with Lincoln on August 14, 1862, he told them, "I suppose one of the principal difficulties in the way of colonization is that the free colored man cannot see that his comfort would be advanced by it. You may believe you can live in Washington or elsewhere in the United States the remainder of your life [as easily], perhaps more so than you can in any foreign country, and hence you may come to the conclusion that you have nothing to do with the idea of going to a foreign country. This is (I speak in no unkind sense) an extremely selfish view of the case," he told them. "But you ought to do something to help those who are not so fortunate as yourselves." Abraham Lincoln, "Address on Colonization to a Deputation of Colored Men," August 14, 1862, in *Abraham Lincoln: Complete Works*, vol. 2, ed. John G. Nicolay and John Hay (New York: Century, 1920), 222–23.

8. Brath's language here is intentionally harsh, but it is also offensive. "Handkerchief heads" is a reference to filmed mammies, a female version of Uncle Tom. See Jonathon Green, *Cassell's Dictionary of Slang* (London: Weidenfeld & Nicolson, 2005), 674. Brath was in no way the only one to use the term. Joseph Lowery argued in 2011 about Black apathy, "We are wearing a kente cloth headpiece with a handkerchief head mentality." Joseph E. Lowery, *Singing the Lord's Song in a Strange Land* (Nashville: Abingdon Press, 2011), 148.

9. For more on Garvey and his legacy, see introduction.

10. Herzl is considered the father of modern Zionism and a spiritual father of Israel, even though he died in 1904 and never lived to see its formation. He was the founder of the Zionist Organization, and in his book *Der Judenstaat*, he explained, "The Jewish question persists wherever Jews live in appreciable numbers. Wherever it does not exist, it is brought in together with Jewish immigrants. We are naturally drawn into those places where we are not persecuted, and our appearance there gives rise to persecution. This is the case, and will inevitably be so, everywhere, even in highly civilised countries—see, for instance, France—so long as the Jewish question is not solved on the political level." Theodor Herzl, *Der Judenstaat* (Leipzig: Verlags-Buchhandlung, 1896), quote from translation in Arthur Hertzberg, *The Zionist Idea: A Historical Analysis and Reader* (1959; repr., Lincoln: University of Nebraska Press, 1997), 209.

11. This is another problematic statement that plays to the stereotype of Jewish finance and wealth.

12. The comparison with Nazism of radical right-wing organization's like the John Birch Society or out-and-out racist organizations like the White Citizens Council was not new, but was typically made in metaphor. The strength of Brath's critique is his assertion that all such groups are engaged in something functionally similar to that of the Nazis.

13. For more on Lumumba and his legacy, see introduction.

14. There is no evidence that the United States participated in the capture or execution of Patrice Lumumba. Rumors of that possibility, however, were real, spurred in large measure by Lumumba's willingness to turn to the Soviet Union for help in

suppressing a Belgian-supported coup attempt, despite the fact that he only did so after being refused aid by the United States and United Nations. He was killed by the Joseph-Désiré Mobutu government after his successful coup, based largely on his opposition to Lumumba's Soviet ties. Lumumba's falling-out with the United States led to the assumption by many in the Republic of the Congo that he was expendable. See Richard Mahoney, *JFK: Ordeal in Africa* (New York: Oxford University Press, 1983); and Robin McKown, *Lumumba: A Biography* (Garden City, NY: Doubleday, 1969).

15. Jomo Kenyatta helped lead the push for Kenya's independence from the colonial thumb of Britain and, as Brath intimates, was a Pan-Africanist nationalist. He was influenced by George Padmore, along with Garvey, while in England, and helped organize the 1945 Pan-African Congress in Manchester. His anticolonial political career in Kenya began in 1947 when he became President of the Kenya Africa Union. He helped organize the Mau Mau Uprising. He became Prime Minister of Kenya in June 1963, and just months after the publication of *Color Us Cullud!*, in December 1964, he became the country's president, where he would serve until his death in 1978. See W. O. Maloba, *The Anatomy of Neo-Colonialism in Kenya: British Imperialism and Kenyatta, 1963–1978* (London: Palgrave Macmillan, 2017); W. O. Maloba, *Kenyatta and Britain: An Account of Political Transformation, 1929–1963* (London: Palgrave Macmillan, 2018); and Donald C. Savage, "Kenyatta and the Development of African Nationalism in Kenya," *International Journal* 25 (Summer 1970): 518–37.

16. That "Gikuyu tribal girl" was Ngina Muhoho, Kenyatta's fourth wife, from Ngenda in Kenya's Central Province, a member of the Kikuyu, the largest ethnic group in the nation. Known after Kenyatta's ascendance as Mama Ngina Kenyatta, she was almost forty years younger than her husband, married to him when she was eighteen years old. For more on Mama Ngina, see Maloba's two-volume Kenyatta biography.

17. Thomas Gangemi became Jersey City's mayor in July 1961, but the Italian immigrant had never become a citizen. The resulting controversy forced his resignation in September 1963. *New York Times*, September 26, 1963, 1; November 13, 1963, 1; 29 August 29, 1964, 23.

9. ANNOTATIONS TO THE COLORING BOOK

1. For more on the Du Bois-Washington feud, see Thomas Aiello, *The Battle for the Souls of Black Folk: W. E. B. Du Bois, Booker T. Washington, and the Debate That Shaped the Course of Civil Rights* (Westport, CT: Praeger, 2016).

2. Jervis Anderson, *A. Philip Randolph: A Biographical Portrait* (Berkeley: University of California Press, 1986), 120–37, quote from 127; and A. Philip Randolph, "The Only Way to Redeem Africa," in *For Jobs and Freedom: Selected Speeches and Writings of A. Philip Randolph*, ed. Andrew E. Kersten and David Lucander (Amherst: University of Massachusetts Press, 2014), 323–32.

3. David Wright, "The Use of Race and Racial Perceptions among Asians and Blacks: The Case of the Japanese and African Americans," *Hitotsubashi Journal of Social Studies* 30 (1998): 143. See also Gerald Horne, "Race from Power: US Foreign Policy and the General Crisis of 'White Supremacy,'" in *The Ambiguous Legacy: US Foreign Relations in the "American Century,"* ed. Michael J. Hogan (New York: Cambridge University Press, 1999), 318.

4. For more on the Porters, see Eric Arnesen, *Brotherhoods of Color: Black Railroad Workers and the Struggle for Equality* (Cambridge, MA: Harvard University Press, 2001); Beth Tompkins Bates, *Pullman Porters and the Rise of Protest Politics in Black America, 1925–1945* (Chapel Hill: University of North Carolina Press, 2001); and William H. Harris, *Keeping the Faith: A. Philip Randolph, Milton P. Webster, and the Brotherhood of Sleeping Car Porters, 1925–37* (Urbana: University of Illinois Press, 1977). For more on the NALC, see Anderson, *A. Philip Randolph*, 305–10; Paula F. Pfeffer, *A. Philip Randolph, Pioneer of the Civil Rights Movement* (Baton Rouge: Louisiana State University

Press, 1990); and Herbert Hill, "The Racial Practices of Organized Labor: The Contemporary Record," in *The Negro and the American Labor Movement*, ed. Julius Jacobson (New York: Anchor, 1968), 286–357.

5. Harvard Sitkoff, *King: Pilgrimage to the Mountaintop* (New York: Hill and Wang, 2008), 76; and Derek Charles Catsam, *Freedom's Main Line: The Journey of Reconciliation and the Freedom Rides* (Lexington: University Press of Kentucky, 2009), 236.

6. Sitkoff, *King*, 78–86; Clayborne Carson, "SNCC and the Albany Movement," *Journal of Southwest Georgia History* 2 (1984): 15–25; and Martin Luther King, *The Autobiography of Martin Luther King Jr.*, ed. Clayborne Carson (New York: Warner Books, 1998), 151–69.

7. For more on Birmingham 1963 and the church bombing that served as a grim exclamation point on the sentence that was the violence that summer, see Glenn T. Eskew, *But for Birmingham: The Local and National Movements in the Civil Rights Struggle* (Chapel Hill: University of North Carolina Press, 1997); David Garrow, ed., *Birmingham, Alabama, 1956–1963: The Black Struggle for Civil Rights* (Brooklyn: Carlson Publishing, 1989); Diane McWhorter, *Carry Me Home: Birmingham, Alabama, the Climactic Battle of the Civil Rights Revolution* (New York: Simon & Schuster, 2001); and Frank Sikora, *Until Justice Rolls Down: The Birmingham Church Bombing Case* (Tuscaloosa: University of Alabama Press, 1991).

8. "Never Again Where He Was," *Time*, January 3, 1964, 22.

9. *New York Times*, September 22, 1963, 1, 72; *Chicago Defender*, October 2, 1963, 5; *Pittsburgh Courier*, October 5, 1963, 11; *Afro-American*, October 5, 1963, 14; and Robert E. Weems, *Desegregating the Dollar: African American Consumerism in the Twentieth Century* (New York: New York University Press, 1998), 67.

10. *Pittsburgh Courier*, October 5, 1963, 11; and *Chicago Defender*, October 7, 1963, 4.

11. There were local efforts at Christmas boycotts, but they too were unable to meet the mark they set for themselves. In Jackson, Mississippi, boycott efforts did prompt the mayor and other officials to create incentives for downtown shopping, which at least demonstrated an acknowledgment of the boycott, but those incentives also largely ended it. There was limited success in Danville, Virginia, Cambridge, Maryland, and in Birmingham. *Washington Post*, January 2, 1964, A6; and Manning Marable, *Malcolm X: A Life of Reinvention* (New York: Viking, 2011), 163.

12. See Irving A. Falk, *Prophecy for the Year 2000* (New York: Julian Messner, 1970).

13. John R. Shillady, *Planning Public Expenditures to Compensate for Decreased Private Employment During Business Depressions* (New York: Mayor's Committee on Unemployment, November 1916); NAACP, *The Mobbing of John R. Shillady, Secretary for the National Association for the Advancement of Colored People, Austin, Texas, Aug. 22, 1919* (New York: NAACP, October 1919); and Hubert Harrison, "Shillady Resigns," *Negro World* 8 (June 19, 1920): 2.

14. G. Marc Hamburger, "Jewish Rush in the Bible Belt," *Vanderbilt Magazine*, August 5, 2009, https://news.vanderbilt.edu/vanderbiltmagazine/jewish-rush-in-the-bible-belt/, accessed April 5, 2019. For more on Wilkins, see Yvonne Ryan, *Roy Wilkins: The Quiet Revolutionary and the NAACP* (Lexington: University Press of Kentucky, 2014); and Roy Wilkins, *Standing Fast: The Autobiography of Roy Wilkins*, ed. Tom Mathews (New York: Da Capo Press, 1994).

15. The Clark Atlanta University School of Social Work is now named in honor of Young. For more on Young and his emphasis on Black job creation, see Nancy J. Weiss, *Whitney M. Young Jr. and the Struggle for Civil Rights* (Princeton, NJ: Princeton University Press, 1990); and Dennis C. Dickerson, *Militant Mediator: Whitney M. Young Jr.* (Lexington: University Press of Kentucky, 2015).

16. See Leah Platt Boustan, *Competition in the Promised Land: Black Migrants in Northern Cities and Labor Markets* (Princeton, NJ: Princeton University Press, 2016); Isabel Wilkinson, *The Warmth of Other Suns: The Epic Story of America's Great Migration* (New York: Vintage Books, 2011);

and John R. Commons, "Labor Conditions in Meat Packing and the Recent Strike," *Quarterly Journal of Economics* 19 (November 1904): 1–32.

17. Victor Oliveira, "Trends in the Hired Farm Work Force, 1945–1987" (Washington: USDA/ERS, 1989); and David G. Gutiérrez, "Migration, Emergent Ethnicity, and the 'Third Space': The Shifting Politics of Nationalism in Greater Mexico," *Journal of American History* 86 (September 1999): 481–517. See also Kunal M. Parker, *Making Foreigners: Immigration and Citizenship Law in America, 1600–2000* (New York: Cambridge University Press, 2015); John Bodnar, *The Transplanted: A History of Immigrants in Urban America* (Bloomington: Indiana University Press, 1985); David Reimers, *Still the Golden Door: The Third World Comes to America* (New York: Columbia University Press, 1985); and Alejandro Portes and Robert L. Bach, *Latin Journey: Cuban and Mexican Immigrants in the United States* (Berkeley: University of California Press, 1985).

18. See Raymond Arsenault, *Freedom Riders 1961 and the Struggle for Racial Justice* (New York: Oxford University Press, 2006); James Farmer, *Lay Bare the Heart: An Autobiography of the Civil Rights Movement* (Ft. Worth: Texas Christian University Press, 1985); Ben Voth, *James Farmer Jr.: The Great Debater* (Lanham, MD: Lexington Books, 2017); and August Meier and Elliott Rudwick, *CORE: A Study in the Civil Rights Movement, 1942–1968* (New York: Oxford University Press, 1973).

19. See Christopher W. Schmidt, *The Sit-Ins: Protest and Legal Change in the Civil Rights Era* (Chicago: University of Chicago Press, 2018); and Iwan Morgan and Philip Davis, *From Sit-Ins to SNCC: The Student Civil Rights Movement in the 1960s* (Gainesville: University Press of Florida, 2013).

20. Raymond Arsenault, *Freedom Riders: 1961 and the Struggle for Racial Justice* (New York: Oxford University Press, 2007); and Derek Charles Catsam, *Freedom's Main Line: The Journey of Reconciliation and the Freedom Rides* (Lexington: University Press of Kentucky, 2009).

21. For more on James and Lula Farmer, see the James Leonard Farmer Jr. and Lula Peterson Farmer Papers, Dolph Briscoe Center for American History, University of Texas, Austin.

22. Clayborne Carson, *In Struggle: SNCC and the Black Awakening of the 1960s* (Cambridge, MA: Harvard University Press, 1995); James Forman, *The Making of Black Revolutionaries* (1972; Seattle: University of Washington Press, 1997); and Vanessa Murphree, *The Selling of Civil Rights: The Student Nonviolent Coordinating Committee and the Use of Public Relations* (New York: Routledge, 2006).

23. John Lewis and Michael D'Orso, *Walking with the Wind: A Memoir of the Movement* (New York: Simon & Schuster, 1998), 219–27; and William P. Jones, *The March on Washington: Jobs, Freedom, and the Forgotten History of Civil Rights* (New York: W.W. Norton, 2013), 193–95.

24. See Larry S. Gibson, *Young Thurgood: The Making of a Supreme Court Justice* (New York: Prometheus Books, 2012); Mark V. Tushnet, *Making Civil Rights Law: Thurgood Marshall and the Supreme Court, 1936–1961* (New York: Oxford University Press, 1994); and Juan Williams, *Thurgood Marshall: American Revolutionary* (New York: New York Times, 1998). For more on Houston, see Genna Rae McNeil, *Groundwork: Charles Hamilton Houston and the Struggle for Civil Rights* (Philadelphia: University of Pennsylvania Press, 1983).

25. See Mark V. Tushnet, *Making Constitutional Law: Thurgood Marshall and the Supreme Court, 1961–1991* (New York: Oxford University Press, 1997); and Michael D. Davis and Hunter R. Clark, *Thurgood Marshall: Warrior at the Bar, Rebel on the Bench* (Secaucus, NJ: Carol Publishing, 1992).

26. For more on the Tuskegee Syphilis Experiment, see Allan M. Brandt, "Racism and Research: The Case of the Tuskegee Syphilis Study," **Hastings Center Report** 8 (December 1978): 21–29; Susan M. Reverby, *Examining Tuskegee: The Infamous Syphilis Study and Its Legacy* (Chapel Hill: University of North Carolina Press, 2009); and James Jones, *Bad Blood: The Tuskegee Syphilis Experiment* (New York: Free Press, 1981).

27. For more on Marshall's wives, see the biographies in previous notes, as well as DeNeen L. Brown,

"Thurgood Marshall's Interracial Love," *Washington Post*, online edition, August 18, 2016, https://www .washingtonpost.com/local/thurgood-marshalls -interracial-love-i-dont-care-what-people-think-im -marrying-you/2016/08/18/84f636be-54d5–11e6 -bbf5–957ad17b4385_story.html?utm_term=.9950 b1ff9de7, accessed March 21, 2019.

28. For more on Powell, see Charles V. Hamilton, *Adam Clayton Powell Jr.: The Political Biography of an American Dilemma* (New York: Atheneum, 1991); and Wil Haygood, *King of the Cats: The Life and Times of Adam Clayton Powell Jr.* (Boston: Houghton Mifflin, 1993).

29. Lawrence Rushing, "The Racial Identity of Adam Clayton Powell Jr.: A Case Study in Racial Ambivalence and Redefinition," *Afro-Americans in New York Life and History* 34 (January 2010): 7–33.

30. Powell's personal life is chronicled in the biographies listed above. See also "Investigations: Adam and Yvette," *Time*, February 24, 1967, 36; and "Congressional Witness: Yvette Diago Powell," *New York Times*, February 17, 1967, 26.

31. See Brian Urquhart, *Ralph Bunche: An American Life* (New York: W.W. Norton, 1993); Charles P. Henry, *Ralph Bunche: Model Negro or American Other?* (New York: New York University Press, 1999); and Elad Ben-Dror, *Ralph Bunche and the Arab-Israeli Conflict: Mediation and the UN, 1947–1949* (New York: Routledge, 2016).

32. For more on the Suez Crisis, see Michael N. Barnett, *Confronting the Costs of War: Military Power, State, and Society in Egypt and Israel* (Princeton, NJ: Princeton University Press, 1992); and Donald Neff, *Warriors at Suez: Eisenhower Takes America into the Middle East* (New York: Simon & Schuster, 1981). For more on the Congo Crisis, see Herbert Weiss, "The Congo's Independence Struggle Viewed Fifty Years Later," *African Studies Review* 55 (April 2012): 109–15; and Lise Namikas, *Battleground Africa: Cold War in the Congo, 1960–1965* (Washington, DC: Woodrow Wilson Center Press, 2013).

33. Urquhart, *Ralph Bunche*, 431; and Fred Ferretti, "Black Gains Membership at Forest Hills," *New York Times*, June 27, 1978, C11.

34. See David Leeming, *James Baldwin: A Biography* (New York: Simon & Schuster, 2015); James Campbell, *Talking at the Gate: A Life of James Baldwin* (Berkeley: University of California Press, 2002); and Herb Boyd, *Baldwin's Harlem: A Biography of James Baldwin* (New York: Simon & Schuster, 2008).

35. See James Baldwin, *Giovanni's Room* (New York: Dial Press, 1956); Michele Wallace, *Black Macho and the Myth of the Superwoman* (New York: Dial Press, 1979); Rachel Corbman, "'Next Time, The Fire In Giovanni's Room': The Critical Reception of James Baldwin's Second Novel in the Black Press," *Zeteo* (Spring 2012), available at http://zeteojournal .com/2012/04/11/james-baldwin-and-the-black-press/, accessed April 7, 2019; and Georges-Michel Sarotte, *Like a Brother, Like a Lover: Male Homosexuality in the American Novel and Theatre from Herman Melville to James Baldwin* (New York: Doubleday, 1978).

36. See James Baldwin, *The Fire Next Time* (New York: Dial Press, 1963); and James Baldwin, "A Letter to My Nephew," *The Progressive* 26 (December 1962): 19–20.

37. For more on Belafonte's career in music and civil rights, see Judith Smith, *Becoming Belafonte: Black Artist, Public Radical* (Austin: University of Texas Press, 2014); Genia Fogelson, *Harry Belafonte* (Los Angeles: Melrose Square, 1991); and Harry Belafonte and Michael Shnayerso, *My Song: A Memoir* (New York: Knopf, 2011).

38. Hank Bordowitz, "Miriam Makeba," in *The Outlaw Bible of American Essays*, ed. Alan Kaufman (New York: Thunder's Mouth Press, 2006), 313–34; Ruth Feldstein, *How It Feels to Be Free: Black Women Entertainers and the Civil Rights Movement* (New York: Oxford University Press, 2013), 51–52; Tyler Fleming, "A Marriage of Inconvenience: Miriam Makeba's Relationship with Stokely Carmichael and her Music Career in the United States," *Safundi: The Journal of South African and American Studies* 17 (May 2016): 312–38; and April Sizemore-Barber, "The Voice of (Which?) Africa: Miriam Makeba in America," *Safundi: The Journal of South African and American Studies* 13 (July-October 2012): 251–76.

39. Jeff Sharlet, "Voice and Hammer: Harry Belafonte's Unfinished Fight," *Virginia Quarterly Review* (Fall 2013): 24–41; and Henry Louis Gates, "Belafonte's Balancing Act," *New Yorker* 72 (August 26, 1996): 132–38.

40. See James Gavin, *Stormy Weather: The Life of Lena Horne* (New York: Atria, 2009); and James Haskins and Kathleen Benson, *Lena: A Personal and Professional Biography of Lena Horne* (New York: Stein and Day, 1984). In addition, the year following Brath's account, Horne wrote her own. See Lena Horne and Richard Schickel, *Lena* (New York: Doubleday, 1965).

41. Stories of Hayton can be found in accounts of his movies or in accounts of Horne's life, above.

42. *New York Times*, February 17, 1960, 30.

43. See John L. Williams, *America's Mistress: The Life and Times of Eartha Kitt* (New York: Quercus, 2013).

44. Williams, *America's Mistress*, 218–21, 223–241; and Eartha Kitt, "Eartha Kitt Tells Why Her Marriage Has Broken Up," *Jet* 24 (October 10, 1963): 22–24.

45. Eartha Kitt, "My Baby Travels with Me," *Ebony* 18 (January 1963): 93–98.

46. See Eartha Kitt, *Thursday's Child* (New York: Four Square Books, 1956); Eartha Kitt, *Alone with Me: A New Autobiography* (New York: Regnery, 1976); and Eartha Kitt, *I'm Still Here: Confessions of a Sex Kitten* (New York: Barricade Books, 1993).

47. See Will Haygood, *In Black and White: The Life of Sammy Davis Jr.* (New York: Knopf, 2003); and Matt Birkbeck, *Deconstructing Sammy: Music, Money, and Madness* (New York: Amistad, 2008). For King quote, see "Martin Luther King Jr. to Sammy Davis Jr., 20 December 1960," in *The Papers of Martin Luther King Jr.*, vol. V, *Threshold of a New Decade, January 1959–December 1960*, eds. Clayborne Carson, Tenisha Armstrong, Susan Carson, Adrienne Clay, and Kieran Taylor (Berkeley: University of California Press, 2005), 582–83.

48. "Sammy Davis Will Make Second Command Performance," New York *Amsterdam News*, October 21, 1961, 17.

49. For more on Davis's love live and its consequences for his career, see biographical treatments above.

50. "Religion: Jewish Negro," *Time*, February 1, 1960, 40.

51. Zionism, as described above, began as a concentrated effort to create a Jewish homeland. After Israel's founding, it became a more sustained effort to advocate for the sustainability of Israel and for Jewish interests.

52. New York *Amsterdam News*, September 15, 1979, 21; and September 22, 1979, 16.

53. There are dozens of book-length treatments of Robinson's life, but for the most complete and influential, see Jules Tygiel, *Baseball's Great Experiment: Jackie Robinson and His Legacy* (New York: Oxford University Press, 1983); Jonathan Eig, *Opening Day: The Story of Jackie Robinson's First Season* (New York: Simon & Schuster, 2007); David Falkner, *Great Time Coming: The Life of Jackie Robinson, from Baseball to Birmingham* (New York: Simon & Schuster, 1995); and Arnold Rampersad, *Jackie Robinson: A Biography* (New York: Alfred A. Knopf, 1997).

54. See biographical treatments above, from which this account is culled.

55. See biographical treatments above, from which this account is culled.

56. See W. K. Stratton, *Floyd Patterson: The Fighting Life of Boxing's Invisible Champion* (Boston: Houghton Mifflin, 2012); and Alan H. Levy, *Floyd Patterson: A Boxer and a Gentleman* (Jefferson, NC: McFarland, 2008).

57. Stratton, *Floyd Patterson*, 140–42; and Levy, *Floyd Patterson*, 140.

58. Stratton, *Floyd Patterson*, 129–30.

59. See Gerald Nachman, *Seriously Funny: The Rebel Comedians of the 1950s and 1960s* (New York: Pantheon, 2003), 480–508; and Dick Gregory and Robert Lipsyte, *Nigger: An Autobiography* (New York: E.P. Dutton, 1964).

60. See Dick Gregory and Sheila P. Moses, *Callus on My Soul: A Memoir* (New York: Kensington Books, 2000).

61. See John D'Emilio, *Lost Prophet: The Life and Times of Bayard Rustin* (Chicago: University of Chicago Press, 2004); Jervis Anderson, *Bayard Rustin: Troubles I've Seen* (New York: HarperCollins, 1997); and Daniel Levine, *Bayard Rustin and the Civil Rights Movement* (New Brunswick, NJ: Rutgers University Press, 2000).

62. See biographical treatment listed above.

63. Rustin's quote was part of a research interview for Robert Penn Warren's *Who Speaks for the Negro?*, published in 1965. It can be accessed at the *Who Speaks for the Negro?* Archives at the Robert Penn Warren Center for the Humanities at Vanderbilt University, or online at https://whospeaks.library.vanderbilt.edu/.

64. Louis E. Lomax, "Georgia Boy Goes Home," *Harper's* 230 (April 1965): 152–59. For a full biographical treatment of Lomax, see Thomas Aiello, *The Life and Times of Louis Lomax: The Art of Deliberate Disunity* (Durham, NC: Duke University Press, 2021).

65. Louis E. Lomax, *To Kill a Black Man* (Los Angeles: Holloway House, 1968), 52–63; and Peter Goldman, *The Death and Life of Malcolm X* (Urbana: University of Illinois Press, 2013), 61–62.

66. Louis E. Lomax, *The Reluctant African* (New York: Harper, 1960).

67. Marable, *Malcolm X*, 303.

68. See John Morrow, *Finding W. D. Fard: Unveiling the Identity of the Founder of the Nation of Islam* (Newcastle-upon-Tyne, UK: Cambridge Scholars, 2019); Erdmann Doane Beynon, "The Voodoo Cult among Negro Migrants in Detroit," *American Journal of Sociology* 43 (May 1938): 894–907; and Fard's FBI file, which can be found online at the FBI's Freedom of Information Act Vault, https://vault.fbi.gov/Wallace%20Fard%20Muhammed.

69. See Karl Evanzz, *The Messenger: The Rise and Fall of Elijah Muhammad* (New York: Vintage, 2001); Herbert Berg, *Elijah Muhammad and Islam* (New York: New York University Press, 2009); and Claude Andrew Clegg, *An Original Man: The Life and Times of Elijah Muhammad* (New York: Macmillan, 1998).

70. See Marable, *Malcolm X*; Jared A. Ball and Todd Steven Burroughs, eds., *A Lie of Reinvention: Correcting Manning Marable's Malcolm X* (Baltimore: Black Classic Press, 2012); Louis A. DeCaro, *Malcolm and the Cross: The Nation of Islam, Malcolm X, and Christianity* (New York: New York University Press, 1998); Michael Eric Dyson, *Making Malcolm: The Myth and Meaning of Malcolm X* (Oxford: Oxford University Press, 1995); and Alex Haley and Malcolm X, *The Autobiography of Malcolm X* (1965; New York: One World Press, 1992).

71. "'And This Happened in Los Angeles:' Malcolm X Describes Police Brutality Against Members of the Nation of Islam," Malcolm X interviewed by Dick Elman, 1962, History Matters, George Mason University, http://historymatters.gmu.edu/d/7041/.

72. New York *Amsterdam News*, March 14, 1964, 20.

73. New York *Amsterdam News*, February 3, 1990, 8; November 28, 1992, 8, 31; and *New York Times*, August 9, 1991, B1, B2; August 21, 1994, CY7.

74. For more on the Ole Miss War to contextualize Brath's poem and accompanying illustrations, see Frank Lambert, *The Battle of Ole Miss: Civil Rights v. States' Rights* (New York: Oxford University Press, 2010).

10. MISCELLANEOUS ACTIVIST ART, 1963–1970

1. Cecil Elombe Brath, "Of Land, Lunatics & the Cosmos," *Journal of Black Poetry*, 1st Pan-African Issue 1 (Winter-Spring 1970): 89–93. For more on the Black Arts Movement, see James Edward Smethurst, *The Black Arts Movement: Literary Nationalism in the 1960s and 1970s* (Chapel Hill: University of North Carolina Press, 2005); Lisa Gail Collins and Margo Natalie Crawford, eds., *New Thoughts on the Black Arts Movement* (Piscataway, NJ: Rutgers University Press, 2006); and Larry Neal, "The Black Arts Movement," *Drama Review* 12 (Summer 1968): 29–39.

11. ESSAYS, 1963–1970

1. Originally published in New York *Amsterdam News*, November 10, 1979, 18.

2. Originally published in New York *Amsterdam News*, July 12, 1980, 15.

3. Essay published in *Elombe Brath: Selected Writings and Essays*, ed. Herb Boyd (New York: Elombe Brath Foundation, 2018), 152–61.

4. Essay published in *Elombe Brath: Selected Writings and Essays*, 193–204.

Bibliography

NEWSPAPERS

Atlanta Daily World
Baltimore *Afro-American*
Barbados Herald
Chicago Defender
Los Angeles Sentinel
Negro World
New York *Amsterdam News*
New York *Citizen-Call*
New York *Herald Tribune*
New York Times
Pittsburgh Courier
Washington Post

ARCHIVAL SOURCES

Chuck Stone Papers, 1931–2007, RL.01259, David M. Rubenstein Rare Book and Manuscript Library, Duke University, Durham, North Carolina.

E.S. Reddy Papers, MS1499, Manuscripts and Archives, Yale University Library, New Haven, CT.

Extra: African Nationalist Pioneer Movement News, Sc Micro RS-999, Schomburg Center for Research in Black Culture, New York.

Fard, Wallace D. File no. 25–20607, Federal Bureau of Investigation, FOIA, available online at https://vault.fbi.gov/Wallace%20Fard%20Muhammed. Accessed March 15, 2019.

Garvey, Marcus. File no. 190–1781–6, Federal Bureau of Investigation, FOIA, available online at https://vault.fbi.gov/marcus-garvey. Accessed March 12, 2019.

Grandassa Models Collection, 1963–1968, Sc MG 822, Schomburg Center for Research in Black Culture, New York.

The James Leonard Farmer Jr. and Lula Peterson Farmer Papers, Dolph Briscoe Center for American History, University of Texas, Austin.

Lieber, Larry. *Your Future Rests . . . In Your Hands*. New York: NAACP, 1964. GLC09640.160, Gilder Lehrman Collection, Gilder Lehrman Institute of American History, New York.

Moore (Richard B.) Papers, 1902–1978, Sc MG 397, Schomburg Center for Research in Black Culture, New York Public Library, New York.

New York *Citizen-Call*, Sc Micro RS-934, Schomburg Center for Research in Black Culture, New York Public Library, New York.

"Pamphlet about the Patrice Lumumba Coalition." 2015.97.27.1, Collection of the Smithsonian National Museum of African American History and Culture, Washington, DC, available online at https://nmaahc.si.edu/object/nmaahc_2015.97.27.1. Accessed March 31, 2019.

Patrice Lumumba Coalition, African Activist Archive, Michigan State University Libraries, available online at http://africanactivist.msu.edu/browse_results.php?category=all&member=Patrice%20Lumumba%20Coalition&org=Patrice%20Lumumba%20Coalition. Accessed March 22, 2019.

Photographs [graphic]/Kwame Brathwaite, Sc Photo Portfolio (Brathwaite, K.), Schomburg Center for Research in Black Culture, New York.

The Street Speaker, Sc Micro RS-513, Schomburg Center for Research in Black Culture, New York.

Who Speaks for the Negro? Archives. Robert Penn Warren Center for the Humanities, Vanderbilt University, Nashville, Tennessee. Available online at https://whospeaks.library.vanderbilt.edu/.

OTHER PRIMARY SOURCES

"'And This Happened in Los Angeles:' Malcolm X Describes Police Brutality Against Members of the Nation of Islam." Malcolm X interviewed by Dick Elman, 1962, History Matters, George Mason University, http://historymatters.gmu.edu/d/7041/. Accessed April 12, 2019.

Baldwin, James. *The Fire Next Time.* New York: Dial Press, 1963.

Baldwin, James. *Giovanni's Room.* New York: Dial Press, 1956.

Baldwin, James. "A Letter to My Nephew." *The Progressive* 26 (December 1962): 19–20.

Belafonte, Harry, and Michael Shnayerso. *My Song: A Memoir.* New York: Knopf, 2011.

"Benjamin Banneker to Thomas Jefferson, 19 August 1791." In *The Papers of Thomas Jefferson*, Vol. 22, *6 August 1791–31 December 1791*, ed. Charles T. Cullen, 49–54. Princeton, NJ: Princeton University Press, 1986.

Brath, Cecil Elombe. "Of Land, Lunatics & the Cosmos." *Journal of Black Poetry*, 1st Pan-African Issue 1 (Winter-Spring 1970): 89–93.

Brath, Elombe. *Elombe Brath: Selected Writings and Essays*, ed. Herb Boyd. New York: Elombe Brath Foundation, 2018.

Brathwaite, Dr. Noel. Obituary, in possession of the author.

Brown, Sterling A. "Negro Character as Seen by White Authors." *Journal of Negro Education* 2 (April 1933): 179–203.

Brown, William Wells. *Clotel, or the President's Daughter.* London: Partridge and Oakey, 1853.

Campbell, T. Boyer. *Black Sadie.* Boston: Houghton Mifflin, 1928.

Campbell, T. Boyer. *White Nigger.* London: W. Collins, 1932.

Carlson, John Roy. *Under Cover: My Four Years in the Nazi Underworld of America.* New York: E.P. Dutton, 1943.

Chesnutt, Charles. *The House Behind the Cedars.* New York: Houghton, Mifflin, 1900.

Chesnutt, Charles. *The Marrow of Tradition.* New York: Houghton, Mifflin, 1901.

Commons, John R. "Labor Conditions in Meat Packing and the Recent Strike." *Quarterly Journal of Economics* 19 (November 1904): 1–32.

Falk, Irving A. *Prophecy for the Year 2000.* New York: Julian Messner, 1970.

Farmer, James. *Lay Bare the Heart: An Autobiography of the Civil Rights Movement.* Ft. Worth: Texas Christian University Press, 1985.

Fisher, Rudolph. "The City of Refuge." *Atlantic Monthly* (February 1925). Reprinted in *The City of Refuge: The Collected Stories of Rudolph Fisher*, ed. John McCluskey, 3–16. Columbia: University of Missouri Press, 1987.

Fisher, Rudolph. *The Walls of Jericho.* New York: Alfred A. Knopf, 1928.

Fitzgerald, F. Scott. *Tales of the Jazz Age.* New York: Charles Scribner's Sons, 1922.

Forman, James. *The Making of Black Revolutionaries.* 1972; Seattle: University of Washington Press, 1997.

Garvey, Marcus. "Capitalism and the State." In *Philosophy and Opinions of Marcus Garvey*, ed. Amy Jacques-Garvey. Vol. 2, 72–73. New York: Universal Publishing House, 1925.

Garvey, Marcus. *Message to the People: The Course of African Philosophy*, ed. Tony Martin. Dover, MA: Majority Press, 1986.

Garvey, Marcus. "The Negro, Communism, and His Friend." In *Philosophy and Opinions of Marcus Garvey*, ed. Amy Jacques-Garvey. Vol. 2, 69–71. New York: Universal Publishing House, 1925.

Gregory, Dick, and Robert Lipsyte. *Nigger: An Auto-biography*. New York: E.P. Dutton, 1964.

Gregory, Dick, and Sheila P. Moses. *Callus on My Soul: A Memoir*. New York: Kensington Books, 2000.

Harris, Robert, Nyota Harris, and Grandassa Harris, eds. *Carlos Cooks and Black Nationalism from Garvey to Malcolm*. Dover, MA: Majority Press, 1992.

Haley, Alex, and Malcolm X. *The Autobiography of Malcolm X*. 1965; New York: One World Press, 1992.

Herzl, Theodor. *Der Judenstaat*. Leipzig: Verlags-Buchhandlung, 1896.

Hill, Robert A., ed. *The Marcus Garvey and Universal Negro Improvement Association Papers*, 13 vols. Berkeley: University of California Press; Durham, NC: Duke University Press, 1983–2016.

Hill, Robert A., and Barbara Bair, eds. *Marcus Garvey, Life and Lessons: A Centennial Companion to the Marcus Garvey and Universal Negro Improvement Association Papers*. Berkeley: University of California Press, 1987.

Hopkins, Pauline. *Contending Forces: A Romance Illustrative of Negro Life North and South*. Boston: Colored Co-operative Publishing, 1900.

Hopkins, Pauline. *Of One Blood: Or, the Hidden Self*. In *The Colored American* (November 1902; December 1902; January 1903).

Horton, George M. *The Poetical Works of George M. Horton, the Colored Bard of North Carolina, to which Is Prefixed the Life of the Author, Written by Himself*. Hillsborough, NC: Heartt, 1845.

Horne, Lena, and Richard Schickel. *Lena*. New York: Doubleday, 1965.

Hughes, Langston. *The Best of Simple*. New York: Hill and Wang, 1961.

Hughes, Langston. *The First Book of Jazz*. New York: Franklin Watts, 1955.

Hughes, Langston. "The Negro Artist and the Racial Mountain." *Nation* 122 (June 23, 1926): 692–94.

Hughes, Langston. *Not Without Laughter*. New York: Random House, 1930.

Hughes, Langston. *The Return of Simple*. New York: Hill and Wang, 1994.

Hughes, Langston. *Simple Speaks His Mind*. New York: Simon & Schuster, 1950.

Hughes, Langston. *Simple Stakes a Claim*. New York: Rinehart, 1950.

Hughes, Langston. *The Weary Blues*. New York: Alfred A. Knopf, 1926.

"Investigations: Adam and Yvette." *Time*, February 24, 1967, 36.

Jacques-Garvey, Amy, ed. *Philosophy and Opinions of Marcus Garvey*. Vol. 1. New York: Universal Publishing House, 1923.

Jacques-Garvey, Amy, ed. *Philosophy and Opinions of Marcus Garvey*. Vol. 2. New York: Universal Publishing House, 1925.

James, C. L. R. *Beyond a Boundary*. London: Hutchinson, 1963.

Jefferson, Thomas. *The Autobiography of Thomas Jefferson, 1743–1790: Together with a Summary of the Chief Events in Jefferson's Life*, ed. Paul Leicester Ford. Philadelphia: University of Pennsylvania Press, 2005.

Johnson, James Weldon. *Autobiography of an Ex-Colored Man*. Boston: Sherman, French, 1912.

Johnson, James Weldon. *Black Manhattan*. New York: Perseus Books, 1930.

Juangu, Sabamya. "A Tribute to Elombe Brath: Pan-African Revolutionary Teacher." Unpublished reflection in possession of the author.

King, Martin Luther. *The Autobiography of Martin Luther King Jr.*, ed. Clayborne Carson. New York: Warner Books, 1998.

Kitt, Eartha. *Alone with Me: A New Autobiography*. New York: Regnery, 1976.

Kitt, Eartha. "Eartha Kitt Tells Why Her Marriage Has Broken Up." *Jet* 24 (October 10, 1963): 22–24.

Kitt, Eartha. *I'm Still Here: Confessions of a Sex Kitten*. New York: Barricade Books, 1993.

Kitt, Eartha. "My Baby Travels with Me." *Ebony* 18 (January 1963): 93–98.

Kitt, Eartha. *Thursday's Child*. New York: Four Square Books, 1956.

Larsen, Nella. *Passing*. New York: Alfred A. Knopf, 1929.

Lewis, John, and Michael D'Orso. *Walking with the Wind: A Memoir of the Movement*. New York: Simon & Schuster, 1998.

Lewis, Theophilus. "The Theater: The Souls of Black Folks." *The Messenger* (July 1926): 214–15.

Lincoln, Abraham. "Address on Colonization to a Deputation of Colored Men," August 14, 1862. In *Abraham Lincoln: Complete Works*, ed. John G. Nicolay and John Hay. Vol. 2, 222–23. New York: Century, 1920.

"Little Ol' Bosko and the Pirates." Metro Goldwyn Mayer, 1937. Available at https://www.youtube.com/watch?v=0Vyvk_TshcI. Accessed March 22, 2020.

Lomax, Louis E. "Georgia Boy Goes Home." *Harper's* 230 (April 1965): 152–59.

Lomax, Louis E. *To Kill a Black Man*. Los Angeles: Holloway House, 1968.

Lomax, Louis E. *The Reluctant African*. New York: Harper & Bros., 1960.

"Martin Luther King Jr. to Sammy Davis Jr., 20 December 1960." In *The Papers of Martin Luther King Jr.*, Vol. V, *Threshold of a New Decade, January 1959-December 1960*, eds. Clayborne Carson, Tenisha Armstrong, Susan Carson, Adrienne Clay, and Kieran Taylor, 582–83. Berkeley: University of California Press, 2005.

Moore, Richard B. *The Name "Negro": Its Origin and Evil Use*. 1960; Baltimore: Black Classic Press, 1992.

NAACP. *The Mobbing of John R. Shillady, Secretary for the National Association for the Advancement of Colored People, Austin, Texas, Aug. 22, 1919*. New York: NAACP, October 1919.

Neal, Larry. "The Black Arts Movement." *Drama Review* 12 (Summer 1968): 29–39.

"Never Again Where He Was." *Time*, January 3, 1964, 19–30.

"New York Beat." *Jet*, March 5, 1964, 63.

Nugent, Richard Bruce. *Gentleman Jigger*. New York: Da Capo Press, 2008.

"The Old Mill Pond." Metro Goldwyn Mayer, 1936, Available at https://www.youtube.com/watch?v=CQbbADi60og. Accessed March 22, 2020.

Oliveira, Victor. "Trends in the Hired Farm Work Force, 1945–1987." Washington: USDA/ERS, 1989.

Randolph, A. Philip. "The Only Way to Redeem Africa." In *For Jobs and Freedom: Selected Speeches and Writings of A. Philip Randolph*, ed. Andrew E. Kersten and David Lucander, 323–32. Amherst: University of Massachusetts Press, 2014.

Rangel, Charles B. "In Honor of Elombe Brath." *Congressional Record*, May 13, 2013, E644–45.

"Religion: Jewish Negro." *Time*, February 1, 1960, 40.

Schuyler, George S. *Black No More*. New York: Macaulay, 1931.

Schuyler, George S. "The Negro-Art Hokum." *Nation* 122 (June 16, 1926): 662–63.

Shillady, John R. *Planning Public Expenditures to Compensate for Decreased Private Employment During Business Depressions*. New York: Mayor's Committee on Unemployment, November 1916.

Thurman, Wallace. *The Blacker the Berry*. New York: Macaulay, 1929.

Thurman, Wallace. *Infants of the Spring*. New York: Macaulay, 1932.

West, Dorothy. *The Living Is Easy*. 1948; New York: Feminist Press at City University of New York, 2013.

Wilkins, Roy. *Standing Fast: The Autobiography of Roy Wilkins*, ed. Tom Mathews. New York: Da Capo Press, 1994.

Williams, R. Waldo. "The Awakening Call." *The Black Challenge*, Freedom Archives. https://www.freedomarchives.org/Documents/Finder/DOC32_scans/32.Various.BLM.The.Black.Challenge.pdf. Accessed March 10, 2019.

Wilson, Harriet E. *Our Nig: Or, Sketches from the Life of a Free Black, in a Two-Story White House, North*. Boston: George C. Rand and Avery, 1859.

Wright, Richard. "Blueprint for Negro Writing." *New Challenge* 2 (Fall 1937). Reprinted in *The Richard*

Wright Reader, eds. Ellen Wright and Michel Fabre, 36–49. New York: Harper and Row, 1978.

SECONDARY SOURCES

Abdelwahid, Mustafa. *Dusé Mohamed Ali (1866–1945): The Autobiography of a Pioneer Pan African and Afro-Asian Activist.* Trenton, NJ: Red Sea Press, 2011.

Adeleke, Tunde. *The Case Against Afrocentrism.* Jackson: University Press of Mississippi, 2009.

Aiello, Thomas. *The Life and Times of Louis Lomax: The Art of Deliberate Disunity.* Durham, NC: Duke University Press, 2021.

Aiello, Thomas. *The Battle for the Souls of Black Folk: W. E. B. Du Bois, Booker T. Washington, and the Debate That Shaped the Course of Civil Rights.* Westport, CT: Praeger, 2016.

Ampiah, Kweku. *The Political and Moral Imperatives of the Bandung Conference of 1955: The Reactions of the US, UK and Japan.* Folkestone, UK: Global Oriental, 2007.

Anderson, Jervis. *Bayard Rustin: Troubles I've Seen.* New York: HarperCollins, 1997.

Anderson, Jervis. *A. Philip Randolph: A Biographical Portrait.* Berkeley: University of California Press, 1986.

Anderson, Jervis. *This Was Harlem: A Cultural Portrait, 1900–1950.* New York: Farrar, Straus and Giroux, 1991.

Andrews, William. *The Literary Career of Charles W. Chesnutt.* Baton Rouge: Louisiana State University Press, 1980.

Apap, Chris. "'Let no man of us budge one step': David Walker and the Rhetoric African American Emplacement." *Early American Literature* 46 (June 2011): 319–50.

Arnesen, Eric. *Brotherhoods of Color: Black Railroad Workers and the Struggle for Equality.* Cambridge, MA: Harvard University Press, 2001.

Arsenault, Raymond. *Freedom Riders 1961 and the Struggle for Racial Justice.* New York: Oxford University Press, 2006.

Asukile, Thabiti. "Joel Augustus Rogers: Black International Journalism, Archival Research, and Black Print Culture." *Journal of African American History* 95 (Summer-Fall 2010): 322–47.

Asukile, Thabiti. "Joel Augustus Rogers' Race Vindication: A Chicago Pullman Porter and The Making of *From Superman to Man* (1917)." *Western Journal of Black Studies* 35 (Fall 2011): 281–93.

Ball, Jared A., and Todd Steven Burroughs, eds. *A Lie of Reinvention: Correcting Manning Marable's Malcolm X.* Baltimore: Black Classic Press, 2012.

Barnett, Michael N. *Confronting the Costs of War: Military Power, State, and Society in Egypt and Israel.* Princeton, NJ: Princeton University Press, 1992.

Bates, Beth Tompkins. *Pullman Porters and the Rise of Protest Politics in Black America, 1925–1945.* Chapel Hill: University of North Carolina Press, 2001.

Beatty, Paul, ed. *Hokum: An Anthology of African-American Humor.* New York: Bloomsbury, 2006.

Ben-Dror, Elad. *Ralph Bunche and the Arab-Israeli Conflict: Mediation and the UN, 1947–1949.* New York: Routledge, 2016.

Berg, Herbert. *Elijah Muhammad and Islam.* New York: New York University Press, 2009.

Bernstein, Irving. *Promises Kept: John F. Kennedy's New Frontier.* New York: Oxford University Press, 1991.

Beynon, Erdmann Doane. "The Voodoo Cult among Negro Migrants in Detroit." *American Journal of Sociology* 43 (May 1938): 894–907.

Birkbeck, Matt. *Deconstructing Sammy: Music, Money, and Madness.* New York: Amistad, 2008.

Bodnar, John. *The Transplanted: A History of Immigrants in Urban America.* Bloomington: Indiana University Press, 1985.

Bordowitz, Hank. "Miriam Makeba." In *The Outlaw Bible of American Essays*, ed. Alan Kaufman, 313–34. New York: Thunder's Mouth Press, 2006.

Boustan, Leah Platt. *Competition in the Promised Land: Black Migrants in Northern Cities and Labor Markets.* Princeton, NJ: Princeton University Press, 2016.

Boyd, Herb. *Baldwin's Harlem: A Biography of James Baldwin*. New York: Simon & Schuster, 2008.

Brandt, Allan M. "Racism and Research: The Case of the Tuskegee Syphilis Study." *Hastings Center Report* 8 (December 1978): 21–29.

Brown, Lois. *Pauline Elizabeth Hopkins: Black Daughter of the Revolution*. Chapel Hill: University of North Carolina Press, 2008.

Burns, Sarah. *The Central Park Five: A Chronicle of a City Wilding*. New York: Knopf, 2011.

Campbell, James. *Talking at the Gate: A Life of James Baldwin*. Berkeley: University of California Press, 2002.

Carey, Julian C. "Jesse B. Semple Revisited and Revised." *Phylon* 32 (2nd Qtr. 1971): 158–63.

Carpio, Glenda. *Laughing Fit to Kill: Black Humor in the Fictions of Slavery*. London: Oxford University Press, 2008.

Carroll, Jimbe. "Activist Elombe Brath Goes Home to the Ancestors." *New York Beacon* 21 (June 5, 2014–June 11, 2014): 5.

Carson, Clayborne. *In Struggle: SNCC and the Black Awakening of the 1960s*. Cambridge, MA: Harvard University Press, 1995.

Carson, Clayborne. "SNCC and the Albany Movement." *Journal of Southwest Georgia History* 2 (1984): 15–25.

Catsam, Derek Charles. *Freedom's Main Line: The Journey of Reconciliation and the Freedom Rides*. Lexington: University Press of Kentucky, 2009.

Clegg, Claude Andrew. *An Original Man: The Life and Times of Elijah Muhammad*. New York: Macmillan, 1998.

Cobb, Jelani. "The Path Cleared by Amiri Baraka." *New Yorker*, January 15, 2014, https://www.newyorker.com/news/news-desk/the-path-cleared-by-amiri-baraka. Accessed July 6, 2020.

Collins, Lisa Gail, and Margo Natalie Crawford, eds. *New Thoughts on the Black Arts Movement*. Piscataway, NJ: Rutgers University Press, 2006.

Corbman, Rachel. "'Next Time, The Fire In Giovanni's Room': The Critical Reception of James Baldwin's Second Novel in the Black Press."

Zeteo (Spring 2012), available at http://zeteo journal.com/2012/04/11/james-baldwin-and-the-black-press/. Accessed April 7, 2019.

Cronon, Edmund David. *Black Moses: The Story of Marcus Garvey and the Universal Negro Improvement Association*. Madison: University of Wisconsin Press, 1955.

Cruse, Harold. *The Crisis of the Negro Intellectual: A Historical Analysis of the Failure of Black Leadership*. 1967; New York: New York Review of Books Classical, 2005.

Davis, Arthur P. "Jesse B. Semple: Negro American." *Phylon* 15 (1st Qtr. 1954): 21–28.

Davis, Michael D., and Hunter R. Clark. *Thurgood Marshall: Warrior at the Bar, Rebel on the Bench*. Secaucus, NJ: Carol Publishing, 1992.

DeCaro, Louis A. *Malcolm and the Cross: The Nation of Islam, Malcolm X, and Christianity*. New York: New York University Press, 1998.

D'Emilio, John. *Lost Prophet: The Life and Times of Bayard Rustin*. Chicago: University of Chicago Press, 2004.

Dickerson, Dennis C. *Militant Mediator: Whitney M. Young Jr*. Lexington: University Press of Kentucky, 2015.

Dickson-Carr, Darryl. *Spoofing the Modern: Satire in the Harlem Renaissance*. Columbia: University of South Carolina Press, 2014.

Duffield, Ian. "Duse Mohamed Ali and the Development of Pan-Africanism 1866–1945." PhD diss., Edinburgh University, 1971.

Dworkin, Ira. *Congo Love Song: African American Culture and the Crisis of the Colonial State*. Chapel Hill: University of North Carolina Press, 2017.

Dyson, Michael Eric. *Making Malcolm: The Myth and Meaning of Malcolm X*. Oxford: Oxford University Press, 1995.

Eig, Jonathan. *Opening Day: The Story of Jackie Robinson's First Season*. New York: Simon & Schuster, 2007.

Ellis, Sylvia. *Freedom's Pragmatist: Lyndon Johnson and Civil Rights*. Gainesville: University Press of Florida, 2013.

Esedebe, Peter Olisanwuche. *Pan-Africanism: The Idea and Movement, 1776–1963*. Washington, DC: Howard University Press, 1982.

Eskew, Glenn T. *But for Birmingham: The Local and National Movements in the Civil Rights Struggle*. Chapel Hill: University of North Carolina Press, 1997.

Evanzz, Karl. *The Messenger: The Rise and Fall of Elijah Muhammad*. New York: Vintage, 2001.

Ewing, Adam. *The Age of Garvey: How a Jamaican Activist Created a Mass Movement and Changed Global Black Politics*. Princeton, NJ: Princeton University Press, 2014.

Falkner, David. *Great Time Coming: The Life of Jackie Robinson, from Baseball to Birmingham*. New York: Simon & Schuster, 1995.

Farrison, W. Edward. "William Wells Brown, Social Reformer." *Journal of Negro Education* 18 (Winter 1949): 29–39.

Feldstein, Ruth. *How It Feels to Be Free: Black Women Entertainers and the Civil Rights Movement*. New York: Oxford University Press, 2013.

Ferguson, Jeffrey. *The Sage of Sugar Hill: George S. Schuyler and the Harlem Renaissance*. New Haven, CT: Yale University Press, 2005.

Field, Corinne T. "Frances E. W. Harper and the Politics of Intellectual Maturity." In *Toward an Intellectual History of Black Women*, eds. Mia Bay, Farah J. Griffin, Martha S. Jones, and Barbara D. Savage, 110–26. Chapel Hill: University of North Carolina Press, 2015.

Fitzgerald, Michael W. "'We Have Found a Moses': Theodore Bilbo, Black Nationalism, and the Greater Liberia Bill of 1939." *Journal of Southern History* 63 (May 1997): 293–320.

Fleming, Tyler. "A Marriage of Inconvenience: Miriam Makeba's Relationship with Stokely Carmichael and Her Music Career in the United States." *Safundi: The Journal of South African and American Studies* 17 (May 2016): 312–38.

Fogelson, Genia. *Harry Belafonte*. Los Angeles: Melrose Square, 1991.

Frankel, Philip. *An Ordinary Atrocity: Sharpeville and Its Massacre*. New Haven: Yale University Press, 2001.

Gaither, Renoir W. "The Moment of Revision: A Reappraisal of Wallace Thurman's Aesthetics in *The Blacker the Berry* and *Infants of the Spring*." *CLA Journal* 37 (September 1993): 81–93.

Gardner, Eric. "'This Attempt of Their Sister': Harriet Wilson's *Our Nig* from Printer to Readers." *New England Quarterly* 66 (June 1993): 226–46.

Garrow, David, ed. *Birmingham, Alabama, 1956–1963: The Black Struggle for Civil Rights*. Brooklyn: Carlson Publishing, 1989.

Gates, Henry Louis. "Belafonte's Balancing Act." *New Yorker* 72 (August 26, 1996): 132–38.

Gavin, James. *Stormy Weather: The Life of Lena Horne*. New York: Atria, 2009.

Gerard, Emmanuel, and Bruce Kuklick. *Death in the Congo: Murdering Patrice Lumumba*. Cambridge, MA: Harvard University Press, 2015.

Gibson, Larry S. *Young Thurgood: The Making of a Supreme Court Justice*. New York: Prometheus Books, 2012.

Gill, Johnathan. *Harlem: The Four-Hundred Year History from Dutch Village to Capital of Black America*. New York: Grove Press, 2011.

Goldman, Peter. *The Death and Life of Malcolm X*. Urbana: University of Illinois Press, 2013.

Goldstein, Brian D. *The Roots of Urban Renaissance: Gentrification and the Struggle over Harlem*. Cambridge, MA: Harvard University Press, 2017.

Green, Jonathon. *Cassell's Dictionary of Slang*. London: Weidenfeld & Nicolson, 2005.

Gutiérrez, David G. "Migration, Emergent Ethnicity, and the 'Third Space': The Shifting Politics of Nationalism in Greater Mexico." *Journal of American History* 86 (September 1999): 481–517.

Gwin, Minrose. *Remembering Medgar Evers: Writing the Long Civil Rights Movement*. Athens: University of Georgia Press, 2013.

Haggins, Bambi. *Laughing Mad: The Black Comic Persona in Post-Soul America*. New Brunswick, NJ: Rutgers University Press, 2007.

Hamburger, G. Marc. "Jewish Rush in the Bible Belt." *Vanderbilt Magazine*, August 5, 2009. https://news.vanderbilt.edu/vanderbiltmagazine/jewish-rush-in-the-bible-belt/. Accessed April 5, 2019.

Hamilton, Charles V. *Adam Clayton Powell Jr.: The Political Biography of an American Dilemma.* New York: Atheneum, 1991.

Harlan, Louis R. *Booker T. Washington: Wizard of Tuskegee, 1901–1915.* New York: Oxford University Press, 1986.

Harper, Donna Akiba Sullivan. *Not So Simple: The "Simple" Stories by Langston Hughes.* Columbia: University of Missouri Press, 1995.

Harris, William H. *Keeping the Faith: A. Philip Randolph, Milton P. Webster, and the Brotherhood of Sleeping Car Porters, 1925–37.* Urbana: University of Illinois Press, 1977.

Haskins, James, and Kathleen Benson. *Lena: A Personal and Professional Biography of Lena Horne.* New York: Stein and Day, 1984.

Haygood, Will. *In Black and White: The Life of Sammy Davis Jr.* New York: Knopf, 2003.

Haygood, Will. *King of the Cats: The Life and Times of Adam Clayton Powell Jr.* Boston: Houghton Mifflin, 1993.

Henry, Charles P. *Ralph Bunche: Model Negro or American Other?* New York: New York University Press, 1999.

Hertzberg, Arthur. *The Zionist Idea: A Historical Analysis and Reader.* 1959; Lincoln: University of Nebraska Press, 1997.

Hill, Herbert. "The Racial Practices of Organized Labor: The Contemporary Record." In *The Negro and the American Labor Movement*, ed. Julius Jacobson, 286–357. New York: Anchor, 1968.

Hills, Patricia. *Painting Harlem Modern: The Art of Jacob Lawrence.* Berkeley: University of California Press, 2009.

Horne, Gerald. "Race from Power: US Foreign Policy and the General Crisis of 'White Supremacy.'" In *The Ambiguous Legacy: US Foreign Relations in the "American Century,"* ed. Michael J. Hogan, 302–36. New York: Cambridge University Press, 1999.

Howe, Glenford D. "De(Re) Constructing Identities: World War I and the Growth of Barbadian/West Indian Nationalism." In *The Empowering Impulse: The Nationalist Tradition of Barbados*, eds. Don D. Marshall and Glenford D. Howe, 110–27. Kingston, Jamaica: Canoe Press, University of the West Indies, 2001.

Hoyos, F. A. *Barbados: A History from the Amerindians to Independence.* London: Macmillan, 1978.

Hoyos, F. A. *Builders of Barbados.* London: Macmillan, 1972.

Huggins, Nathan Irvin. *Harlem Renaissance.* New York: Columbia University Press, 1974.

Hunte, Keith. "The Struggle for Political Democracy: Charles Duncan O'Neal and the Democratic League." In *Emancipation XI: Aspects of the Post-Slavery Experience of Barbados*, ed. W. K. Marshall, 20–38. Bridgetown, Barbados: National Cultural Foundation and Department of History, University of the West Indies, 1988.

"Introduction." *Journal for the Study of Radicalism* 1 (Spring 2007): vii–viii.

Jackson, Blyden. "A Word about Simple." *CLA Journal* 11 (June 1968): 310–18.

Jackson, Tim. *Pioneering Cartoonists of Color.* Jackson: University Press of Mississippi, 2016.

James, Winston. *Holding Aloft the Banner of Ethiopia: Caribbean Radicalism in Early Twentieth-Century America.* New York: Verso, 1999.

Jones, Doug. *Bending Toward Justice: The Birmingham Church Bombing That Changed the Course of Civil Rights.* New York: All Points Books, 2019.

Jones, James. *Bad Blood: The Tuskegee Syphilis Experiment.* New York: Free Press, 1981.

Jones, William P. *The March on Washington: Jobs, Freedom, and the Forgotten History of Civil Rights.* New York: W.W. Norton, 2013.

Joseph, Peniel E. "Malcolm X's Harlem and Early Black Power Activism." In *Neighborhood Rebels: Black Power at the Local Level*, ed. Peniel E. Joseph, 21–43. New York: Palgrave Macmillan, 2010.

Joseph, Peniel E. *The Sword and the Shield: The Revolutionary Lives of Malcolm X and Martin Luther King Jr.* New York: Basic Books, 2020.

Kirschke, Amy Helene. *Aaron Douglas: Art, Race, and the Harlem Renaissance.* Jackson: University Press of Mississippi, 1995.

Klotman, Phyllis R. "Jesse B. Semple and the Narrative Art of Langston Hughes." *Journal of Narrative Technique* 3 (January 1973): 66–75.

Kornweibel, Theodore. *No Crystal Stair: Black Life and ⊠The Messenger," 1917–1928.* Westport, CT: Greenwood Press, 1975.

Kornweibel, Theodore. *Seeing Red: Federal Campaigns Against Black Militancy, 1919–1925.* Bloomington: Indiana University Press, 1999.

Kotz, Nick. *Judgment Days: Lyndon Baines Johnson, Martin Luther King Jr., and the Laws That Changed America.* Boston: Houghton Mifflin, 2005.

Kuenz, Jane. "American Racial Discourse, 1900–1930: Schuyler's *Black No More.*" *NOVEL: A Forum on Fiction* 30 (Winter 1997): 170–92.

Kuykendall, Ronald A. "The African Blood Brotherhood, Independent Marxist During the Harlem Renaissance." *Western Journal of Black Studies* 26, no. 1 (2002): 16–21.

Lambert, Frank. *The Battle of Ole Miss: Civil Rights v. States' Rights.* New York: Oxford University Press, 2010.

Leeming, David. *James Baldwin: A Biography.* New York: Simon & Schuster, 2015.

Levine, Daniel. *Bayard Rustin and the Civil Rights Movement.* New Brunswick, NJ: Rutgers University Press, 2000.

Levine, Robert Steven. *Martin Delany, Frederick Douglass, and the Politics of Representative Identity.* Chapel Hill: University of North Carolina Press, 1997.

Levy, Alan H. *Floyd Patterson: A Boxer and a Gentleman.* Jefferson, NC: McFarland, 2008.

Lewis, David Levering. *When Harlem Was in Vogue.* New York: Oxford University Press, 1989.

Locke, Alain. *The New Negro: An Interpretation.* 1925; New York: Simon & Schuster, 1992.

Lodge, Tom. *Sharpeville: An Apartheid Massacre and Its Consequences.* New York: Oxford University Press, 2011.

Lowery, Joseph E. *Singing the Lord's Song in a Strange Land.* Nashville: Abingdon Press, 2011.

Mahoney, Richard. *JFK: Ordeal in Africa.* New York: Oxford University Press, 1983.

Makalani, Minkah. *For the Liberation of Black People Everywhere: The African Blood Brotherhood, Black Radicalism, and Pan-African Liberation in the New Negro Movement, 1917–1936.* PhD diss., University of Illinois at Urbana-Champaign, 2004.

Maloba, W. O. *The Anatomy of Neo-Colonialism in Kenya: British Imperialism and Kenyatta, 1963–1978.* London: Palgrave Macmillan, 2017.

Maloba, W. O. *Kenyatta and Britain: An Account of Political Transformation, 1929–1963.* London: Palgrave Macmillan, 2018.

Marable, Manning. *Malcolm X: A Life of Reinvention.* New York: Viking, 2011.

Marshall, Don D., and Glenford D. Howe, eds. *The Empowering Impulse: The Nationalist Tradition of Barbados.* Kingston, Jamaica: Canoe Press, University of the West Indies, 2001.

Martin, Tony. *Race First: The Ideological and Organizational Struggle of Marcus Garvey and the Universal Negro Improvement Association.* Westport, CT: Greenwood Press, 1976.

Maus, Derek C., and James J. Donahue. *Post-Soul Satire: Black Identity after Civil Rights.* Jackson: University Press of Mississippi, 2014.

McGruder, Kevin. *Race and Real Estate: Conflict and Cooperation in Harlem, 1890–1920.* New York: Columbia University Press, 2015.

McKown, Robin. *Lumumba: A Biography.* Garden City, NY: Doubleday, 1969.

McNeil, Genna Rae. *Groundwork: Charles Hamilton Houston and the Struggle for Civil Rights.* Philadelphia: University of Pennsylvania Press, 1983.

McWhorter, Diane. *Carry Me Home: Birmingham, Alabama, the Climactic Battle of the Civil Rights Revolution.* New York: Simon & Schuster, 2001.

Meier, August, and Elliott Rudwick. *CORE: A Study in the Civil Rights Movement, 1942–1968.* New York: Oxford University Press, 1973.

Mitchell, Verner, and Cynthia Davis. *Literary Sisters: Dorothy West and Her Circle, A Biography of the Harlem Renaissance.* New Brunswick, NJ: Rutgers University Press, 2011.

Morgan, Iwan, and Philip Davis. *From Sit-Ins to SNCC: The Student Civil Rights Movement in the 1960s.* Gainesville: University Press of Florida, 2013.

Morgan, Stacy. "'The Strange and Wonderful Workings of Science': Race Science and Essentialism in George Schuyler's *Black No More.*" *CLA Journal* 42 (March 1999): 331–52.

Morrow, John. *Finding W. D. Fard: Unveiling the Identity of the Founder of the Nation of Islam.* Newcastle-upon-Tyne, UK: Cambridge Scholars, 2019.

Moses, Wilson Jeremiah, ed. *Classical Black Nationalism: From the American Revolution to Marcus Garvey.* New York: New York University Press, 1996.

Moses, Wilson Jeremiah. *The Golden Age of Black Nationalism, 1850–1925.* 1978; New York: Oxford University Press, 1988.

Murphree, Vanessa. *The Selling of Civil Rights: The Student Nonviolent Coordinating Committee and the Use of Public Relations.* New York: Routledge, 2006.

Nachman, Gerald. *Seriously Funny: The Rebel Comedians of the 1950s and 1960s.* New York: Pantheon, 2003.

Namikas, Lise. *Battleground Africa: Cold War in the Congo, 1960–1965.* Washington, DC: Woodrow Wilson Center Press, 2013.

Neff, Donald. *Warriors at Suez: Eisenhower takes America into the Middle East.* New York: Simon & Schuster, 1981.

Osofsky, Gilbert. *Harlem, The Making of a Ghetto: Negro New York, 1890–1930.* New York: Harper & Row, 1966.

Parker, Jason C. "Small Victory, Missed Chance: The Eisenhower Administration, the Bandung Conference, and the Turning of the Cold War." In *The Eisenhower Administration, the Third World, and the Globalization of the Cold War,* eds. Kathryn C. Statler and Andrew L. Johns, 153–74. Lanham, MD: Rowman & Littlefield, 2006.

Parker, Kunal M. *Making Foreigners: Immigration and Citizenship Law in America, 1600–2000.* New York: Cambridge University Press, 2015.

Perry, Jeffrey B. *Hubert Harrison: The Voice of Harlem Radicalism, 1883–1918.* New York: Columbia University Press, 2009.

Perry, Jeffrey B. *Hubert Harrison: The Struggle for Equality, 1918–1927.* New York: Columbia University Press, 2020.

Pfeffer, Paula F. *A. Philip Randolph, Pioneer of the Civil Rights Movement.* Baton Rouge: Louisiana State University Press, 1990.

"Policing Masculinities and Femininities." In *The SAGE Encyclopedia of LGBTQ Studies,* ed. Abbie E. Goldberg, 859–63. Thousand Oaks, CA: SAGE Publications, 2016.

Portes, Alejandro, and Robert L. Bach. *Latin Journey: Cuban and Mexican Immigrants in the United States.* Berkeley: University of California Press, 1985.

Presley, James. "The Birth of Jesse B. Semple." *Southwest Review* 58 (Summer 1973): 219–25.

Putnam, Aric. "Ethiopia Is Now: J. A. Rogers and the Rhetoric of Black Anticolonialism During the Great Depression." *Rhetoric and Public Affairs* 10 (Fall 2007): 419–44.

Rampersad, Arnold. *Jackie Robinson: A Biography.* New York: Alfred A. Knopf, 1997.

Rampersad, Arnold. *The Life of Langston Hughes.* Vol. 1, *I, Too, Sing America.* New York: Oxford University Press, 1986.

Rampersad, Arnold. *The Life of Langston Hughes.* Vol. 2, *I Dream a World.* New York: Oxford University Press, 1988.

Reimers, David. *Still the Golden Door: The Third World Comes to America.* New York: Columbia University Press, 1985.

Reverby, Susan M. *Examining Tuskegee: The Infamous Syphilis Study and Its Legacy.* Chapel Hill: University of North Carolina Press, 2009.

Riley, Sam G. "Langston Hughes's Jesse B. Semple Columns as Literary Journalism." *American Periodicals* 10 (2000): 63–78.

Risen, Clay. *The Bill of the Century: The Epic Battle for the Civil Rights Act*. New York: Bloomsbury, 2014.

Rivera, Pedro R. *Carlos Cooks and Garveyism: Bridging Two Eras of Black Nationalism*. PhD diss., Howard University, 2012.

Roberts, Brian Russell. *Artistic Ambassadors: Literary and International Representation of the New Negro Era*. Charlottesville: University of Virginia Press, 2013.

Rodgers, Lawrence R. "Dorothy West's the Living is Easy and the Ideal of Southern Folk Community." *African American Review* 26 (Spring 1992): 161–172.

Rushing, Lawrence. "The Racial Identity of Adam Clayton Powell Jr.: A Case Study in Racial Ambivalence and Redefinition." *Afro-Americans in New York Life and History* 34 (January 2010): 7–33.

Russell, Heather. "Revising Critical Judgments of *The Autobiography of an Ex-Colored Man*." *African American Review* 40 (Summer 2006): 257–70.

Ryan, Yvonne. *Roy Wilkins: The Quiet Revolutionary and the NAACP*. Lexington: University Press of Kentucky, 2014.

Sanders, Pamela Peden. "The Feminism of Dorothy West's *The Living Is Easy*: A Critique of the Limitations of the Female Sphere through Performative Gender Roles." *African American Review* 36 (Autumn 2002): 435–46.

Sarotte, Georges-Michel. *Like a Brother, Like a Lover: Male Homosexuality in the American Novel and Theatre from Herman Melville to James Baldwin*. New York: Doubleday, 1978.

Savage, Donald C. "Kenyatta and the Development of African Nationalism in Kenya." *International Journal* 25 (Summer 1970): 518–37.

Schmidt, Christopher W. *The Sit-Ins: Protest and Legal Change in the Civil Rights Era*. Chicago: University of Chicago Press, 2018.

Shabazz, Saaed. "What Is the Future of Pan African, Black Nationalist Movements?" *BlackPress USA*, July 8, 2014. https://www.blackpressusa.com/what-is-the-future-of-pan-african-black-nationalist-movements/. Accessed March 15, 2019.

Sharlet, Jeff. "Voice and Hammer: Harry Belafonte's Unfinished Fight." *Virginia Quarterly Review* (Fall 2013): 24–41.

Sherman, Joan R. "James Monroe Whitfield, Poet and Emigrationist: A Voice of Protest and Despair." *Journal of Negro History* 57 (April 1972): 169–76.

Sikora, Frank. *Until Justice Rolls Down: The Birmingham Church Bombing Case*. Tuscaloosa: University of Alabama Press, 1991.

Sitkoff, Harvard. *King: Pilgrimage to the Mountaintop*. New York: Hill and Wang, 2008.

Sizemore-Barber, April. "The Voice of (Which?) Africa: Miriam Makeba in America." *Safundi: The Journal of South African and American Studies* 13 (July-October 2012): 251–76.

Smethurst, James Edward. *The Black Arts Movement: Literary Nationalism in the 1960s and 1970s*. Chapel Hill: University of North Carolina Press, 2005.

Smith, Judith. *Becoming Belafonte: Black Artist, Public Radical*. Austin: University of Texas Press, 2014.

Solomon, Mark I. *The Cry Was Unity: Communists and African Americans, 1917–36*. Jackson: University Press of Mississippi, 1998.

Stratton, W. K. *Floyd Patterson: The Fighting Life of Boxing's Invisible Champion*. Boston: Houghton Mifflin, 2012.

Sullivan, Timothy. *Unequal Verdicts: The Central Park Jogger Trials*. New York: Simon & Schuster, 1992.

Taylor, Theman Ray. *Cyril Briggs and the African Blood Brotherhood: Another Radical View of Race and Class in the 1920s*. PhD diss., University of California at Santa Barbara, 1981.

Tucker, Terrence T. *Furiously Funny: Comic Rage from Ralph Ellison to Chris Rock*. Gainesville: University Press of Florida, 2017.

Turner, Joyce Moore. *Caribbean Crusaders and the Harlem Renaissance.* Urbana: University of Illinois Press, 2005.

Turner, Joyce Moore. "Richard B. Moore and His Works." In *Richard B. Moore, Caribbean Militant in Harlem: Collected Writings, 1920–1972,* eds. W. Burghardt Turner and Joyce Moore Turner, 3–39. Bloomington: Indiana University Press, 1988.

Turner, Joyce Moore, and W. Burghart Turner. *Richard B. Moore, Caribbean Militant in Harlem: Collected Writings, 1920–1972.* Bloomington: Indiana University Press, 1988.

Tushnet, Mark V. *Making Civil Rights Law: Thurgood Marshall and the Supreme Court, 1936–1961.* New York: Oxford University Press, 1994.

Tushnet, Mark V. *Making Constitutional Law: Thurgood Marshall and the Supreme Court, 1961–1991.* New York: Oxford University Press, 1997.

Tygiel, Jules. *Baseball's Great Experiment: Jackie Robinson and His Legacy.* New York: Oxford University Press, 1983.

Urquhart, Brian. *Ralph Bunche: An American Life.* New York: W.W. Norton, 1993.

Van Deburg, William L., ed. *Modern Black Nationalism from Marcus Garvey to Louis Farrakhan.* New York: New York University Press, 1997.

Van Deburg, William L. *New Day in Babylon: The Black Power Movement and American Culture, 1965–1975.* Chicago: University of Chicago Press, 1992.

Vollers, Maryanne. *Ghosts of Mississippi: The Murder of Medgar Evers, The Trials of Byron de la Beckwith, and the Haunting of the New South.* New York: Little, Brown, 1995.

Voth, Ben. *James Farmer Jr.: The Great Debater.* Lanham, MD: Lexington Books, 2017.

Wallace, Michele. *Black Macho and the Myth of the Superwoman.* New York: Dial Press, 1979.

Watkins, Charles A. "Simple: The Alter Ego of Langston Hughes." *The Black Scholar* 2 (June 1971): 18–26.

Watkins-Owens, Irma. *Blood Relations: Caribbean Immigrants and the Harlem Community, 1900–1930.* Bloomington: Indiana University Press, 1996.

Weems, Robert E. *Desegregating the Dollar: African American Consumerism in the Twentieth Century.* New York: New York University Press, 1998.

Weiss, Herbert. "The Congo's Independence Struggle Viewed Fifty Years Later." *African Studies Review* 55 (April 2012): 109–15.

Weiss, Nancy J. *Whitney M. Young Jr. and the Struggle for Civil Rights.* Princeton, NJ: Princeton University Press, 1990.

"Who Was Elombe Brath?" Elombe Brath Foundation. https://www.elombebrathfoundation.org/legacy. Accessed March 2, 2019.

Wilkinson, Isabel. *The Warmth of Other Suns: The Epic Story of America's Great Migration.* New York: Vintage Books, 2011.

Williams, Dana A., ed. *African American Humor, Irony, and Satire.* Newcastle upon Tyne, UK: Cambridge Scholars, 2007.

Williams, John L. *America's Mistress: The Life and Times of Eartha Kitt.* New York: Quercus, 2013.

Williams, Juan. *Thurgood Marshall: American Revolutionary.* New York: New York Times, 1998.

Williams, Melvin G. "Langston Hughes's Jesse B. Semple: A Black Walter Mitty." *Negro American Literature Forum* 10 (Summer 1976): 66–69.

Williams, Oscar R. *George S. Schuyler: Portrait of a Black Conservative.* Knoxville: University of Tennessee Press, 2007.

Wirth, Thomas H. *Gay Rebel of the Harlem Renaissance: Selections from the Work of Richard Bruce Nugent.* Durham, NC: Duke University Press, 2002.

Worrell, Rodney. "Pan-Africanism in Barbados." In *The Empowering Impulse: The Nationalist Tradition of Barbados,* eds. Don D. Marshall and Glenford D. Howe, 200–204. Kingston, Jamaica: Canoe Press, University of the West Indies, 2001.

Wright, David. "The Use of Race and Racial Perceptions among Asians and Blacks: The Case of the Japanese and African Americans." *Hitotsubashi Journal of Social Studies* 30 (1998): 135–52.

Youman, Mary Mabel. "Nella Larsen's *Passing*: A Study in Irony." *CLA Journal* 18 (December 1974): 235–41.

Zumoff, J. A. "The African Blood Brotherhood: From Caribbean Nationalism to Communism." *Journal of Caribbean History* 41 (January 2007): 200–226.

Index

to come

About the Author

Photo by: Kate Heine Elliott

Thomas Aiello is a professor of history and African American studies at Valdosta State University. He is the author of almost twenty books, including *The Life and Times of Louis Lomax: The Art of Deliberate Disunity* (Duke University Press, 2021) and dozens of peer-reviewed journal articles. His work helped amend the Louisiana constitution to make nonunanimous juries illegal and was cited in the United States Supreme Court as part of its decision ruling them unconstitutional. His work was also included as part of the effort that led Major League Baseball to include Negro Leagues statistics in its historical record. Learn more at www.thomasaiellobooks.com.

CPSIA information can be obtained
at www.ICGtesting.com
Printed in the USA
BVHW090625130921
616608BV00003BB/46